Expert Swift

First Edition

By Ehab Amer, Marin Benčević, Ray Fix & Shai Mishali

Expert Swift

Ehab Amer, Marin Benčević, Ray Fix & Shai Mishali

Copyright ©2021 Razeware LLC.

Notice of Rights

Notice of Liability

Trademarks

ISBN: 978-1-950325-44-3

Table of Contents

Book License

By purchasing *Expert Swift*, you have the following license:

- You are allowed to use and/or modify the source code in *Expert Swift* in as many apps as you want, with no attribution required.

- You are allowed to use and/or modify all art, images and designs that are included in *Expert Swift* in as many apps as you want, but must include this attribution line somewhere inside your app: "Artwork/images/designs: from *Expert Swift*, available at www.raywenderlich.com".

- The source code included in *Expert Swift* is for your personal use only. You are NOT allowed to distribute or sell the source code in *Expert Swift* without prior authorization.

- This book is for your personal use only. You are NOT allowed to sell this book without prior authorization, or distribute it to friends, coworkers or students; they would need to purchase their own copies.

Before You Begin

This section tells you a few things you need to know before you get started, such as what you'll need for hardware and software, where to find the project files for this book, and more.

What You Need

To follow along with this book, you'll need the following:

- A Mac running macOS Catalina 10.15 or later, with the latest point release and security patches installed. This is so you can install the latest version of the required development tool: Xcode.

- Xcode 12.5 or later. You can download the latest version of Xcode for free from the Mac App Store, here: apple.co/1FLn51R

If you haven't installed the latest version of Xcode, be sure to do that before continuing with the book. The code covered in this book depends on Swift 5.4 and Xcode 12.5 — you may get lost if you try to work with an older version or work outside the playground environment that this book assumes.

Book Source Code &
Forums

Where to download the materials for this book

The materials for this book can be cloned or downloaded from the GitHub book materials repository:

- https://github.com/raywenderlich/advs-materials/tree/editions/1.0

Forums

We've also set up an official forum for the book at https://forums.raywenderlich.com/c/books/expert-swift/78. This is a great place to ask questions about the book or to submit any errors you may find.

"Thanks to my family for their unconditional support, and my beautiful wife Merche for being a wonderful blessing."

— *Ehab Amer*

"To my dad, for teaching me all of the things I thought were too hard to know."

— *Marin Bencevic*

"To my friends and family and the Swift community of dreamers, inventors, teachers, learners and doers. You guys make this place awesome."

— *Ray Fix*

"For my beautiful family: Elia and Baby Ethan. You're everything to me: my love, inspiration, and rock 🩶. To my family and friends for their support, you're the best!"

— *Shai Mishali*

About the Authors

Ehab Amer is an author of this book. He is a very enthusiastic Lead iOS developer with a very diverse experience from building games to enterprise applications and POCs with new technologies. In his spare time, TV shows take the majority of his time, followed by video games. When away from the screen, he goes with his wife and friends to explore the underwater world through diving.

Marin Bencevic is a computer vision researcher working on medical images. He is also an iOS developer who likes to work on cool iOS apps and games, nerd out about programming, learn new things and then blog about it. He also has a chubby cat.

Ray Fix works on next-generation microscopes made for iPad at Discover Echo Inc. in San Diego, California. Ray enjoys learning new things and is excited about math, data, visualization, machine learning and computer vision. Swift is his problem-solving language of choice and he has been using it and teaching others about it since its 2014 public release.

Shai Mishali is an author on this book. He's an experienced, award-winning iOS specialist; as well as an international speaker, and a highly active open-source contributor and maintainer on several high-profile projects - namely, the RxSwift Community and RxSwift projects, but also releases many open-source endeavors around Combine such as CombineCocoa, RxCombine and more. As an avid enthusiast of hackathons, Shai took 1st place at BattleHack Tel-Aviv 2014, BattleHack World Finals San Jose 2014, and Ford's Developer Challenge Tel-Aviv 2015. You can find him on GitHub and Twitter as @freak4pc.

About the Editors

 **Morten Faarkrog** is the technical editor of this book. He is a Technical Director & Solution Architect at a consultancy in Denmark, where he works with architecting larger software solutions across a range of companies. Morten has a background as an iOS developer and still loves tinkering with the Swift language in his spare time.

 **Daniel Souza** comes from Cascavel-Ceara - a small city in Brazil.He started his career as a generalist and worked as a Backend, Frontend, and Android.But then he decided to focus on iOS Development and he couldn't be happier. He loves the iOS Dev Community and how much you can learn from it.

 **John Hagemann** is the English language editor of this book. He is a communications specialist and analyst who enjoys putting technical subject matter into plain talk. He lives in Washington state with his son.

 **Eli Ganim** is the final pass editor for this book. He is an iOS engineer from Israel, who's passionate about teaching, writing and sharing knowledge with others.

About the Artist

 **Vicki Wenderlich** is the designer and artist of the cover of this book. She is Ray's wife and business partner. She is a digital artist who creates illustrations, game art and a lot of other art or design work for the tutorials and books on raywenderlich.com. When she's not making art, she loves hiking, a good glass of wine and attempting to create the perfect cheese plate.

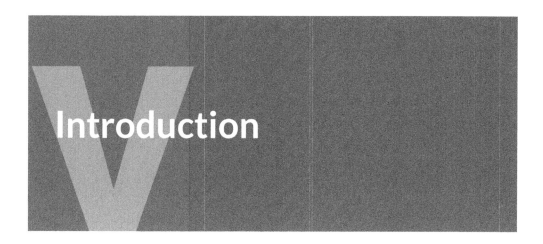

Introduction

Welcome to Expert Swift! The book for intermediate Swift developers looking to enhance their skills and understanding of the language.

Swift is a powerful and wonderful language, used by many developers around the world to build iOS, macOS, tvOS and watchOS apps. If you're reading this book, then you've probably built a few apps yourself.

Most of the books from raywanderlich.com are "By Tutorials", however this book is a little different. Since this is an advanced book, we didn't build a tutorial to accompany each chapter. Instead, we go deep by covering low-level concepts as well as high-level abstractions, by using sample projects to illustrate how the advanced topic might be used in real life.

You should expect some longer chapters. Trying to explain advanced topics, like the ones this book covers, is not an easy task. Acquiring this advanced knowledge is worth it though, and as you read through the book, you'll find yourself wanting to jump to your existing apps and implement the techniques you learn.

Take a deep breath and enjoy the ride!

How to read this book

Each chapter of this book presents some theory on the topic at hand, along with Swift code to demonstrate the practical applications of what you're learning.

The chapters are independent, meaning you can read them in any order you'd like. The only exception to this are the Protocols (chapter 3) and Generics (chapter 4) chapters, which share one sample project.

Some chapters provide a starter project, while in some you'll use playgrounds to write code from scratch.

This book is split into three main sections:

Section I: Core Concepts

The first section of this book covers the basic building blocks of the Swift language: The type system (enums, structs and classes), Protocols and Generics. We'll start with a brief refresher of each topic and then jump right into the behind-the-scenes implementations.

The content of this section will expose the inner workings of the type system, as well as get you intimately familiar with protocols and generics.

Section II: Standard Library

This section covers the base layer of writing Swift programs: Numerics, Ranges, Strings, Sequences, Collections, Codable and the less obvious, but very important topic - Unsafe.

As you'd expect from an advanced book, we don't only explain these topics, but also investigate how they're built, how they're represented, and how to use them effectively.

Section III: Techniques

The final section of this book covers advanced techniques to super-charge your Swift powers, and use all of what Swift has to offer.

We'll cover topics like Higher order functions, Functional reactive programming, Objective-C interoperability, using Instrumentation, and API design.

Section I: Core Concepts

The first section of this book covers the basic building blocks of the Swift language: The type system (enums, structs and classes), Protocols and Generics. We'll start with a brief refresher of each topic and then jump right into the behind-the-scenes implementations.

The content of this section will expose the inner workings of the type system, as well as get you intimately familiar with protocols and generics.

Chapter 1: Introduction

By Ray Fix

In 2010, Chris Lattner typed `mkdir shiny` on his laptop, and what would ultimately become the Swift language was born. Shiny started as a personal project he worked on during evenings and weekends.

The project had many ambitious goals. Lattner has mentioned some of them in interviews and podcasts, including:

- Adopting modern language features that allow new programming paradigms.

- Using automatic memory management to avoid the overhead of garbage collection.

- Defining as much of the language as possible in the library instead of the compiler.

- Making the language defaults safe to avoid costly undefined behavior.

- Making it easy to learn for beginners.

But perhaps most of all, he wanted this new language to be "real". Using it should feel like using a scripting language but be suitable for everything from app development to system-level programming. Half-jokingly, he has called this, "world domination".

Swift released

Shiny transitioned to Swift and officially became real in the summer of 2014 at Apple's Worldwide Developer Conference (WWDC). It was real in the sense that, out of the box, it had full interoperability with Objective-C and could leverage battle-tested frameworks such as UIKit for building apps. The iOS community embraced it quickly and wholeheartedly, with little exception.

The following year's WWDC came with another seismic announcement. Swift would become an open-source project and expand beyond Apple platforms. Apple made good on that promise by the end of the year, setting up https://swift.org/, a website to find toolchain downloads for platforms such as Linux and ultimately Windows as well as discussion and links to complete source code with history hosted at GitHub (https://github.com/apple/swift). Here, Apple and the community would continue to develop Swift in the open.

Swift.org established a language evolution process in which the community could propose and implement changes to the language. To date, 311 change proposals have been made, all of which (accepted or not) have pushed the language forward.

Easy onboarding

It was imperative to the design of Swift that this one-liner compiled and run as a valid program:

```
print("Hello, world!")
```

Despite being a strongly typed language that can catch all kinds of errors at compile-time, you can write programs like this. Robust type inference and lack of boilerplate make it pleasant to use and feel almost like a scripting language.

Swift embraces the philosophy of progressive disclosure, which means you're exposed to only the language complexity you need. You can learn about things like modules, access control, objects, static methods, protocols, generics and escaped characters as they become necessary to what you're trying to do.

Additionally, Swift allows this to work out of the box:

```
let pointer = malloc(100)
defer {
  free(pointer)
}
// work with raw memory
```

Swift strives to be a "language without borders" or "infinitely hackable" so it can support seamless interoperability between low-level C and scripting environments, such as Python. Interoperability with other environments continues to be a theme as the language evolves. You'll learn about interoperability with Objective-C in Chapter 12, "Objective-C Interoperability".

Multi-paradigm

Apple demonstrated Swift's modern language features at that first WWDC. In the first live demo, they functionally mapped strings to SpriteKit images. In addition to handling the intricacies of giant, legacy object-oriented frameworks, such as UIKit, CoreData and SpriteKit, Swift can also speak functionally with sequences of values using map, reduce and filter. Chapter 10, "Higher-Order Functions", covers these in detail.

Consider the problem of a sequence of numbers you want to add so you can compare using imperative and functional styles.

You can follow along with the starter playground **Multi-paradigm.playground**. This includes an example() function that scopes the example so you can use the same variable names repeatedly in the same playground.

Start by adding and running this:

```
let numbers = [1, 2, 4, 10, -1, 2, -10]

example("imperative") {
  var total = 0
  for value in numbers {
    total += value
  }
  print(total)
}
```

As the example's title suggests, this adds the numbers and stores the result in the mutable variable total in an imperative style.

Now, add a functional version:

```
example("functional") {
  let total = numbers.reduce(0, +)
  print(total)
}
```

This functional version is intoxicatingly simple. The method is descriptive, and it allows total to be an immutable value that you don't need to worry about changing later in your code. Experience suggests going functional can be beneficial for your code. You'll learn more about these techniques in Chapter 10, "Higher-Order Functions".

Suppose the task is to add a number sequence from left to right but to stop when a negative number appears. One possible, functional version might look like this:

```
example("functional, early-exit") {
  let total = numbers.reduce((accumulating: true, total: 0))
    { (state, value) in
      if state.accumulating && value >= 0 {
        return (accumulating: true, state.total + value)
      }
      else {
        return (accumulating: false, state.total)
      }
    }.total
  print(total)
}
```

This code is more complex but calls the same reduce function and uses a tuple to control whether values accumulate and keep the running total. It works, although the compiler needs to work hard to figure out that an early exit is possible.

Although you can solve this problem functionally in other ways (such as finding the sub-sequence and then summing), you can do it in a straightforward way imperatively:

```
example("imperative, early-exit") {
  var total = 0
  for value in numbers {
    guard value >= 0 else { break }
    total += value
  }
  print(total)
}
```

This code is easy to follow because it more directly describes the problem statement. It also maps directly to actual computer hardware so the optimizer doesn't have to work nearly as hard.

One downside of the above code is that total leaks out as a mutable variable. However, thanks to Swift's mutation model, you can fix that:

```
example("imperative, early-exit with just-in-time mutability") {
  let total: Int = {
    // same-old imperative code
    var total = 0
    for value in numbers {
      guard value >= 0 else { break }
      total += value
    }
    return total
  }()
  print(total)
}
```

This code wraps the imperative code in a closure and calls it to assign the outer immutable total. In this way, Swift gives you "mutation when you need it." It lets you express algorithms with local mutation when that's the most natural solution.

The Swift compiler

Central to the Swift toolchain is the Swift compiler. It's responsible for turning source code into object code you can link into an executable. It runs on the LLVM compiler infrastructure, and the data flow looks like this:

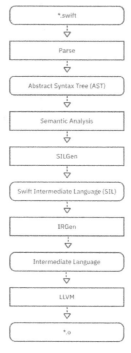

The Swift toolchain pipeline

The process of taking a high-level language such as Swift and transforming it into machine code that can run efficiently on actual hardware is called **lowering**. The rounded rectangles shown above are data that are inputs or outputs of the phases represented by rectangles. It's worth understanding each one of the steps from a high level:

1. **Parse**: Swift source code is first parsed into tokens and put into an **abstract syntax tree** or **AST**. You can think of this being a tree in which each expression is a node. The nodes also hold source location information so, if an error is detected, the node can tell you exactly where the problem occurred.

2. **Semantic Analysis (Sema)**: In this step, the compiler uses the AST to analyze your program's meaning. This is where **type checking** occurs. It passes the type-checked AST to the **SILGen** phase.

3. **SILGen**: This phase departs from previous compiler pipelines such as **Clang**, which didn't have this step. The AST gets lowered into **Swift Intermediate Language** (**SIL**). SIL contains **basic blocks** of computation and understands Swift Types, reference counting and dispatch rules. There are two flavors of SIL: raw and canonical. Canonical SIL results from raw SIL run through a minimum set of optimization passes (even when all optimizations are turned off). SIL also contains source location information so it can produce meaningful errors.

4. **IRGen**: This tool lowers SIL to LLVM's intermediate representation. At this point, the instructions are no longer Swift specific. (Every LLVM-based uses this representation.) IR is still quite abstract. Like SIL, IR is in Static single assignment (SSA) form. It models machines as having an unlimited number of registers, making it easier to find optimizations. It doesn't know anything about Swift types.

5. **LLVM**: This final step optimizes the IR and lowers it to machine instructions for a particular platform. Backends (which output machine instructions) include ARM, x86, Wasm and more.

The diagram above shows how the Swift compiler generates object code. Other tools, such as source code formatters, refactoring tools, documentation generators and syntax highlighters can tap into the intermediate results, such as the AST, making the final results more robust and consistent.

> **Historical note**: Before Apple adopted LLVM and Clang for Xcode's compiler technology, the syntax highlighting, document generation, debugging and compiling all used different parsers. Most of the time, this worked fine. But things could also get weird if they got out of sync.

The magic of SIL

The idea of creating an intermediate language that keeps all the type semantics of the source language was new with the development of Swift. Unlike other LLVM compilers that need to take an extremely circuitous route to show specific diagnostics and perform higher-level optimizations, SILGen can produce them directly in a testable way.

Overflow detection

Check out the power of SIL in action. Consider the following playground error:

```
let x = Int8(15)+115    🚫   Arithmetic operation '15 + 115' (on type 'Int8') results in an overflow
```

Thanks to a SILGen pass, the compiler statically analyzes (checks at compile-time) your source and sees that the number 130 can't fit in an Int8 that can go up to only 127.

Definite initialization

Swift is a safe language that by default makes it hard to access uninitialized memory. SILGen provides guarantee through a checking process called definite initialization. Consider this example:

```swift
final class Printer {
  var value: Int
  init(value: Int) { self.value = value }
  func print() { Swift.print(value) }
}

func printTest() {
  var printer: Printer
  if .random() {
    printer = Printer(value: 1)
  }
  else {
    printer = Printer(value: 2)
  }
  printer.print()
}

printTest()
```

This code compiles and runs fine. But if you comment out the else clause, the compiler correctly flags an error (Variable 'printer' used before being initialized) thanks to the SIL. This error is possible because SIL understands the semantics of method calls to `Printer`.

Allocation and devirtualization

SILGen helps with the optimization of allocations and method calls. Take the following code and put it in a file called **magic.swift**, using your favorite plain text editor:

```swift
class Magic {
  func number() -> Int { return 0 }
```

```
}

final class SpecialMagic: Magic {
  override func number() -> Int { return 42 }
}

public var number: Int = -1

func magicTest() {
  let specialMagic = SpecialMagic()
  let magic: Magic = specialMagic
  number = magic.number()
}
```

This code is probably the most contrived example you'll ever see for setting a number. In the function `magicTest`, you create a `SpecialMagic` type and then assign it to a base class reference and call `number()` to set the global number. Conceptually, it uses the class's virtual table to look up the correct function, which returns the value 42.

Raw SIL

From a terminal window, change to the source directory where **magic.swift** lives and run this command:

```
swiftc -O -emit-silgen magic.swift > magic.rawsil
```

This runs the Swift compiler with optimization and creates raw SIL, outputting it to the file *magic.rawsil*.

Take a deep breath, don't panic and open **magic.rawsil** in your text editor. If you scroll down to the bottom, you find this definition of the function `magicTest()`:

```
// magicTest()
sil hidden [ossa] @$s5magic0A4TestyyF : $@convention(thin) () ->
() {
bb0:
  %0 = global_addr @$s5magic6numberSivp : $*Int    // user: %14
  %1 = metatype $@thick SpecialMagic.Type          // user: %3
  // function_ref SpecialMagic.__allocating_init()
  %2 = function_ref @$s5magic12SpecialMagicCACycfC :
$@convention(method) (@thick SpecialMagic.Type) -> @owned
SpecialMagic // user: %3
  %3 = apply %2(%1) : $@convention(method) (@thick
SpecialMagic.Type) -> @owned SpecialMagic // users: %18, %5, %4
  debug_value %3 : $SpecialMagic, let, name "specialMagic" //
id: %4
  %5 = begin_borrow %3 : $SpecialMagic              // users: %9,
```

```
%6
  %6 = copy_value %5 : $SpecialMagic                    // user: %7
  %7 = upcast %6 : $SpecialMagic to $Magic              // users: %17,
%10, %8
  debug_value %7 : $Magic, let, name "magic"            // id: %8
  end_borrow %5 : $SpecialMagic                         // id: %9
  %10 = begin_borrow %7 : $Magic                        // users: %13,
%12, %11
  %11 = class_method %10 : $Magic, #Magic.number : (Magic) -> ()
-> Int, $@convention(method) (@guaranteed Magic) -> Int // user:
%12
  %12 = apply %11(%10) : $@convention(method) (@guaranteed
Magic) -> Int // user: %15
  end_borrow %10 : $Magic                               // id: %13
  %14 = begin_access [modify] [dynamic] %0 : $*Int // users:
%16, %15
  assign %12 to %14 : $*Int                             // id: %15
  end_access %14 : $*Int                                // id: %16
  destroy_value %7 : $Magic                             // id: %17
  destroy_value %3 : $SpecialMagic                      // id: %18
  %19 = tuple ()                                        // user: %20
  return %19 : $()                                      // id: %20
} // end sil function '$s5magic0A4TestyyF'
```

This excerpt is the SIL definition of the three-line function magicTest(). The label bb0 stands for basic block 0 and is a unit of computation. (If you had an if/else statement, there would be two basic blocks, bb1 and bb2 created for each possible path.) The %1, %2, etc. values are virtual registers. SIL is in Single Static Assignment form so registers are unlimited and never reused. There are many more small details that aren't important to the discussion here. Reading through it, you should roughly see how it's allocating, assigning, calling and deallocating the objects. This expresses the full semantics of the Swift language.

Canonical SIL

Canonical SIL includes optimizations, including a minimum set of optimization passes when optimization is turned off with −Onone. Run this Terminal command:

```
swiftc −O −emit−sil magic.swift > magic.sil
```

This command creates the file **magic.sil**, which contains canonical SIL. Scroll toward the end of the file to find magicTest():

```
// magicTest()
sil hidden @$s5magic0A4TestyyF : $@convention(thin) () -> () {
bb0:
  %0 = global_addr @$s5magic6numberSivp : $*Int   // user: %3
  %1 = integer_literal $Builtin.Int64, 42         // user: %2
```

```
    %2 = struct $Int (%1 : $Builtin.Int64)           // user: %4
    %3 = begin_access [modify] [dynamic] [no_nested_conflict] %0 :
 $*Int // users: %4, %5
    store %2 to %3 : $*Int                           // id: %4
    end_access %3 : $*Int                            // id: %5
    %6 = tuple ()                                    // user: %7
    return %6 : $()                                  // id: %7
 } // end sil function '$s5magic0A4TestyyF'
```

This excerpt is a lot more concise than the raw SIL, even though it represents the same thing. The main work is to store the integer literal 42 into a global address location store %2 to %3 : $*Int. No classes are being initialized or de-initialized, nor are any virtual methods being called. When you hear that structures use the stack and classes use the heap, keep in mind this is a generalization.

In Swift, everything starts off being initialized on the heap, and a SIL analysis can move the allocation to the stack or even get rid of it altogether. Virtual function calls can also be devirtualized through the optimization process and called directly or even inlined.

Implementing a language feature

Swift pushes the implementation of as many features as possible from the compiler into the library. You might be aware, for example, that Optional is just a generic enumeration. The truth is that most of the fundamental types are part of the standard library and not baked into the compiler. This includes Bool, Int, Double, String, Array, Set, Dictionary, Range and many more. In an October 2020 Lex Fridman interview, Lattner said he regards this kind of expressive library design as *the most beautiful* feature of a programming language.

A great way to learn about some of the more esoteric features of Swift or gain a better appreciation of some of the basic ones is to do this yourself — to build a language-like feature. You'll do that now.

Building ifelse

For this coding experiment, you'll implement an ifelse() statement like the statistical programming language **R** uses. The function looks like this:

```
ifelse(condition, valueTrue, valueFalse)
```

It does the same thing as the Swift ternary operator `condition ? valueTrue : valueFalse`, which some don't like because of aesthetic objections.

Start by typing this into a playground:

```
func ifelse(condition: Bool,
            valueTrue: Int,
            valueFalse: Int) -> Int {
  if condition {
    return valueTrue
  } else {
    return valueFalse
  }
}
let value = ifelse(condition: Bool.random(),
                   valueTrue: 100,
                   valueFalse: 0)
```

What's wrong with this solution? Maybe nothing. If it solves your problem and you're working with only `Int`, this might even be a good place to stop. But because you're trying to make a general-purpose language feature for everyone, you can make several improvements. First, refine the interface a little:

```
func ifelse(_ condition: Bool,
            _ valueTrue: Int,
            _ valueFalse: Int) -> Int {
  condition ? valueTrue : valueFalse
}

let value = ifelse(.random(), 100, 0)
```

For a language construct that's going to be used often, removing the argument labels makes sense. The wildcard label _ gives you the ability to remove them. For brevity, implement the feature in terms of the less verbose ternary operator. (You might wonder why you shouldn't use the camel-case name `ifElse`. There's precedent for keywords being simple concatenations, such as `typealias` and `associatedtype`, so stay with the original **R** language naming.)

The next obvious problem is that this works only for `Int` types. You could replace it with a lot of overloads for the important types you want:

```
func ifelse(_ condition: Bool,
            _ valueTrue: Int,
            _ valueFalse: Int) -> Int {
  condition ? valueTrue : valueFalse
}
func ifelse(_ condition: Bool,
            _ valueTrue: String,
```

```
                    _ valueFalse: String) -> String {
    condition ? valueTrue : valueFalse
  }
  func ifelse(_ condition: Bool,
              _ valueTrue: Double,
              _ valueFalse: Double) -> Double {
    condition ? valueTrue : valueFalse
  }
  func ifelse(_ condition: Bool,
              _ valueTrue: [Int],
              _ valueFalse: [Int]) -> [Int] {
    condition ? valueTrue : valueFalse
  }
```

It's easy to see this doesn't scale. As soon as you think you're done, there's another type your users want support for. And each overload repeats the implementation, which is not great.

As an alternative, you could use the type Any, a type-erased, stand-in for any Swift type:

```
  func ifelse(_ condition: Bool,
              _ valueTrue: Any,
              _ valueFalse: Any) -> Any {
    condition ? valueTrue : valueFalse
  }

  let value = ifelse(.random(), 100, 0) as! Int
```

This code works for any type, but there's an important caveat you have to cast back to the original type you want. Using the Any type doesn't protect you from a situation like this where you mix types:

```
  let value = ifelse(.random(), "100", 0) as! Int
```

This statement might work in testing but crash in production if the random number comes up true. Any is super versatile but also error-prone to use.

A better answer, as you might have guessed, is to use generics. Change the code to this:

```
  func ifelse<V>(_ condition: Bool,
                 _ valueTrue: V,
                 _ valueFalse: V) -> V {
    condition ? valueTrue : valueFalse
  }

  // let value = ifelse(.random(), "100", 0)  // doesn't compile
```

```
anymore
let value = ifelse(.random(), 100, 0)
```

This design both preserves type information and constrains the arguments to be the same type as the return type. Generics are such an essential part of the Swift language that Chapter 4, "Generics" is dedicated to them. You'll use generics throughout the book.

Note: The Swift standard library uses generics extensively to eliminate code duplication, as in the example above. In some cases where the generic system is not *yet* strong enough, the library uses a python script, gyb (or generate-your-boilerplate), to generate the code for a family of types.

Deferring execution

The feature is looking good, but it's still not done. Consider this usage:

```
func expensiveValue1() -> Int {
  print("side-effect-1")
  return 2
}

func expensiveValue2() -> Int {
  print("side-effect-2")
  return 1729
}

let taxicab = ifelse(.random(),
                     expensiveValue1(),
                     expensiveValue2())
```

If you run this, you see *both* functions are always called. As a language feature, you would hope that only the expression you use gets evaluated. You can fix this by passing a closure that defers execution:

```
func ifelse<V>(_ condition: Bool,
               _ valueTrue: () -> V,
               _ valueFalse: () -> V) -> V {
  condition ? valueTrue() : valueFalse()
}
```

This code defers the execution but changes how you need to call the function.Now, you have to call it like this:

```
let value = ifelse(.random(), { 100 }, { 0 })

let taxicab = ifelse(.random(),
                     { expensiveValue1() },
                     { expensiveValue2() })
```

Only one function gets called, but having to wrap your arguments in a closure is pretty annoying. Fortunately, Swift has a way to fix it:

```
func ifelse<V>(_ condition: Bool,
               _ valueTrue: @autoclosure () -> V,
               _ valueFalse: @autoclosure () -> V) -> V {
  condition ? valueTrue() : valueFalse()
}

let value = ifelse(.random(), 100, 0 )

let taxicab = ifelse(.random(),
                     expensiveValue1(),
                     expensiveValue2())
```

Decorating a parameter type with `@autoclosure` causes the compiler to wrap arguments in a closure automatically. This change restores the call sites to what they used to be and still defers execution so only the used argument evaluates.

Using expressions that can fail

Things are going well, but there's still one more small problem. What if you want to use expressions that can fail?

Consider the following example:

```
func expensiveFailingValue1() throws -> Int {
  print("side-effect-1")
  return 2
}

func expensiveFailingValue2() throws -> Int {
  print("side-effect-2")
  return 1729
}

let failableTaxicab = ifelse(.random(),
                             try expensiveFailingValue1(),
                             try expensiveFailingValue2())
```

This fails to compile because the autoclosures aren't expecting a throwing closure. Without any special help from the compiler, you might think to solve it by creating another function version like this:

```
func ifelseThrows<V>(_ condition: Bool,
            _ valueTrue: @autoclosure () throws -> V,
            _ valueFalse: @autoclosure () throws -> V) throws
  -> V {
  condition ? try valueTrue() : try valueFalse()
}

let taxicab2 = try ifelseThrows(.random(),
                                try expensiveFailingValue1(),
                                try expensiveFailingValue2())
```

This code works, but the situation is worse than initially described. Suppose only the first expression throws or suppose only the second throws. Do you need to make four versions of the same function to handle all the cases? Because the keyword throws does not figure into the signature of a Swift function, you would need to have four flavors of ifelse, all with slightly different names.

Fortunately, there's a better way. You can write one version of the function that handles all these cases:

```
func ifelse<V>(_ condition: Bool,
            _ valueTrue: @autoclosure () throws -> V,
            _ valueFalse: @autoclosure () throws -> V)
  rethrows -> V {
  condition ? try valueTrue() : try valueFalse()
}
```

The key is using rethrows. Rethrows propagates the error of any failing closure to the caller. If none of the closure parameters throw, it deduces the function is non-throwing and doesn't need to be marked with try.

With this single version, all these variants work:

```
let value = ifelse(.random(), 100, 0 )
let taxicab = ifelse(.random(),
                      expensiveValue1(),
                      expensiveValue2())
let taxicab2 = try ifelse(.random(),
                            try expensiveFailingValue1(),
                            try expensiveFailingValue2())
let taxicab3 = try ifelse(.random(),
                            expensiveValue1(),
                            try expensiveFailingValue2())
let taxicab4 = try ifelse(.random(),
```

```
        try expensiveFailingValue1(),
        expensiveValue2())
```

You're getting close to finishing `ifelse`. You don't want to pay the cost of an extra layer of abstraction, and the implementation will never change, so it makes sense to mark the function `@inlinable`. This added keyword hints to the compiler that the body of the method should be directly included in the client code without the overhead of calling a function.

```
@inlinable
func ifelse<V>(_ condition: Bool,
               _ valueTrue: @autoclosure () throws -> V,
               _ valueFalse: @autoclosure () throws -> V)
rethrows -> V {
  condition ? try valueTrue() : try valueFalse()
}
```

> **Note**: There are stronger forms of @inlinable available privately. You'll see these if you browse the Swift source. One such attribute is @_transparent, which always "sees through" to the underlying implementation. It will inline even with −Onone and not include a stack frame when debugging. Check out the details here: https://github.com/apple/swift/blob/main/docs/ TransparentAttr.md

Performance

One of the cool things about writing programs with an optimizing compiler is that the abstraction cost of making code clear and maintainable is often nothing or close to nothing.

To look at how you did here, put this code into a text file called **ifelse.swift**:

```
@inlinable
func ifelse<V>(_ condition: Bool,
               _ valueTrue: @autoclosure () throws -> V,
               _ valueFalse: @autoclosure () throws -> V)
rethrows -> V {
  condition ? try valueTrue() : try valueFalse()
}

func ifelseTest1() -> Int {
  if .random() {
      return 100
  } else {
```

```
      return 200
  }
}

func ifelseTest2() -> Int {
  Bool.random() ? 300 : 400
}

func ifelseTest3() -> Int {
  ifelse(.random(), 500, 600)
}
```

Take this code and run the compiler on it directly with this command:

```
swiftc -O -emit-assembly ifelse.swift > ifelse.asm
```

Take another deep breath and open the assembly file. Keep in mind these assembly files contain a ton of boilerplate ceremony around calling conventions and entry points. Don't let that discourage you from looking. Trimming off the unneeded stuff, here are the good parts:

```
_$s6ifelse0A5Test1SiyF:
    :
    callq   _swift_stdlib_random
    testl   $131072, -8(%rbp)
    movl    $100, %ecx
    movl    $200, %eax
    cmoveq  %rcx, %rax
    :

_$s6ifelse0A5Test2SiyF:
    :
    callq   _swift_stdlib_random
    testl   $131072, -8(%rbp)
    movl    $300, %ecx
    movl    $400, %eax
    cmoveq  %rcx, %rax
    :

_$s6ifelse0A5Test3SiyF:
    :
    callq   _swift_stdlib_random
    testl   $131072, -8(%rbp)
    movl    $500, %ecx
    movl    $600, %eax
    cmoveq  %rcx, %rax
    :
```

These are the assembly instructions for your three test functions. It might look like gibberish to you. The important thing is that this is the *same* gibberish for ifelseTest1(), ifelseTest2() and ifelseTest3(). In other words, there's zero abstraction penalty for the three ways of writing the code. Choose what looks most beautiful to you.

Now, demystifying the above assembly, the callq instruction calls the function to get a random number. Next, the testl instruction gets the random number return value (located at the address pointed to by the 64-bit base pointer - 8). It checks this against 131072, which is 0x20000 or the 17th bit. If you look at the Swift source for Bool.random, you find this:

```
@inlinable
public static func random<T: RandomNumberGenerator>(
  using generator: inout T
) -> Bool {
  return (generator.next() >> 17) & 1 == 0
}
```

That explains the 131072 mystery: It's shifting over the 17th bit, masking it and testing it all in one instruction. Next, the two possible outcome values of the function are moved (using the movl instruction) into the registers cx and ax. The prefix "e" stands for extended 32-bit versions of the registers. The rest of the bits are zero-extended to fill all 64-bits. Finally, the "conditional move if equal" or cmoveq instruction uses the result of the earlier test instruction to move the cx register to the ax register. The prefix r on rcx and rax indicates you use the full 64-bits of the registers.

> **Note**: The **mangled** symbol _$s6ifelse0A5Test1SiyF: is the unique symbol name for the ifelse.ifelseTest1() -> Int. (The leading "ifelse." is the module name, or in this case, the filename.) The linker needs short, guaranteed unique names for all the external symbols in your program. You can find the specification for mangling here: https://github.com/apple/swift/blob/main/docs/ABI/Mangling.rst. You can also run the command line tool swift-demangle found in /Library/Developer/CommandLineTools/usr/bin/. For example, swift-demangle _\$s6ifelseAAyxSb_xyKXKxyKXKtKlF corresponds to the symbol ifelse.ifelse<A>(Swift.Bool, @autoclosure () throws -> A, @autoclosure () throws -> A) throws -> A.

That completes the discussion and implementation of `ifelse`. It would be best if you asked the question posed by Swift core team member John McCall: "Is this an abstraction that pays for itself?" In this case, probably not. The ternary operator already exists, which does essentially the same thing. Nevertheless, going through this example hopefully reminded you of some of the capabilities Swift offers when building language-like features as part of a library.

Key points

This chapter talked about some of the motivations for building the Swift language and how Swift's libraries and compiler work together to make powerful abstractions. Here are some key takeaways:

- Swift is a multi-paradigm language that supports many programming styles, including imperative, functional, object-oriented, protocol-oriented and generic paradigms.

- Swift aims to pick reasonable defaults, making undefined behavior hard to trigger.

- Swift embraces the idea of progressive disclosure. You only need to learn about more advanced language features when you need them.

- Swift is a general-purpose programming language that features a powerful type system and type inference.

- Much of Swift is defined in its expressive, standard library and not as part of the compiler.

- The Swift compiler phases are parse, semantic analysis, SILGen, IRGen and LLVM.

- Source location information resides in AST and SIL, making better error reporting possible.

- SIL is a low-level description using basic blocks of instructions written in SSA form. It understands the semantics of Swift types, which enables many optimizations not possible with pure LLVM IR.

- SIL helps support definite initialization, memory allocation optimizations and devirtualization.

- Any is the ultimate type-erasure in Swift, but it can be error-prone to use. Generics are usually a better alternative.

- Pass a closure as a parameter that returns a value to defer evaluation of the argument until within the body of a function.

- `@autoclosure` is a way to implement short-circuit behavior because it defers execution of expression arguments.

- `rethrow` is a way to propagate errors from closures that might or might not be marked `throws`.

- `@inlinable` hints to the compiler that the instructions for a function should be emitted into the call site.

- Compilers remove much if not all the abstraction costs of your source code. If different source code has the same semantics, the compiler likely will emit identical machine instructions.

- Abstractions should pay for themselves. Think hard before creating new language features.

Where to go from here?

Much of this chapter discussed how the Swift compiler lowers high-level types and statements to efficient machine representation through SIL. Lowering is an intense (and niche) topic. If you're interested in knowing more, check out this slightly old but still quite relevant blog post by compiler engineer Slava Pestov http://bit.ly/slava-types. It's an *extremely* deep dive into Swift types and lowering, so you might want to read the rest of this section on types, protocols and generics before tackling it.

Members of the Swift compiler team, including Chris Lattner, Slava Pestov, Joseph Groff, John McCall and Doug Gregor, appear in LLVM conference talks about compiler implementation. A good one to start with is http://bit.ly/swift-sil.

Finally, check out the online tool https://godbolt.org, which lets you edit code in the web browser for many different languages (including Swift) and see how they lower. You might want to experiment around with compiler flags –O, –Onone, –Ounchecked. Under **Output settings** in the web interface, you might want to uncheck "Intel asm syntax" to get assembly output like in this chapter.

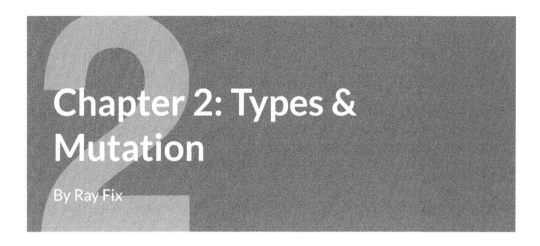

Chapter 2: Types & Mutation

By Ray Fix

What's a type? It's a logical grouping of data along with a set of operations you can perform with it. You use both standard types and custom types to build your programs in Swift. The Swift compiler often can guarantee correctness using type information in a process known as **type checking** before your program even runs.

Beginners, who are dealing with unfamiliar types such as Optional for the first time, might find type checking errors burdensome and slightly mysterious. But by type-checking your program, the type system makes sure you use the software correctly and enables many optimizations. Swift's type system is the key to safe and efficient code. As you become a more advanced practitioner, your programming perspective likely will become more type-centric.

Swift emphasizes **mutable value semantics** for its types. In this chapter, you'll review the important nominal types that Swift offers. Value types (enumerations and structures), reference types (classes) and the mutation rules all work together to allow mutable value semantics, which you can adopt in your own Swift types.

The fundamental types

The Swift type system consists of a small number of fundamental types. These types include the so-called **named types** (protocols, enumerations, structures and classes) as well as **compound types** (functions and tuples). Each of these types has a unique set of properties that make it useful for a particular situation.

As discussed in the previous chapter, it's pretty incredible that all the standard library types such as `Bool`, `Int`, `Double`, `String`, `Optional`, `Array` and `Dictionary` are clever compositions of these fundamental types. It speaks to the power of what you can do with them.

> **Note**: Protocols and generics also are amazing. This book has whole chapters for protocol types and generic types because they're so powerful and important. You'll also briefly look at types of types, or metatypes, in Chapter 4, "Generics".

In this chapter, you'll explore the properties of named concrete types created from classes, structures and enumerations. Although some of this might be a review, it will provide a platform to explore some more advanced topics.

Modeling with types

Two-dimensional geometry is a great problem domain for exploring the type system because it's well defined mathematically and easy to visualize. Start by opening the **Geometry** starter playground and adding the following two definitions for a point type:

```
struct StructPoint {
  var x, y: Double
}

class ClassPoint {
  var x, y: Double
  init(x: Double, y: Double) { (self.x, self.y) = (x, y) }
}
```

Both of these types model a point in the x-y plane. But already there are five essential differences you should be aware of.

Difference 1: Automatic initialization

The first, most obvious difference is the need for an initializer in the class type. If you don't declare one, the compiler will declare an internal **member-wise initializer** for structures. This initializer simply assigns the member properties one by one. You must define an initializer for your class because x and y need to be initialized.

> **Note:** If you define an initializer for a structure, the compiler won't define the member-wise one for you. A common trick is to define your initializer in an extension if you want both the compiler-generated one and a custom one.

Difference 2: Copy semantics

The second major and probably most important difference is copy semantics. Classes have **reference semantics** and structures have **value semantics**. Value semantics says that given two instances **A** and **B**, it's impossible to affect the value **B** by making changes to **A** and vice versa.

With reference semantics, you can affect one object from the other. Check out an example by adding this to the end of your playground and running it:

```
let structPointA = StructPoint(x: 0, y: 0)
var structPointB = structPointA
structPointB.x += 10
print(structPointA.x) // not affected, prints 0.0

let classPointA = ClassPoint(x: 0, y: 0)
let classPointB = classPointA
classPointB.x += 10
print(classPointA.x) // affected, prints 10.0
```

With reference semantics, changing classPointB affects classPointA because both variables point to the same underlying memory. This phenomenon is not the case with the structure in which structPointA and structPointB are independent copies with value semantics.

Difference 3: Scope of mutation

Swift supports an **instance-level** mutation model. This means that by using the introducer keyword `let` instead of `var`, you can lock down an instance from mutation. This is why you must declare `structPointB` in the code above with a `var`. If you didn't, you wouldn't be able to add 10 to the x coordinate. The compiler would prevent this with an error.

Notice that you can modify the x coordinate with the class version even though `let` introduces `classPointB`. The mutation control applies to the reference itself, not the underlying property data.

Value semantics through immutability

You know from the example above that classes are reference types with reference semantics. Is it possible to give a class value semantics? The answer is yes, and the easiest way is through immutability. Simply make all the properties immutable by declaring them with `let`. Because you can't modify anything from anywhere, this satisfies the definition for value semantics. Functional languages often use strict immutability at the cost of performance to achieve value semantics.

> **Note**: Objective-C uses a **type-level** mutation model. For example, `NSString` is immutable. But `NSMutableString`, which derives from `NSString`, adds mutability. However, if you have a pointer to an `NSString`, you can't be 100 percent sure it doesn't point to an `NSMutableString` that another client could modify. Defensive copies become necessary, making this a less efficient, less safe and more error-prone programming model.

The beautiful thing about declaring the x and y properties with `var` in `StructPoint` is that they can be mutable if you declare the instance with `var` and immutable with `let`. That is why you usually want to declare properties with `var` for structures, because you can control mutability for each instance at the point of use.

Difference 4: Heap versus stack

A general rule of thumb is that classes use heap memory but structures and enumerations use stack memory. Because stack allocations are orders of magnitude faster than heap allocations, this is where value types get their fast reputation.

Each thread of execution has its own stack, and stacks only change by modifying the top-most element. As a result, allocating and deallocating onto a stack doesn't require expensive concurrency locks or fancy allocation strategies. Allocation and deallocation can be performed with a single add or subtract instruction in a single clock tick.

The heap, by contrast, is shared by multiple threads and needs to be protected by concurrency locks. The operating system must protect against **heap fragmentation**, which can happen if you allocate and deallocate different size memory blocks. As a result, even though heap allocation has been highly optimized, it's ultimately non-deterministic and could require thousands or even millions of instructions to perform.

Here's a diagram of how the above code might look like allocated in memory:

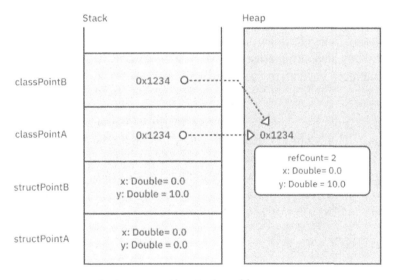

Instances on the stack and heap

The structures are put on the stack, whereas the classes are put on both the stack and the heap. The reference count in heap memory keeps track of the object's lifetime because reference types are shared. Only when the reference count drops to zero does deinit get called and the memory deallocated.

> **Note**: Heap for classes vs. stack for structures and enumerations is just a general rule of thumb. As you saw in the previous chapter, the Swift compiler starts by allocating everything on the heap and then reasons about the object's lifetime to determine whether it can be allocated on the stack. For example, an escaping closure that closes over a local structure will need to put that object on the heap to extend the structure's lifetime beyond its scope. On the other hand, a class that is created, that performs some action and then goes out of scope might be optimized away entirely and just include the instructions necessary to complete the operation.

Difference 5: Lifetime and identity

Value types, such as structures and enumerations, generally live on the stack and are cheap to copy. Values don't have the notion of a lifetime or intrinsic identity. References do have lifetimes, and because of that, you can define a `deinit` function for them. They also automatically have an identity because they reside at a specific place in memory you can use to identify them.

> **Note**: It's possible to give a value type identity by specifying a unique property attribute. The `Identifiable` protocol, which adds a `Hashable` (and `Equatable`) id property, does this. The SwiftUI framework defines property wrappers, such as `@State`, which among other things imbue lifetime into simple value types.

More differences

There are other differences between classes and structures that this simple example doesn't illuminate. The most glaring one is inheritance, which classes use to realize runtime polymorphism. Classes dispatch their methods dynamically, whereas this doesn't happen for structures unless you're using a protocol. Dispatch happens statically for structure methods not part of a protocol. You'll learn more about protocol dispatch in the next chapter.

> **Note**: You can mark methods in classes as `final`, which can have a side effect of devirtualizing them and making them run faster. The compiler can use hints from access control and whole module optimization to prove that a method can't be overridden and optimize it.

Defining a Point

Given the differences above, having a lightweight value representing your `Point` is likely a good choice. Go with that design. Add this to the playground:

```swift
struct Point: Equatable {
  var x, y: Double
}

struct Size: Equatable {
  var width, height: Double
}

struct Rectangle: Equatable {
  var origin: Point
  var size: Size
}
```

This defines `Point`, `Size` and `Rectangle` with `Equatable` conformance. For value types, the compiler will generate the required `==` method for you if the stored properties are also `Equatable` types. Reference types (aka classes) require you to write `==` for `Equatable` and `hash(into:)` for `Hashable` yourself.

Another essential characteristic of value semantics is that they compose. `Rectangle` has value semantics because it's a value type and both `Point` and `Size` have value semantics. Further, because Swift arrays have value semantics, an array of `Rectangle` will also have value semantics.

> **Note**: Code synthesis happens during the type-checking phase of the compiler. When you adopt a protocol, the compiler checks to see whether the type fulfills (witnesses) the protocol. If it doesn't, it typically emits an error. In the special cases of `Equatable`, if the type is a value type, it will attempt to synthesize `==` if all the stored properties are also `Equatable`. A similar process happens for `Hashable`, `Codable` and `CaseIterable`. Unlike the others, `Codable` synthesizes code for both value types and reference types.

Functions and methods

The custom types so far only have data in the form of stored properties. But things get interesting when you add operations. To warm up, add a couple of methods to the Point type:

```
// 1st draft version
extension Point {
  func flipped() -> Self {
    Point(x: self.y, y: self.x)
  }

  mutating func flip() {
    let temp = self
    self.x = temp.y
    self.y = temp.x
  }
}
```

Here are two simple methods for exchanging the x and y coordinates of a point. The names of the methods follow the "fluent" usage of mutating and non-mutating pairs described by the Swift API Design Guidelines (https://swift.org/documentation/api-design-guidelines/).

The function flipped() uses self, and the function flip both uses and modifies self. For that reason, you need to declare it mutating. Both functions contain the exchanging logic, which is repetitious.

Clean things up by replacing the code above with this version:

```
extension Point {
  func flipped() -> Self {
    Point(x: y, y: x)
  }

  mutating func flip() {
    self = flipped()
  }
}
```

The unnecessary references to self are gone, and the exchanging logic is *only* in flipped. In this case, the implementation is trivial, so the duplication wasn't a big deal. But when you have non-mutating and mutating function pairs that are more complicated, you'll appreciate this pattern.

Mutating and self

With a type method, the Swift compiler passes `self: Self` as an invisible parameter. That's why you can use it in the function body. With a `mutating` method, Swift passes an invisible `self: inout Self`. If you recall, the semantics of `inout` make a copy on entry into the function and then make a copy on exit. This timing corresponds to the property observers `willSet` and `didSet` getting called. Further, `inout` effectively makes an input and extra return value from your function.

> **Note**: Methods on classes (i.e., reference types) don't use `inout`. If you think about what `self: inout Self` does, that makes sense. `inout` on a reference type would only prevent the entire instance from being reassigned to another instance.

Static methods and properties

Add a static property and method to your point type using an extension by adding this to the playground:

```
extension Point {
  static var zero: Point {
    Point(x: 0, y: 0)
  }

  static func random(inRadius radius: Double) -> Point {
    guard radius >= 0 else {
      return .zero
    }

    let x = Double.random(in: -radius ... radius)
    let maxY = (radius * radius - x * x).squareRoot()
    let y = Double.random(in: -maxY ... maxY)
    return Point(x: x, y: y)
  }
}
```

This code creates a static property `zero`, which is just a point at the origin. The static method `random` creates a random point bounded by the specified radius. The x value is first pinned down, and you use the Pythagorean theorem to determine the maximum bounds of allowed y values so it stays in the circle.

Going deterministic

Swift's default `Double.random(in:)` uses `SystemRandomNumberGenerator()`, which is cryptographically secure. This choice is a great default because it prevents would-be attackers from guessing your random numbers.

Sometimes, you want your random values to be deterministic and repeatable. This importance is especially true for continuous integration tests. You want these types of tests to fail in response to a code change (bad merge or refactoring), not because of a new, untried input value. Fortunately, the Swift standard library supports your own generators with the overloaded method `Double.random(in:using:)`, where the `using` parameter takes a pseudo-random number generator of your choice.

Although the standard library doesn't include one of these seedable pseudo-random sources, it's easy to make one yourself. There's a lot of research about making "good" random generators on the web. Here is a decent one from Wikipedia. The Permuted Congruential Generator (https://en.wikipedia.org/wiki/Permuted_congruential_generator) can be translated to Swift from the listed C code. Add this to your playground:

```swift
struct PermutedCongruential: RandomNumberGenerator {
  private var state: UInt64
  private let multiplier: UInt64 = 6364136223846793005
  private let increment: UInt64 = 1442695040888963407

  private func rotr32(x: UInt32, r: UInt32) -> UInt32 {
    (x &>> r) | x &<< ((~r &+ 1) & 31)
  }

  private mutating func next32() -> UInt32 {
    var x = state
    let count = UInt32(x &>> 59)
    state = x &* multiplier &+ increment
    x ^= x &>> 18
    return rotr32(x: UInt32(truncatingIfNeeded: x &>> 27),
                          r: count)
  }

  mutating func next() -> UInt64 {
    UInt64(next32()) << 32 | UInt64(next32())
  }

  init(seed: UInt64) {
    state = seed &+ increment
    _ = next()
  }
}
```

This code contains some math details that aren't important for this book. (However, you will see more about C-style unsafe binary arithmetic such as &>>, &* and &+ in Chapter 5, "Numerics & Ranges".) The critical thing to notice is how you can mark the internal details and state as private. As a user of this type, you only need to know that it's seeded with a 64-bit integer and that it produces a deterministic stream of pseudo-random 64-bit integers. This hiding is **encapsulation** in action; it tames complexity and makes the type easy to use and reason about. You'll see encapsulation used throughout this book and discussed further in Chapter 14, "API Design Tips & Tricks".

To use this pseudo-random source, create an overload of `Point.random`. Add this to your playground:

```swift
extension Point {
  static func random(inRadius radius: Double,
                     using randomSource:
                           inout PermutedCongruential) -> Point {
    guard radius >= 0 else {
      return .zero
    }

    let x = Double.random(in: -radius...radius,
                          using: &randomSource)
    let maxY = (radius * radius - x * x).squareRoot()
    let y = Double.random(in: -maxY...maxY,
                          using: &randomSource)
    return Point(x: x, y: y)
  }
}
```

It's quite like the previous version that uses the system random number generator. As a static method, `random(in:using:)` also doesn't touch an instance of `Point`. But notice how mutable state can flow through the function because `randomSource` is an `inout` parameter. This way to handle a side-effect via parameters is a much better design than, say, using a global variable to track the pseudo-random state. It explicitly surfaces the side-effect to the user, allowing it to be controlled.

> **Note**: This random function is unfortunately specific to the concrete type `PermutedCongruential`. In Chapter 4, "Generics", you'll see the techniques for working with any type conforming to `RandomNumberGenerator`, including `SystemRandomNumberGenerator()`. If you want to see this function written generically and without logic duplication, check out the playground **RandomPointGeneric** in this chapter's final resources folder.

Test deterministic random numbers with this code in your playground:

```
var pcg = PermutedCongruential(seed: 1234)
for _ in 1...10 {
  print(Point.random(inRadius: 1, using: &pcg))
}
```

These look like random numbers but are reproducible. The tenth random point will always be Point(x: 0.43091531644250813, y: 0.3236366519677818) given a starting seed of 1234.

Enumerations

Swift enumerations are another powerful value type that lets you model a finite set of states. Add this to your playground:

```
enum Quadrant: CaseIterable, Hashable {
  case i, ii, iii, iv

  init?(_ point: Point) {
    guard !point.x.isZero && !point.y.isZero else {
      return nil
    }

    switch (point.x.sign, point.y.sign) {
    case (.plus, .plus):
      self = .i
    case (.minus, .plus):
      self = .ii
    case (.minus, .minus):
      self = .iii
    case (.plus, .minus):
      self = .iv
    }
  }
}
```

This code creates an abstraction for quadrants in the two-dimensional plane. The CaseIterable conformance lets you access an array, allCases. Hashable means you can use it as an element of a Set or key of as the key of a Dictionary. You can make the initializer failable because points on the x- or y-axis aren't defined to be in a quadrant. An optional initializer lets you document this possibility naturally.

Try it out with this:

```
Quadrant(Point(x: 10, y: -3)) // evaluates to .iv
Quadrant(.zero) // evaluates to nil
```

Types as documentation

Types can serve as documentation. For example, if you have a function that returns an Int, you don't need to worry if the function will return 3.14159 or "Giraffe". It just can't happen. In a sense, the compiler rules out all those crazy possibilities.

> **Historical note**: One of the more famous software engineering failures came in 1999 with the Mars Climate Orbiter. Engineers at the Jet Propulsion Lab in California wrote their functions with metric impulse values measured in newton-seconds. In contrast, engineers at Lockheed Martin Astronautics in Colorado wrote their functions with English units of pound-seconds. Imagine if the two groups had made units explicit with a type. Doing so might have prevented the costly ($125M+) error that caused the space probe to skip off (or burn up in) the Mars atmosphere.

Foundation has an extensible set of types for dealing with common physical units, such as length, temperature and angle. Consider angles, which can be expressed in a variety of units. Add this to the playground:

```swift
let a = Measurement(value: .pi/2,
                    unit: UnitAngle.radians)

let b = Measurement(value: 90,
                    unit: UnitAngle.degrees)

a + b  // 180 degrees
```

The variable a is a right angle expressed in radians, and b is a right angle expressed in degrees. You can add them together to see that they're 180 degrees. The + operator converts them to a base unit before adding the values.

Of course, Swift lets you define overloads of standard math functions. You can make a type-safe version of cos() and sin().

```swift
func cos(_ angle: Measurement<UnitAngle>) -> Double {
  cos(angle.converted(to: .radians).value)
}

func sin(_ angle: Measurement<UnitAngle>) -> Double {
  sin(angle.converted(to: .radians).value)
}

cos(a)  // 0
cos(b)  // 0
```

```
sin(a)  // 1
sin(b)  // 1
```

The function takes an angle and converts it explicitly to radians before passing it to the standard transcendental `cos()` and `sin()` functions. With this new API, the compiler can check to make sure you're passing angle types instead of something nonsensical.

> **Note**: Several popular frameworks take care of angle types. In addition to the Foundation's `Measurement` type, SwiftUI also defines an `Angle` that explicitly initializes with degrees or radians. A generic version that abstracts across all the different floating-point types is proposed for the official Swift numerics package.

Improving type ergonomics

One of the great things about Swift is how you can extend the functionality and interoperability of existing types that you don't even have the source for. For example, suppose you wanted your program to deal with polar coordinates. You'll use angles a lot, so add this:

```
typealias Angle = Measurement<UnitAngle>

extension Angle {
  init(radians: Double) {
    self = Angle(value: radians, unit: .radians)
  }
  init(degrees: Double) {
    self = Angle(value: degrees, unit: .degrees)
  }
  var radians: Double {
    converted(to: .radians).value
  }
  var degrees: Double {
    converted(to: .degrees).value
  }
}
```

`typealias` gives you a shorter, descriptive spelling for angles. You can now go back and improve your `sin` and `cos` implementations like this:

```
func cos(_ angle: Angle) -> Double {
  cos(angle.radians)
}
```

```
func sin(_ angle: Angle) -> Double {
  sin(angle.radians)
}
```

You'll probably agree that those look much nicer. Now, you can define a polar coordinate type:

```
struct Polar: Equatable {
  var angle: Angle
  var distance: Double
}
```

Because you'll want to flip between xy coordinates and polar coordinates easily, you can add type converting initializers for those:

```
// Convert polar-coordinates to xy-coordinates
extension Point {
  init(_ polar: Polar) {
    self.init(x: polar.distance * cos(polar.angle),
              y: polar.distance * sin(polar.angle))
  }
}

// Convert xy-coordinates to polar coordinates
extension Polar {
  init(_ point: Point) {
    self.init(angle: Angle(radians: atan2(point.y, point.x)),
              distance: hypot(point.x, point.y))
  }
}
```

Notice how your abstractions build on one another, making an even more powerful environment to work with. Your types are letting you hide complexity layer-by-layer.

Now, you can easily go from xy coordinates to polar coordinates and vice-versa like this:

```
let coord = Point(x: 4, y: 3)
Polar(coord).angle.degrees // 36.87
Polar(coord).distance      // 5
```

Strong types mean you can't accidentally mix up polar coordinates and xy coordinates, but you can still easily switch between the two when that is what you intend.

Associated values

Enumerations in Swift are quite powerful because they let you associate information with a particular case. For example, you can create a fixed set of shapes:

```
enum Shape {
  case point(Point)
  case segment(start: Point, end: Point)
  case circle(center: Point, radius: Double)
  case rectangle(Rectangle)
}
```

As you can see, it's easy to compose types. You can succinctly model the valid states in your app and even prevent invalid states from being representable and thus compiling.

Using RawRepresentable

There's another essential tool for your tool chest. You have probably used RawRepresentable for enumerations without realizing it. Open the starter playground **RawRepresentable** and add the following:

```
enum Coin {
  case penny, nickel, dime, quarter
}
```

When you back the enumeration with an integer, character or string, it becomes RawRepresentable thanks to compiler magic. Replace the previous definition with this:

```
enum Coin: Int {
  case penny = 1, nickel = 5, dime = 10, quarter = 25
}
```

Being RawRepresentable means you can create and get the raw value. It also means that the type is Equatable, Hashable and Codable for free.

```
let lucky = Coin(rawValue: 1)
lucky?.rawValue  // returns Optional(1)
let notSoMuch = Coin(rawValue: 2)
```

You can use `RawRepresentable` directly to create simple checked types. Consider this example:

```
struct Email: RawRepresentable {
  var rawValue: String

  init?(rawValue: String) {
    guard rawValue.contains("@") else {
      return nil
    }
    self.rawValue = rawValue
  }
}
```

This simple type provides a form of documentation. Consider the signature of a function that uses it:

```
func send(message: String, to recipient: Email) throws {
  // some implementation
}
```

This function's easier to use because the parameter labels make it clear where `message` and `recipient` go and hard to misuse because of the specific types that the compiler can check. The type for `Email` means that it's only possible to pass around well-formed email addresses. (For this example, the check simply looks to make sure there is an @ in the address, but you can make it arbitrarily strict.)

Rather than having a property like `isValid`, it's better if you can make your custom type's initializer failable either by returning nil or throwing a more specific error when a valid instance can't be created. This explicit failure mode allows you to set up your code so the compiler forces you to check for errors. The reward is this: When you write a function that uses a type, you don't have to worry about half-baked instances that might not be valid. This pattern pushes data validation and error handling to your software stack's upper layers and lets the lower levels run efficiently without extra checks.

Exercises

Here are a few quick exercises to check your understanding. You can use the starter playground **Exercises** to get you started. It imports the types you've made so far. As always, it's best to give it an honest try before looking at the answers in the final version.

1. Generate 100 random points in the unit circle. How many does the second quadrant contain? Demonstrate the solution with code. Use `PermutedCongruential` with the seed 4321 to make your answer repeatable.

2. How many cups are in 1.5 liters? Use Foundation's `Measurement` types to figure it out.

3. Create an initializer for `Quadrant` that takes a polar coordinate.

QuadTree

Now, you'll get a little more experience with types by building a `QuadTree` type for `CGPoints`. This example will show you how to implement mutable value semantics when using class types for storage.

A `QuadTree` is an efficient tree data structure for finding points in a region. Instead of requiring **O(n)** to find points in a matching region, it only takes **O(log n)**. It does this by putting the points in nodes (or buckets). When a node reaches maximum capacity and overflows, it creates new child nodes that split the space into four equal parts. When it comes time to find points, you can binary search these nodes efficiently.

The final demo app will let you add some points and then find points in a region by dragging your finger around.

It will look like this:

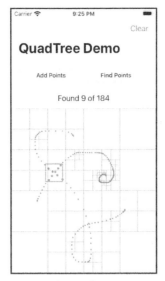

QuadTree demo app

The dots are points in QuadTree, and the rectangles show how the tree partitions the space. The heavier square and larger dots are a set of found points that you can move around.

When drawn as a traditional tree, the QuadTree data structure looks something like this:

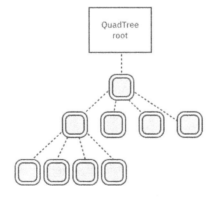

Single instance of a QuadTree

Each node has either zero or four children. The QuadTree type itself is a lightweight value type. It has a private property root to a reference type Node at the top of the tree. It's cheap to copy a QuadTree because copies share the Node reference. Graphically, sharing looks something like this:

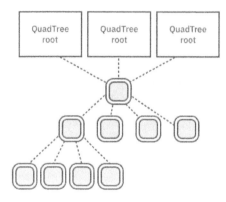

Three QuadTree instances sharing the same node storage

To keep nice value semantics when one of the shared instances decides to modify the tree by adding a point, it must make a deep copy of the tree and add the point. This process is called **copy-on-write** or sometimes **CoW** for short. Graphically, you end up with something that looks like this:

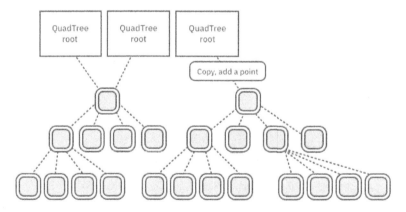

Copy-on-write storage

In this case, you make a copy before adding the new point. The node overflows its capacity and subdivides itself into four new sub-nodes.

Implementing QuadTree

Begin the implementation of QuadTree by opening the **QuadTree** Xcode starter project. Use the file navigator to familiarize yourself with the files in the project. Skim through these five files without worrying too much about the details.

- **AppMain.swift**: Contains the basic definition of the SwiftUI app.

- **ContentView.swift**: The top-level user interface. It defines the picker for adding or finding points, a place to show the number of points found and a clear button. It also contains the drag gesture for inserting and finding points.

- **QuadTree.swift**: Stubs out the definition of QuadTree. This is where you'll do your work.

- **QuadTreeView.swift**: The canvas where points and rectangles are drawn. It finds the size of the view and reports it to the view-model so points can be stored in normalized coordinates ranging from zero to one.

- **QuadTreeViewModel.swift**: Connects the model (your QuadTree instance) to the user interface. This file contains the so-called business logic of your app.

You can build and run the app at this point, but you won't yet be able to insert and find points. To make that happen, you need to fill out the QuadTree type.

Open **QuadTree.swift**, which contains a skeleton definition.

Inside the QuadTree definition, add the private nested class Node:

```swift
private final class Node {
  let maxItemCapacity = 4
  var region: CGRect
  var points: [CGPoint] = []
  var quad: Quad?

  init(region: CGRect, points: [CGPoint] = [], quad: Quad? =
nil) {
    self.region = region
    self.quad = quad
    self.points = points
    self.points.reserveCapacity(maxItemCapacity)
    precondition(points.count <= maxItemCapacity)
  }

  struct Quad {
    // more to come...
  }
}
```

The nested class Node will do the heavy lifting for QuadTree. Each node instance keeps a region and can hold up to four points (the bucket size) before it spills over and subdivides itself into four more nodes contained in Quad's structure.

> **Note**: The bucket size is set to four so you can easily visualize what is happening. An actual implementation would probably have a much higher bucket size based on an analysis of insertion and find times.

Next, add this to the definition of Quad inside Node:

```
var northWest: Node
var northEast: Node
var southWest: Node
var southEast: Node

var all: [Node] { [northWest, northEast, southWest, southEast] }

init(region: CGRect) {
  let halfWidth = region.size.width * 0.5
  let halfHeight = region.size.height * 0.5

  northWest =
    Node(region: CGRect(x: region.origin.x,
                        y: region.origin.y,
                        width: halfWidth, height: halfHeight))
  northEast =
    Node(region: CGRect(x: region.origin.x + halfWidth,
                        y: region.origin.y,
                        width: halfWidth, height: halfHeight))
  southWest =
    Node(region: CGRect(x: region.origin.x, y:
                        region.origin.y + halfHeight,
                        width: halfWidth, height: halfHeight))
  southEast =
    Node(region: CGRect(x: region.origin.x + halfWidth,
                        y: region.origin.y + halfHeight,
                        width: halfWidth, height: halfHeight))
}
// more to come...
```

This code defines the four sub-nodes of a Quad. The initializer is verbose, but all it's doing is dividing the parent region into four equal sub-regions.

You need to be able to make a deep copy Node, so add this initializer and copy method to Quad:

```
init(northWest: Node, northEast: Node,
     southWest: Node, southEast: Node) {
  self.northWest = northWest
  self.northEast = northEast
  self.southWest = southWest
  self.southEast = southEast
}

func copy() -> Quad {
  Quad(northWest: northWest.copy(),
       northEast: northEast.copy(),
       southWest: southWest.copy(),
       southEast: southEast.copy())
}
```

That completes the definition of Quad.

Copying

The code above expects a copy() method on Node, so add that now to the body of Node:

```
func copy() -> Node {
  Node(region: region, points: points, quad: quad?.copy())
}
```

This function will resolve the four compiler errors. Somewhat amazingly, adding this allows Node and Quad to recursively copy themselves from a root node, all the way down the tree.

Next, add a helper method to subdivide a Node by adding this to the Node definition:

```
func subdivide() {
  precondition(quad == nil, "Can't subdivide a node already
subdivided")
  quad = Quad(region: region)
}
```

All this does is assign quad to an instance. The initializer that you wrote above does the real work of rectangle division. The precondition makes sure you aren't subdividing a node that has already been subdivided. It's always a good idea to check your assumptions if it's computationally cheap.

Next, write `insert` for `Node`. Add this:

```
@discardableResult
func insert(_ point: CGPoint) -> Bool {
  // 1
  if let quad = quad {
    return quad.northWest.insert(point) ||
      quad.northEast.insert(point) ||
      quad.southWest.insert(point) ||
      quad.southEast.insert(point)
  }
  else {
    // 2
    if points.count == maxItemCapacity {
      subdivide()
      return insert(point)
    }
    else {
      // 3
      guard region.contains(point) else {
        return false
      }
      points.append(point)
      return true
    }
  }
}
```

This function returns a `Bool` that is `true` if it inserts the point and `false` if it doesn't.

Here is a rundown of what the function does:

1. First, it checks whether the node has been subdivided. If it has, the function attempts to insert the point into each one of the nodes in the quad. The logical or `||` short-circuits and stops inserting as soon as it does.

2. If the node is at maximum capacity, it subdivides the node and attempts the insert again.

3. If the node is not at maximum capacity, it first checks whether the point falls inside the region the node is responsible for. If it does, it inserts it into the array of points and returns `true`.

The last method you'll define for `Node` is for finding points in a region. Add this method to the `Node` type:

```
func find(in searchRegion: CGRect) -> [CGPoint] {
  guard region.intersects(searchRegion) else {
```

```
      return []
  }
  var found = points.filter { searchRegion.contains($0) }
  if let quad = quad {
    found += quad.all.flatMap { $0.find(in: searchRegion) }
  }
  return found
}
```

This code first checks whether the search region overlaps with the region the node is responsible for. If it doesn't, it returns no points. This return is the base case of the recursion. Next, it filters the points in the region and adds them to the found list. Finally, if the node has been subdivided, it goes through the quads and recursively calls find(in:) to add points to the found list before returning it.

Implementing QuadTree methods

Now that you have completed the Node type, you can implement QuadTree's methods. First, add a private property to QuadTree right above count:

```
private var root: Node
```

The initializer of QuadTree specifies a region of space it handles. Replace the stubbed out implementation with this:

```
init(region: CGRect) {
    root = Node(region: region)
}
```

Next, replace find(in:) and points() in QuadTree with these:

```
func find(in searchRegion: CGRect) -> [CGPoint] {
    root.find(in: searchRegion)
}

func points() -> [CGPoint] {
    find(in: root.region)
}
```

find(in:) simply delegates to the root node. points() gathers all the points by finding them from the root node down.

Next, replace the placeholder for regions() that returns the region each Node is responsible for:

```
private func collectRegions(from node: Node) -> [CGRect] {
  var results = [node.region]
  if let quad = node.quad {
    results += quad.all.flatMap { collectRegions(from: $0) }
  }
  return results
}

func regions() -> [CGRect] {
  collectRegions(from: root)
}
```

regions() calls the private helper method collectRegions(from:), which recursively gathers all the regions of all the nodes.

Finally, replace an insert method with this implementation:

```
@discardableResult
mutating func insert(_ point: CGPoint) -> Bool {
  if !isKnownUniquelyReferenced(&root) {
    root = root.copy()
  }
  guard root.insert(point) else {
    return false
  }
  count += 1
  return true
}
```

This function is marked with @discardableResult because clients might not wish to check if the insertion succeeded. The only way it can fail is if you try to insert a point that is outside the region specified by the QuadTree initializer.

This code is where the **copy-on-write** magic happens. Swift has a special function, isKnownUniquelyReferenced(), which returns true if there is only one instance. If there is more than one instance, you need to make a copy of the underlying tree. Then, you can add the point.

The property count exists to make it cheap **O(1)** to know QuadTree's point count without recursively traversing all the nodes. It only gets incremented if the insertion succeeds. The success of insertion depends on the original size of the region QuadTree was initialized with.

> **Note**: To maintain value semantics on mutation, you **must make a deep copy** of the underlying storage for every mutating method. It's an *optimization* not to copy with the instance if it's not shared. This optimization can be prevented if extra copies are lying around. The SwiftUI framework has special property wrappers @State and @Published used to manage UI updates. Unfortunately, these wrappers make an extra copy that interferes with the isKnownUniquelyReferenced optimization. If you look closely at **QuadTreeViewModel.swift**, you'll see quadTree is not a @Published property but instead calls objectWillChange.send() directly to handle UI update. Doing this prevents extra copying from happening, which will slow the user interface after a few hundred points are added.

Build and run the app. Drag your finger around to add some points. If you tap to add points one by one, you'll see that a region subdivides itself on the fifth tap because the node overflows maximum capacity. But finding points in a region is where QuadTree shines. Rather than traversing the entire point list, it can focus on a particular region quickly. You can try it out by switching to find mode and dragging the little find box around. Finding points in a region quickly is why QuadTree is used in collision detection and compression applications.

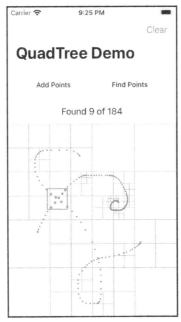

QuadTree demo app

Key points

Swift is a strongly typed language that allows the compiler to check your program's correctness before it runs. The better you get at working with types, the easier it will be to write correct programs.

Here are some key points to keep in mind from this chapter:

- Structures, enumerations and classes are the fundamental named types that Swift uses to make every other concrete type, including `Bool`, `Int`, `Optional`, `String`, `Array`, etc.

- Create custom types to solve problems in your domain elegantly.

- Structures and enumerations are value types. Classes are reference types.

- Any type can be designed to have value semantics.

- The most straightforward way to get value semantics is to use a value type (structure or enumeration) that only contains other types with value semantics.

- All the standard types, including `String`, `Array`, `Set` and `Dictionary`, already have value semantics, making them easy to compose into larger types with value semantics.

- Making a class immutable is one way to give reference types value semantics.

- Value types are generally copied around on the stack, whereas reference types are allocated on the heap and are reference counted.

- Reference types have a built-in notion of lifetime and identity.

- Instance methods secretly pass in self.

- The mutating instance methods of value types pass `inout self`.

- Enumerations model a finite set of states.

- Avoid initializing half-baked, invalid objects. Instead, create failing initializers.

- A good set of types can act as compiler-checkable documentation.

- The foundation `Measurement` types make working with different units less error-prone by defining them as concrete types.

- Swift lets you improve the usage ergonomics for types you don't even own.

- The protocol `RawRepresentable` lets you create simple, expressive types.

- Copy-on-write is a way to give reference types mutating value semantics.

Chapter 3: Protocols

By Marin Benčević

If you've used Swift before, you've probably used protocols. *A lot*. Protocols and **protocol-oriented programming** are built into the DNA of Swift, and it's hard to imagine what Swift would look like without all the power its protocols hold. Because they're an integral part of Swift, this whole chapter focuses on explaining how protocols work and how you can leverage them in your code to produce clean, long-lasting and easy-to-refactor APIs.

As a Swift developer, you probably already know the basics of protocols. Still, it's a good idea to go through a brief refresher on the basics of protocols as well as some of their more rarely used features. Once you remind yourself of everything protocols can do, you'll look at how they work behind the scenes. You'll also learn about common patterns that use protocols as well as some useful gotchas and edge cases to keep in mind.

You'll do this by building a tiny RESTful networking library, which you'll then use to make an app that displays raywenderlich.com articles. Before you get your hands dirty, you'll first go through a brief refresher on Swift's protocols.

Getting started with protocols

To understand why protocols are important, step back and see how statically typed languages work. Look at the following line of code:

```
counter.increment(by: 10)
```

Say that `counter` is an object of a class called `Counter`, and you're calling an instance method called `increment(by:)`. This instance method may or may not exist in the class — maybe you forgot to write it. In a more dynamic language such as Objective-C, the compiler will happily run the code and nothing will happen. Some dynamic languages, such as JavaScript, will run the code but show an error saying that `increment` does not exist. Swift, being a statically typed language, will first check whether `increment(by:)` exists in that class, and if it doesn't, won't even run your code. Although sometimes it seems like the compiler is complaining, really it's saving you from making stupid mistakes.

The compiler knows whether the method exists because it knows the type of `counter` is `Counter`, and it can then query the `Counter` class for a matching `increment` method. But there are cases where neither the compiler nor you is exactly sure which type you'd like to use. What if you want to define a single function that can increment different kinds of counters — not just your own `Counter` but also a `DoubleCounter`, `UserCounter`, etc.?

Consider the following method:

```
func incrementCounters(counters: [?]) {
  for counter in counters {
    counter.increment(by: 1)
  }
}
```

What should be the type of `counters`? It doesn't make sense to limit it to just `[Counter]`, because you want other types to work as well. You could try using `[Any]` but you'd get an error — Swift can't know if an instance of Any will have the `increment(by:)` method. What you need is a way to tell the compiler "I want any type that has an `increment(by:)` method." That's where protocols come in.

A protocol could look as follows:

```
protocol Incrementable {
  func increment(by: Int)
}
```

By defining a protocol with a method requirement, you can use the protocol as a type, saying "This method receives anything that implements Incrementable."

```
func incrementCounters(counters: [Incrementable]) {
  for counter in counters {
    counter.increment(by: 1)
  }
}
```

When you write a concrete implementation of the protocol, Swift will verify that you declared the increment(by:) method. Knowing this, the Swift compiler can guarantee that your function will work for all instances of Incrementable.

Hiding information

Protocols are a tool of the type system that allows you to use multiple types as the same super-type by *hiding* information about a type. For instance, you know that for a square with sides a and b, a == b is true. You also know that a square is a rectangle. By loosening the requirement that a == b, you can treat a square as a rectangle and define a single way to calculate the area. That way, you won't need to write two implementations.

In the same way, protocols hide all other members of a class or struct, except the ones exposed by the protocol. This allows you to use multiple types in the same place.

Another way to look at protocols is as *interfaces* (in fact, many languages call them that). Kitchen appliances, computers and phone chargers are quite different, but they all turn the same interface toward the wall socket: a plug. All a socket knows is that the device is something that needs power and has a plug. In the same way, if you were modeling different devices in Swift, you could make a Pluggable protocol that exposes a plug(into:) method, allowing the Socket to work with all possible devices.

Encoding semantics

So far you read about how a type can conform to a protocol if it implements the required methods and protocols. In Swift, there is another important aspect to protocols: semantics. In programming, there are things that you can't encode in the function signature. For instance, you might want to sort some arrays. To allow for different sorting algorithms, you implement a Sorter protocol with methods to sort an array.

However, you are working on an app with lots of data, and your algorithms need to be very fast, so you might want to limit `Sorter` implementations to those with Big O notation of O(n) or faster. Maybe you also require that the sorting algorithm is stable. A stable algorithm keeps repeated elements in the same order after sorting. These are all examples of things you can't let the compiler check for you. Instead, you have to add these requirements in type names and documentation, so you change your protocol name to `StableEfficientSorter`.

If protocols were only method requirements, it would make it hard to write truly generic functions since implementation details could completely change the way your code works. Protocols are also used to describe semantic requirements. This is exactly the reason why Swift doesn't conform types to protocols automatically. When writing code, you must consider which *semantic* requirements are important for your protocols and clearly document them.

Protocol syntax

Now that you understand the semantics of protocols, it's time for a brief refresher on protocol syntax.

> **Note**: For this section of the chapter, you don't need to type along. But should you wish to do so, start by creating a new empty playground that imports `UIKit` and `SwiftUI`. Alternatively, you can find the code used for this section under **final/Protocols.playground**.

Here's a simple enum and a protocol:

```
enum Language {
  case english, german, croatian
}

protocol Localizable {
  static var supportedLanguages: [Language] { get }
}
```

The protocol has one required member, `supportedLanguages`. In this case, this is a variable (not a function) that needs to have a getter. A setter is not required by the protocol, which means computed variables or variables declared with the `private(set)` access modifier will also satisfy the requirement. It is also marked as `static`, which means that the conforming variable needs to be `static` as well.

Next, take a look at another protocol.

```
protocol ImmutableLocalizable: Localizable {
   func changed(to language: Language) -> Self
}
```

This protocol **inherits** from the one mentioned earlier. Inheritance in protocols works similarly to classes: All the protocol's requirements are passed onto its child protocols. This means the ImmutableLocalizable protocol has *two* required members: supportedLanguages and changed(to:). Unlike supportedLanguages, changed(to:) is a function and must be declared as returning Self, the current type. For instance, if you declare this function inside a class called FeedView, Self will have the value of FeedView.

Next, look at another protocol that inherits from Localizable:

```
protocol MutableLocalizable: Localizable {
   mutating func change(to language: Language)
}
```

This protocol is very similar to the last one, but you'll notice a new keyword: mutating. You're probably familiar with this keyword because you have to use it in a struct's method when the method's body changes a property of that struct. In protocols, it means the same thing. Structs need to implement this method by making it mutating, but classes don't. Classes are already mutable by default, so there's no need for an additional keyword.

Implementing protocols

Now that you've declared three protocols, it's time to implement them in a few of your types. If you're used to other programming languages, you might be surprised to hear that, in Swift, every type can implement a protocol. This includes structs, classes and even enums!

Start by declaring a struct called Text, which will implement one of your protocols:

```
struct Text: ImmutableLocalizable {
   static let supportedLanguages: [Language] =
[.english, .croatian]

   var content = "Help"

   func changed(to language: Language) -> Self {
      let newContent: String
      switch language {
      case .english: newContent = "Help"
```

```
    case .german: newContent = "Hilfe"
    case .croatian: newContent = "Pomoć"
    }
    return Text(content: newContent)
  }
}
```

The Text struct implements the ImmutableLocalizable protocol. This means it needs to implement all members of both the ImmutableLocalizable and Localizable properties because one inherits from the other.

You also can conform types to protocols using extensions:

```
extension UILabel: MutableLocalizable {
  static let supportedLanguages: [Language] =
[.english, .german]

  func change(to language: Language) {
    switch language {
    case .english: text = "Help"
    case .german: text = "Hilfe"
    case .croatian: text = "Pomoć"
    }
  }
}
```

You'll see extensions used to conform a type to a protocol more often than not. Doing so allows you to conform types outside your control, like the ones in SwiftUI or UIKit, to your protocols. It also provides a nice way to structure your files so everything protocol-related is within an extension, giving you an easier overview of the file.

Extending protocols

Not all members of a protocol need to be required. You can provide a default implementation of a protocol's member by extending the protocol itself:

```
extension Localizable {
  static var supportedLanguages: [Language] {
    return [.english]
  }
}
```

> **Note**: There are a few caveats to consider with extending protocols like this. Later in this chapter, you'll learn exactly how this extension works and a few edge cases to be wary of.

Here, you extend `Localizable` with a default implementation of `supportedLanguages`. Each type conforming to `Localizable` now has access to that implementation, so they don't have to define their own.

```
struct Image: Localizable {
  // no need to add `supportedLanguages` here
}
```

So far, you have worked with protocols that any type in your code can implement. You can limit your protocols to be conformed to only by classes. You do this by inheriting the `AnyObject` protocol — a protocol that each class implicitly conforms to.

```
protocol UIKitLocalizable: AnyObject, Localizable {
  func change(to language: Language)
}
```

Note that, although this protocol has the same requirements as `MutableLocalizable`, the `mutating` keyword got lost. Because this protocol can be implemented only by classes, there's no reason to specify that something is mutating: In classes, everything is already mutable by default.

Speaking of limiting the conformance to a protocol, you can also limit a protocol to only subclasses of a specific class.

```
protocol LocalizableViewController where Self: UIViewController
{
  func showLocalizedAlert(text: String)
}
```

Here, your protocol can be used by only `UIViewController` or subclasses thereof.

Protocols are abstract. But that doesn't mean you can't get as specific as required to limit conformance to exactly the types you need.

Now that you have a bunch of types and protocols, you can use them in their full glory. For instance, you can define a single function that works with *all* `MutableLocalizable` types.

```
func localize(
  _ localizables: inout [MutableLocalizable],
  to language: Language
) {
  for var localizable in localizables {
    localizable.change(to: language)
  }
}
```

Note that you use an array of MutableLocalizable, which can be filled with any combination of types as long as they all implement MutableLocalizable.

Protocols have immense power. But it's hard to see just how useful they are until you work on a large codebase and for a long time. Everything protocols offer can be approximated in other ways, using inheritance, generics, function overloading or copying and pasting code. What all those ways lack is clear intentions and semantics, as well as protocol-guaranteed safety and ease of refactoring.

Now that you have the basics down, it's time to get into some nitty-gritty protocol details.

Behind the scenes of protocols

Knowing the surface-level of protocols is enough to go out in the world and use them. But to truly wrap your head around the edge cases and performance considerations of protocols, you need to look deeper into Swift's inner workings.

Static and dynamic dispatch

More specifically, you need to understand what happens when a function is called. Functions seem like compiler magic: You declare them in one place and that code is then somehow executed from another place. However, it's a lot less magical than you might think. What happens is that, at runtime, when Swift finds a function name, it jumps to the address of that function and starts executing the code. But jumping to a function's address is not always straightforward.

There are two main mechanisms for storing and calling functions: static and dynamic dispatch. Static dispatch is fairly straightforward: It happens when you know for sure that a function will never change. Static dispatch is used, among other reasons, for global functions and methods declared in structs as well as methods on final classes.

In those cases, there is no function overriding to worry about, so the compiler can, in a sense, *hard-code* the function's address and hop to that whenever the function is referenced.

> **Note**: Aside from method dispatch, there is also a technique called *inlining* that Swift uses extensively. Inlining replaces a function call with the full body of that function at compile time. This is the fastest way to call a function, but it's only available with static dispatch and under specific conditions.

When you add pesky inheritance and protocols, things get a bit more complicated. A method called on a non-`final` class instance can be declared in multiple possible places. It can be declared inside the class, any of its parent classes, an extension or even a protocol extension. This means the compiler can't know ahead of time what the exact address of a function will be. Instead, it uses something called the **witness table** (sometimes also called the v-table or the virtual table).

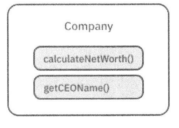
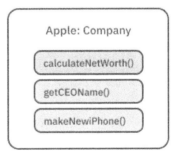

As the compiler goes through your code, it will create a table for each class. This table will have two columns: one for an offset in the table and one for the function at that offset. Each function in the class is stored in the table, which is stored in your working memory. A subclass will get a copy of its parent's table and then replace the rows of the method it wants to override. Now that a witness table is built, Swift can use the table at runtime. When it encounters a method call, Swift knows which offset in the table corresponds to that method.

This allows *dynamic* changing of the implementation of a method with the same name, allowing features like inheritance, polymorphism and even protocols. But these features come at a cost. Calling functions from table rows adds a constant overhead for each function call. It also prevents inlining and other compiler optimizations, making dynamic dispatch slower than static dispatch.

Dispatch in protocols

The whole dispatch story is interesting, but you're probably wondering how this all relates to protocols. I mentioned that inheritance complicates the compiler's life by requiring dynamic dispatch. Well, protocols support inheritance, too. Aside from that, multiple classes and structs can conform to the same protocol and implement the same method. And then they can be used the same way, like in the examples earlier in this chapter. If you're using a protocol as the type of your instance, Swift can't know ahead of time if the Localizable instance will be UILabel or Text. So it needs to dispatch methods dynamically.

Dispatching protocol methods is similar to how classes work. Every type that implements a protocol gets its own **protocol witness table**. The table has two columns again, one with the function and the other with the offset of that function. Each member of the protocol (the methods and variables declared as the protocol requirements) has its own row in the table. This table is then stored together with each instance that implements a protocol. Swift can then, at runtime, look up the correct function in the protocol witness table and call it. If you're using a class instance, Swift can look the function up in both the class and the protocol witness table, dynamically finding the correct implementation.

Dealing with extensions

So far, so good. But there's one feature that can make your head spin when thinking about dispatch: extensions. When you define an extension on a protocol to implement a default method, is that extension stored in the protocol's table or an implementing instance's table? What if you add a protocol extension for a method that is not part of the protocol requirements? Understanding static and dynamic dispatch will help you answer these questions.

First, you'll deal with extending protocols to provide default method implementations. Set up a protocol so it has an extension that provides the default implementation for one of its methods:

```swift
protocol Greetable {
  func greet() -> String
}

extension Greetable {
  func greet() -> String {
    return "Hello"
  }
}
```

Next, create a struct implementing the protocol:

```
struct GermanGreeter: Greetable {
}
```

Then, make an instance of your new struct and call its protocol method:

```
let greeter = GermanGreeter()
print(greeter.greet())
```

As expected, because `GermanGreeter` doesn't implement its own `greet` method, the line above prints out "Hello". The way this works is that the default `greet` implementation is copied to every type that conforms to the protocol and added to their protocol witness table. Note that the protocol itself doesn't have a table. Only concrete types do.

Your greeting is obviously wrong. Translate it to German by implementing the method inside `GermanGreeter`:

```
func greet() -> String {
    return "Hallo"
}
```

One letter is all it takes to make it German. If you run the code again, it'll print "Hallo". This happens because your new implementation replaced the extension method in the protocol witness table. The same thing happens when you override a method in a class.

So far, everything works as expected, right? Now, try to create something unexpected. Add a new method in the protocol extension:

```
func leave() -> String {
    return "Bye"
}
```

This function lives inside the protocol extension, but it's *not* declared as a requirement of the protocol. However, every type implementing the protocol still has access to the method. Verify this by calling the new method:

```
print(greeter.leave())
```

As expected, this outputs "Goodbye". Translate this again by adding a new method in `GermanGreeter`:

```
func leave() -> String {
```

```
    return "Tschüss"
  }
```

If you run the code again, it works just like before: The new method gets called and the output is "Tschüss". However, if you change the declaration of `greeter` to use the protocol:

```
let greeter: Greetable = GermanGreeter()
```

`greet` still outputs "Hallo", but `leave` is now in English and outputs Goodbye!?

Swift seems to entirely bypass the function you declared in the struct and calls the function from the protocol extension. Although this is unexpected, there's a clear reason why it happens. Your first hint is that the called function depends on the variable's declared type. This means polymorphism doesn't work. Earlier, I mentioned that dynamic dispatch enables polymorphism, so `leave` must be called using static dispatch.

Indeed, extension methods rely entirely on static dispatch. There is no table involved in calling `leave` — Swift calls it statically on the variable's type. `greet` works as expected because by adding it to the protocol's requirements, you forced Swift to create a protocol witness table entry for the method, enabling dynamic dispatch.

This is important because adding extension methods to protocols is quite common in Swift. It's a great way to add additional reusable functionality to your structs and classes. But always keep in mind that if you ever want to override the extension method, you need to add it as a protocol requirement. Otherwise, you might end up with very unexpected results.

Protocols and the type system

Protocols really shine when you have a good type system supporting them, and Swift is definitely an example of that. In this section, you'll get into what protocol types are and how to use them most effectively to your advantage.

Existentials

Earlier, you defined a variable as a protocol:

```
let greeter: Greetable = GermanGreeter()
```

This code probably isn't very surprising: You define variables all the time. However, there is a big difference between using `Greetable` here and using a concrete type like `Int`. `Greetable`, though it might look and act as a regular type, is called an **existential type**. Although the name sounds fancy, it's not that complex of a concept: You can think of existential types as placeholders for a real, concrete type. The compiler can interpret them as saying "There exists some type that conforms to this protocol." Existential types allow you to use protocols as types of method parameters, array elements, variables and other data structures without thinking about it.

Using protocols as types

You've already seen a few examples of using protocols as types, such as:

```
func greet(with greeter: Greeter) -> Void
let englishGreeter: Greeter = EnglishGreeter()
let allGreeters: [Greeter] = [englishGreeter]
```

There also are many less-known but useful ways you can use protocols. For instance, you can compose multiple types into a single type using the & operator:

```
func localizedGreet(with greeter: Greeter & Localizable)
```

The `greeter` parameter from above must be a type that conforms to both `Greeter` *and* `Localizable`. You can compose a struct type with protocols (`Date & Codable`), a class type with protocols (`UITableViewCell & Selectable`) or multiple protocols like above. You can also string together as many protocols as you want in the composition. It's not limited to only two members.

However, you can only use these composed types, also called **non-nominal types**, as the type of a variable. You can't, for instance, define an extension on `Greeter & Localizable`. You can do that in other ways, though.

For instance, you can define an extension of all subclasses of a class that also conform to a protocol:

```
extension UITableViewDelegate where Self: UIViewController {
  func showAlertForSelectedCell(at index: IndexPath) {
    // ...
  }
}
```

Here, all `UIViewControllers` that conform to `UITableViewDelegate` automatically get an implementation of `showAlertForSelectedCell`.

You can also drill down to extend generic types where their generic parameter conforms to a protocol:

```
extension Array where Element: Greetable {
  var allGreetings: String {
    self.map { $0.greet() }.joined()
  }
}
```

You can take that a step further and add conformance to a protocol for a generic type whose generic parameter conforms to a protocol:

```
extension Array: Localizable where Element: Localizable {
  static var supportedLanguages: [Language] {
    Element.supportedLanguages
  }
}
```

The extension above makes all arrays `Localizable` as long as their `Element` type is also `Localizable`. This is exactly the way Swift makes an array of `Codable` items also conform to `Codable`, an array of `Equatable` items conform to `Equatable`, etc.

You'll discover more about these sorts of extensions in the next chapter, when you learn about generics in Swift.

Synthesized protocol conformance

If you've used Swift for a while, maybe you've noticed that there are some protocols like `Codable` that magically work as soon as you conform to them. This happens when Swift generates a synthesized protocol implementation for you. Swift does this for `Equatable`, `Hashable`, `Comparable` and the two `Codable` protocols: `Encodable` and `Decodable`.

There are limitations to this for each protocol. Usually, Swift can generate conformance to a protocol only if all your properties also conform to that protocol. In the case of `Hashable`, for instance, all your properties need to be hashable for Swift to synthesize the required methods.

```
struct User: Hashable {
  let name: String
  let email: String
  let id: UUID
}
```

If you add a property that isn't itself `Hashable`, Swift will complain and you'll need to add your implementation.

Protocol-oriented programming

Enough theory! It's time to get your hands dirty and work with protocols to build an easy to use networking library similar to Alamofire. In this part of the chapter, you'll use protocols to make an API nice and clean. In the next chapter, you'll keep working on your library but introduce generics to make it even easier to use.

Start by opening the starter project provided in this chapter's materials. If you build and run the project, you'll see a list of one hard-coded article. You'll change this app so it downloads articles from the raywenderlich.com API, building your own little learning platform! The app already contains the necessary UI in the **Views** group. It also includes an **ArticlesViewModel.swift** file, which you'll modify to load actual data from the API. The model you'll be downloading is inside **Article.swift**: All the decoding code is already written for you.

By the end of this section, you'll have a screen that fetches a list of articles, as well as their images, from the raywenderlich.com API. You'll also use dependency inversion and testing to verify that your code works.

Now that you're familiar with the project, you'll start working on it by defining a protocol that represents a network request. Create a new Swift file called **Request.swift**. Add an enum to the file:

```
enum HTTPMethod: String {
  case get = "GET"
  case post = "POST"
  case put = "PUT"
  case patch = "PATCH"
  case delete = "DELETE"
}
```

According to the REST protocol, when you make a request, you need to tell the server which HTTP REST method you'd like to use for the request. Here, you define a handy enum that will make it easier to select the proper method.

Next, add a protocol to the bottom of the file:

```
protocol Request {
  var url: URL { get }
  var method: HTTPMethod { get }
}
```

This protocol is an abstract representation of an HTTP REST request. It includes the requested URL as well as the method you defined earlier. You can go a step further by adding another property to the request to represent URL parameters or the data to be sent to the server. But for now, you'll keep it simple.

Now, you can create your first Request implementation. You'll create a struct that encompasses a request to fetch a list of articles. Create a new Swift file called **ArticleRequest.swift**, and add the following struct to the file:

```
struct ArticleRequest: Request {
  var url: URL {
    let baseURL = "https://api.raywenderlich.com/api"
    let path = "/contents?filter[content_types][]=article"
    return URL(string: baseURL + path)!
  }

  var method: HTTPMethod { .get }
}
```

You conform to the Request protocol by implementing its two required members. For the URL, you return the appropriate raywenderlich.com API endpoint. Because you're just fetching a list, the proper method to use is GET.

Adding a 'Networker' class

Now, you have a request, but you don't have a way to *do* anything with the request. You'll fix that by adding a `Networker` class that will be responsible for initiating your `Request` implementations.

Create another Swift file called **Networker.swift**. Add the following to the file:

```
import Combine

class Networker {
  func fetch(_ request: Request) -> AnyPublisher<Data, URLError>
{
    var urlRequest = URLRequest(url: request.url)
    urlRequest.httpMethod = request.method.rawValue

    return URLSession.shared
      .dataTaskPublisher(for: urlRequest)
      .compactMap { $0.data }
      .eraseToAnyPublisher()
  }
}
```

First, you import Combine because you'll use it to more easily manage the asynchronous nature of network requests. You define a class called `Networker` with a single method: `fetch(_:)`. This method receives an implementation of your `Request` protocol. It then creates a `URLRequest` based on the request and uses `URLSession` to fetch the request. Instead of returning the requested data, `fetch(_:)` returns a publisher of that data in the form of `AnyPublisher<Data, URLError>`.

You now have all the pieces to fetch the articles. All that's left is to assemble those pieces. Open **ArticlesViewModel.swift** and add a new property to the top of the class:

```
var networker = Networker()
```

The view model's `fetchArticles()` gets called by the view as soon as it appears and is supposed to load articles from the API. Replace its contents with the following code:

```
let request = ArticleRequest()
let decoder = JSONDecoder()
networker.fetch(request)
  .decode(type: Articles.self, decoder: decoder)
  .map { $0.data.map { $0.article } }
  .replaceError(with: [])
  .receive(on: DispatchQueue.main)
```

```
.assign(to: \.articles, on: self)
.store(in: &cancellables)
```

First, you create your article request and a JSON decoder. Next, you call `fetch(_:)` to initiate the request. You wrote a pretty big chain of methods here, but it's fairly readable. `fetch(_:)` gives you a `Publisher` of `Data`, which you decode into `Articles`, a helper struct that's there to match the JSON structure of the API. You then convert your `Articles` instance into an `Article` array in the `map`. After you replace any error you get with an empty array, you switch to the main thread. Finally, you assign the received results to the `articles` property. Because the property is marked as `@Published`, the view will update itself automatically.

Whew! That's a lot of explaining. The good news is, you can now build and run your project to see a list of articles fetched from raywenderlich.com! If you don't see any content, wait for a few seconds while the data is being downloaded.

You should see a bunch of articles presented on your screen. You probably noticed the titles and descriptions are all there but all the images are missing. You don't have to be Sherlock to figure out why: You never wrote any code to download images. It's time to fix that.

Downloading images

To fetch the articles, you created a new Request implementation. Naturally, to download images, you'll do the same. Create a new Swift file called **ImageRequest.swift**. Add the following struct to the file:

```
struct ImageRequest: Request {
  let url: URL
  var method: HTTPMethod { .get }
}
```

Instead of hard-coding a URL like in the article request, this time you'll receive a URL in the initializer. This will make this struct capable of loading any image on the internet.

Next, head back to **ArticlesViewModel.swift** to initiate your new request. Each row in the list will call fetchImage(for:) as soon as it appears. Add the following code inside fetchImage(for:):

```
guard article.downloadedImage == nil,
  let articleIndex = articles.firstIndex(where: { $0.id ==
article.id })
else {
  return
}
```

Because this function is called every time a row appears on the screen, it's important to keep performance in mind, in terms of both scrolling speed and saving the user's bandwidth. You'll do this by caching the results. Once you download an image, store it inside the Article object. Before downloading an image, first check that your Article doesn't already have an image downloaded. This will save you from downloading the same image over and over as the user scrolls.

Still inside fetchImage(for:), continue with the following code to download the image:

```
let request = ImageRequest(url: article.image)
networker.fetch(request)
  .map(UIImage.init)
  .replaceError(with: nil)
  .receive(on: DispatchQueue.main)
  .sink { [weak self] image in
    self?.articles[articleIndex].downloadedImage = image
  }
  .store(in: &cancellables)
```

This code is similar to the code you wrote in `fetchArticles`. This time, instead of decoding JSON, you're converting the data into `UIImage` and replacing any errors with a `nil` image. You then store the image inside the article object.

Build and run your project again.

You have images! It's time to pat yourself on the back and take a breath, but you're only getting started. There's a lot more power to be gained from using protocols.

Getting fancy with extensions

The first change you'll make is to reduce your decoding code in the view model by defining a protocol that handles decoding for you. Create a new Swift file called **URLSessionDecodable.swift**. Then, add a new protocol to the file:

```
protocol URLSessionDecodable {
  init(from output: Data) throws
}
```

This protocol encompasses all structs that can be initialized from `URLSessions`'s output, such as your `Article`.

However, you never actually decode a single `Article` object. You decode *an array* of articles. That's why, instead of conforming `Article` to your new protocol, you'll conform `Array<Article>`.

Open **Article.swift** and add an extension to the bottom of the file:

```
extension Array: URLSessionDecodable where Element == Article {
  init(from output: Data) throws {
    let decoder = JSONDecoder()
    let articlesCollection = try decoder.decode(Articles.self,
from: output)
    let articles = articlesCollection.data.map { $0.article }
    self.init(articles)
  }
}
```

This is about as close as you can get to black magic with Swift extensions. Here's how you should read the first line: "Extend `Array` to conform to `URLSessionDecodable` when its `Element` is `Article`." Earlier, you saw a similar extension when `Element` conforms to a protocol. When you're talking not about conformance but a concrete type, you need to use the == operator to signify that element *is* that type, rather than any subtype of that type.

Inside the extension, you implement the protocol by decoding the data into `Articles`, and then turning that into an array of `Article` by calling a different `Array` initializer.

You can now leverage your decoding by shortening the big method chain sausage in **ArticlesViewModel.swift**. Change the body of `fetchArticles` to the following:

```
let request = ArticleRequest()
networker.fetch(request)
  .tryMap([Article].init)
  .replaceError(with: [])
  .receive(on: DispatchQueue.main)
  .assign(to: \.articles, on: self)
  .store(in: &cancellables)
```

This new method should raise fewer eyebrows when someone else reads your code. Build and run the project to make sure everything still works.

Using dependency inversion to test your code

You now have a working networking library, but that doesn't mean you're done! To verify that your library works and will keep working after you refactor it, it's a good idea to test your code. The starter project already includes a test suite and one test file called **ArticleViewModelTests.swift**. As the name suggests, you'll add a method to test your view model there.

However, before you do so, you first need to make your view model **testable**. A testable class means that the class is decoupled from any outside dependencies that might affect the test results. Like a true scientist in a lab, you need to remove all outside variables that could mess with your results. In your case, the outside variable is the internet.

You don't want to connect to a real server in your tests. Your tests verify that *your* code works. If the server is down or your machine doesn't have a stable internet connection, the tests should still succeed because your code is not the problem.

To decouple your view model from the Internet, you need to add a way to **inject** a different networker, one that returns hard-coded data. This is usually called a **mock object**.

Start by heading back to **Networker.swift** and adding a new protocol:

```
protocol Networking {
  func fetch(_ request: Request) -> AnyPublisher<Data, URLError>
}
```

Instead of using the `Networker` directly, your code will use `Networking`, a protocol that anyone can implement. By doing so, you allow other objects to take `Networkers` place, like the mock object mentioned above.

This is called **dependency inversion**. Instead of depending on a single concrete implementation, your code depends on anything that has the `fetch(_:)` method. In effect, you're hiding details about dependencies, allowing more flexibility in your code.

Then, make sure the class conforms to that protocol:

```
class Networker: Networking {
```

Next, you'll modify **ArticlesViewModel.swift**. First, change the declaration of `networker` to the following:

```
private var networker: Networking
```

Then, add an initializer to the class:

```
init(networker: Networking) {
  self.networker = networker
}
```

Instead of creating a `Networker` itself, your view model now receives a `Networking` instance in its initializer. This is called **dependency injection**: It allows the consumers of a class to *inject* the dependencies into a class. Anyone using the view model can now create their own specific `Networking` implementation and give it to the view model, including your test suite.

Dependency injection and dependency inversion are key principles to make your class more decoupled from its dependencies and to make it testable.

You'll also need to modify **ArticlesView.swift** to pass a networker to its view model. Change the declaration of `viewModel` to this:

```
@ObservedObject private var viewModel = ArticlesViewModel(
  networker: Networker())
```

You've now completely decoupled your view model from any outside dependencies. The project should build without any errors at this point.

Testing your view model

Now that your view model is testable, you can get started with testing it! Open **ArticlesViewModelTests.swift**. Do you remember the mock objects mentioned earlier? You'll create one right now. Add the following class to the top of the file, below the `import` statements:

```
class MockNetworker: Networking {
  func fetch(_ request: Request) -> AnyPublisher<Data, URLError>
{
    let outputData: Data
  }
}
```

This mock networker will implement the `Networking` protocol but return hard-coded values for each request. Continue implementing `fetch(_:)` by adding the following:

```
switch request {
case is ArticleRequest:
  let article = Article(
    name: "Article Name",
    description: "Article Description",
    image: URL(string: "https://image.com")!,
    id: "Article ID",
    downloadedImage: nil)
  let articleData = ArticleData(article: article)
  let articles = Articles(data: [articleData])
  outputData = try! JSONEncoder().encode(articles)
default:
```

```
    outputData = Data()
}
```

If the incoming request is an `ArticleRequest`, you'll create a fake article (sometimes called a **stub**) and encode it into JSON data.

Complete the method with the following code:

```
return Just<Data>(outputData)
  .setFailureType(to: URLError.self)
  .eraseToAnyPublisher()
```

Here, you create a publisher of the encoded data and return it from the method.

With a mock networker in place, you can use it to create a view model instance that you'll test. Add this line to the end of `setUpWithError`:

```
viewModel = ArticlesViewModel(networker: MockNetworker())
```

Before your tests run, you'll create a new view model instance and inject your stub networker.

Now, you can get to writing your test. There's already a method called `testArticlesAreFetchedCorrectly`. As the name suggests, the method will verify that your view model fetches articles and decodes them correctly. Add these lines to the method:

```
XCTAssert(viewModel.articles.isEmpty)
let expectation = XCTestExpectation(description: "Article
received")
```

You'll start your test with a sanity check that the articles array is initially empty. You'll then set up an `XCTestExpectation`. Expectations are used to test asynchronous code. The expectation will keep the test going until the expectation is fulfilled or a timer runs out.

Continue writing the method:

```
viewModel.$articles.sink { articles in
  guard !articles.isEmpty else {
    return
  }
  XCTAssertEqual(articles[0].id, "Article ID")
  expectation.fulfill()
}
.store(in: &cancellables)
```

This is the main part of your test. Here, you subscribe to changes to the articles array and wait until it's not empty. You then grab the first element of the array and verify that the ID matches the one from `MockNetworker`. If it does, you know that the view model decoded the article correctly. You also fulfill your expectation, telling the test it can stop waiting.

Finally, complete the test with the following two lines:

```
viewModel.fetchArticles()
wait(for: [expectation], timeout: 0.1)
```

You call the `fetchArticles` method to start the fetching and decoding process. You also tell XCTest to wait for 0.1 seconds until your expectation is fulfilled.

Run the test suite with **Command-U**.

In the **Test navigator** as well as next to the method you just wrote, you should see a green checkmark, indicating that your test succeeded. Maybe this was the first test you ever wrote! In that case, welcome to a whole new world of having confidence in your code, enabled by clever use of Swift's protocols!

Delegating work

If you've worked with Swift and iOS for a while, I'm sure you've implemented at least one delegate property. Delegates are used across Apple's APIs as well as a plethora of community libraries for a variety of tasks:

- Moving functionality to a different object, *delegating* a piece of work to someone else

- Informing another object of state changes and lifecycle events, such as UITableViewDelegate's `tableView(_:didSelectRowAt:)`

- Asking the delegate to provide information, like `UIScrollViewDelegate`'s `numberOfSections(in:)`

- Adding hooks and ways to influence the default behavior of an object

When designing your APIs, especially if you have a complex object that performs lots of complicated work, adding delegation is a good way to make sure your class remains flexible enough to be used in a variety of contexts in the future.

Adding a delegate protocol

You'll add a delegate protocol to your networker class.

Open **Networker.swift** and add the following protocol to the top of the class:

```
protocol NetworkingDelegate: AnyObject {
  func headers(for networking: Networking) -> [String: String]

  func networking(
    _ networking: Networking,
    transformPublisher: AnyPublisher<Data, URLError>
  ) -> AnyPublisher<Data, URLError>
}
```

Delegates are plain old Swift protocols. But keep in mind a couple of additional pieces of convention when making delegate properties. You defined the NetworkingDelegate as inheriting from AnyObject. As mentioned earlier in this chapter, this restricts the protocol so only classes can conform to it. Because delegates typically are used to affect the behavior of class instances, it makes sense that the delegate is a class as well.

You also might have noticed the slightly weird function signatures. By convention led by Apple's APIs, delegate methods have specific signatures that you should follow. Methods that return a value are named after the value they return, and they receive the source object (the Networking instance in this case) as their first parameter. Following this convention, you define a method that returns the HTTP headers that Networking will use for all of its requests.

Methods that perform side effects, on the other hand, are named after the delegate's source object (networking). The first parameter is usually that source object, while the second parameter gives you a clearer idea of what the delegate does. In this case, you define a function that can perform additional processing on the URLSession publisher before the Networking instance returns it to its consumer.

Next, add the following extension right below the protocol:

```
extension NetworkingDelegate {
  func headers(for networking: Networking) -> [String: String] {
    [:]
  }

  func networking(
    _ networking: Networking,
    transformPublisher publisher: AnyPublisher<Data, URLError>
  ) -> AnyPublisher<Data, URLError> {
    publisher
```

```
    }
  }
```

By implementing protocol methods in an extension, you provide a default implementation to every class conforming to the protocol. This ensures they don't need to have an implementation if they don't want to provide it.

Next, expose the delegate as a settable property requirement inside `Networking`:

```
var delegate: NetworkingDelegate? { get set }
```

There are two implementations of `Networking` in your code. The first is right below the protocol you just defined, `Networker`. Add the delegate property to the class:

```
weak var delegate: NetworkingDelegate?
```

The second implementation is in **ArticlesViewModelTests.swift**. Add the same line to `MockNetworker`.

weak references

You'll notice the variable is marked as `weak`. By default, Swift always keeps strong references between objects. Strong references guarantee that the `delegate` won't get de-initialized while the `Networking` instance is using it. A weak reference has no such guarantees: The `delegate` can get deallocated even if the `Networking` is keeping a reference to it. In the case of delegates, you almost always want the latter behavior.

The reason is to avoid **reference cycles**. Think of the following example: Your `ArticlesViewModel` owns a `Networker` instance. It also sets *itself* as the `Networker`'s `delegate`, which means that the `Networker` now has a reference to the view model.

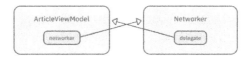

You now have a case where both classes have a strong reference to *each other*. `Networker` won't get deallocated unless `ArticlesViewModel` is deallocated, and vice versa. This means that, even if you set the view model (or the networker) to `nil`, it will still hang around in memory. This is why you have to make one of those references weak. In that case, as far as Swift's memory management is concerned, there's only one reference between the two objects. Therefore, deleting one object will trigger the deletion of the other object, completely freeing up memory.

Using the delegate

Next, hop back to **Networker.swift**. Now that Networker has access to the delegate, it's time to use it. Add the following line inside fetch(_:), right before the return:

```
urlRequest.allHTTPHeaderFields = delegate?.headers(for: self)
```

You make sure to ask the delegate for the headers to add to the URLRequest.

Next, replace the rest of the function with the following:

```
let publisher = URLSession.shared
  .dataTaskPublisher(for: urlRequest)
  .compactMap { $0.data }
  .eraseToAnyPublisher()

if let delegate = delegate {
  return delegate.networking(self, transformPublisher:
publisher)
} else {
  return publisher
}
```

Instead of returning the publisher directly, you store it in a variable. After creating the publisher, you then call the delegate method to transform the publisher if there is a delegate. If there isn't, you directly return the publisher.

Now it's time to implement the delegate protocol. Open **ArticlesViewModel.swift** and add an extension to the bottom of the file:

```
extension ArticlesViewModel: NetworkingDelegate {
  func headers(for networking: Networking) -> [String: String] {
    return ["Content-Type": "application/vnd.api+json;
charset=utf-8"]
  }
}
```

You make the view model the delegate. You also implement the headers(for:) method, where you return a valid Content-Type header that the API expects.

Next, add another method inside the extension:

```
func networking(
  _ networking: Networking,
  transformPublisher publisher: AnyPublisher<Data, URLError>
) -> AnyPublisher<Data, URLError> {
  publisher.receive(on:
DispatchQueue.main).eraseToAnyPublisher()
}
```

`networking(_:transformPublisher:)` might seem weird at first, but here's one of the many ways you can use it. In this case, because the view model always updates `@Published` values, and those updates have to happen on the main thread, you make sure to transform every publisher from the `Networker` to use the main thread. This method can also be used for logging, decoding, re-routing requests and a bunch of other tasks. The best delegate methods are flexible because you can't always predict future requirements.

There's one final step in making the view model the delegate. Add a line of code at the bottom of `init(networker:)`:

```
self.networker.delegate = self
```

This sets the view model as `networker`'s delegate. Now that you transform each publisher inside the delegate, you can remove the two `.receive(on: DispatchQueue.main)` lines in `fetchArticles` and `fetchImage(for:)`.

Run the project one last time and make sure everything works as it worked before.

Key points

- Protocols allow you to **abstract away information** from concrete types, letting you use more types in the same place.

- You can extend existing types to conform to protocols using **extensions** and even limit conformance to specific subtypes.

- Protocols use **dynamic dispatch** to achieve function calls, except for methods defined in protocol extensions that are *not* declared as a protocol requirement.

- Swift will **synthesize protocol conformance** for Equatable, Hashable, Comparable and the two Codable protocols, Encodable and Decodable.

- **Dependency inversion** is a technique to make your code more flexible by declaring your dependencies with the type of a protocol instead of a concrete implementation.

- Using dependency inversion with **dependency injection** can make your code more testable.

- Add **delegates** to complex classes to give them more flexibility. When doing so, keep **strong reference cycles** in mind and use **weak references** to avoid them.

Where to go from here?

Congratulations are in order: You just built a tiny networking library using protocol-oriented programming! You learned how to use protocols to make your code more flexible, how to combine dependency injection and inversion to make your code testable and how to make your own delegates. You also learned about static and dynamic dispatch in protocols and how to use nifty extensions to add protocol conformance to existing types. Pretty good for only one chapter, right?

If you want to learn more about Swift's underbelly and how things are arranged in memory, the Understanding Swift Performance WWDC 2016 session (apple.co/3n01j0w) will clear up a lot of questions you have. If you want to learn more about testing your code, take a look at the Testing in iOS video course (bit.ly/38QLuUG). Finally, if you'd like to know more about the raywenderlich.com API, check out its documentation (bit.ly/3puWr58).

In the next chapter, you'll continue to work on your networking library but add generics into your toolbox to make the library even better, so keep reading!

Chapter 4: Generics

By Marin Benčević

Almost everyone using Swift – from complete beginners to seasoned veterans – has used generics, whether they know it or not. Generics power arrays and dictionaries, JSON decoding, Combine publishers and many other parts of Swift and iOS. Because you have already used many of these features, you know firsthand how powerful generics are. In this chapter, you'll learn how to harness that power to build generics-powered features.

You'll get intimately familiar with generics by continuing to work on the networking library you started in the previous chapter. This time, you'll modify it to use generics to create a nicer API. You'll learn how to write generic functions, classes and structs, how to use protocols with associated types, what type erasure is and how to put all that together to make a coherent API.

Before you do that, though, this chapter front-loads quite a bit of theory, giving you a reference of what generics have to offer. Don't worry — you'll get your hands dirty later in the chapter!

Getting started with generics

Although it's not required, you can follow along with this section by creating a new plain Swift Xcode playground. Begin by writing a generic function:

```
func replaceNilValues<T>(from array: [T?], with element: T) ->
[T] {
  array.compactMap {
    $0 == nil ? element : $0
  }
}
```

The one special bit of syntax that makes this function generic is <T> in the function's prototype. While parentheses (()) surround the function's parameters, angle brackets (‹›) surround the function's **type parameters**. A generic function receives type parameters as part of a function call, just like it receives regular function parameters.

In this case, there is only one type parameter, called T. The name of this parameter isn't some magic, special constant — it's user-defined. In the example above, you could have used Element or anything else. Once you define the type parameter inside the angle brackets, you can use it in the rest of the function's declaration and even inside the function's body.

When you call this function, Swift replaces T with a concrete type that you're calling the function with.

```
let numbers: [Int?] = [32, 3, 24, nil, 4]
let filledNumbers = replaceNilValues(from: numbers, with: 0)
print(filledNumbers) // [32, 3, 24, 0, 4]
```

In the function's prototype, you defined that the function receives an array of optional Ts as well as another T value. When you call the function with numbers, Swift knows that numbers has a type of [Int?] and can figure out that it needs to replace T with Int. Swift is smart like that.

This allows you to create a single function that works across all possible types, saving you from having to copy and paste functions. In a sense, generics are the opposite of protocols. Protocols allow you to call a function on multiple types where each type can specify its implementation of the function. Generics allow you to call a function on multiple types with the *same* implementation of that function.

> **Note**: When your function is *very* generic, and the type can be any type, it's fine to use single letter type parameter names like T and U. But more often than not, your type parameter will have some sort of semantic meaning. In those cases, it's best to use a more descriptive type name that hints at its meaning to the reader. For example, instead of using single letters, you might use Element, Value, Output, etc.

Of course, like regular parameters, you can have multiple comma-separated type parameters:

```
func replaceNils<K, V>(
  from dictionary: [K: V?],
  with element: V) -> [K: V] {
  dictionary.compactMapValues {
    $0 == nil ? element : $0
  }
}
```

However, sometimes instead of a function that works across *all* possible types, you want one that works across only some of them. Swift allows you to add constraints to your generic types:

```
func max<T: Comparable>(lhs: T, rhs: T) -> T {
  return lhs > rhs ? lhs : rhs
}
```

In the example above, you need the ability to compare two values with the > operator. Not every type in Swift can be compared (for example, is one View larger than another?). So you need to specify that T must conform to Comparable. Swift then knows there's a valid implementation of > for T. You're using Comparable as a **generic constraint**: a way to tell Swift which types are accepted for the generic type parameter.

Generic types

Generic functions can take you only so far. At some point, you run into cases where you need a generic class or struct. You already use generic types all the time: Arrays, dictionaries and Combine publishers are all generic types.

Look at a generic struct:

```
struct Preference<T> {
  let key: String
```

```
    var value: T? {
      get {
        UserDefaults.standard.value(forKey: key) as? T
      } set {
        UserDefaults.standard.setValue(newValue, forKey: key)
      }
    }
  }
```

Like generic functions, generic types also have type parameters, declared right next to the type name. The example above shows a generic struct that can store and retrieve any type from UserDefaults.

You can provide a concrete type to a generic type by writing the type inside angle brackets next to the type's name:

```
  var volume = Preference<Float>(key: "audioVolume")
  volume.value = 0.5
```

Here, Swift replaces T with Float. The process of replacing a type parameter with a concrete type value is called **specialization**. In this case, typing <Float> is necessary because Swift doesn't have a way to infer it. In other cases, when you use the type parameter in the initializer, Swift can figure out what your concrete type is without you having to write angle brackets.

Keep in mind, though, that Preference itself *is not a type*. If you try to use Preference as the type of a variable, you get a compiler error. Swift recognizes only specialized variants of the type, such as Preference<String>, as real types. Generic types by themselves are more like a blueprint: a type of scaffolding for you but not of much use for the compiler.

Protocols with associated types

Aside from generic structs, enums and classes, you can also have generic protocols. Except we don't call them that, we call them **protocols with associated types** or PATs for short. PATs are structured a little differently. Instead of the generic type being a parameter of the protocol, it's one of the protocol's requirements, like protocol methods and properties.

```
  protocol Request {
    associatedtype Model
    func fetch() -> AnyPublisher<Model, Error>
  }
```

In the protocol above, Model is simply one of the protocol's requirements. To implement the protocol, you need to declare a concrete Model type by adding a typealias to your implementation:

```
struct TextRequest: Request {
  typealias Model = String

  func fetch() -> AnyPublisher<Model, Error> {
    Just("")
      .setFailureType(to: Error.self)
      .eraseToAnyPublisher()
  }
}
```

In most cases, Swift can figure out the associated type, so you don't need to add a typealias as long as you use the type when implementing one of the protocol's methods:

```
struct TextRequest: Request {
  func fetch() -> AnyPublisher<String, Error> {
    // ...
  }
}
```

In the example above, Swift sees that you use String in the place of Model, so it can infer that String is the associated type.

Like generic types, **PATs are not types**! If you don't believe me, try using a PAT as a type:

The error tells you that Request can be used only *as a generic constraint*, which is mentioned earlier in this section. Implied in that sentence is that it *cannot* be used as a type. The reason has to do with how Swift handles generic types. Swift needs to have a concrete type to work with at compile-time so it can save you from errors and undefined behavior while your program is running. A generic type without all of its type parameters is not a concrete type. Depending on the type parameters, method and property implementations can change, and the object itself can be laid out differently in memory. Because Swift always errs on the side of caution, it forces you to always use concrete, known types in your code.

It's good to be safe, but how the heck do you define an array of PATs, then? The answer is **type erasure**, and you'll see an example later in this chapter.

Extending generics

In the previous chapter, you've seen all the ways you can extend protocols and the types that implement them. Generics are no different! First of all, you can extend generics as any other type, with the added benefit that you get access to the type parameters inside the extension:

```
extension Preference {
  mutating func save(from untypedValue: Any) {
    if let value = untypedValue as? T {
      self.value = value
    }
  }
}
```

In the example above, you have access to `Preferences` type parameter T, which you use to cast the received value.

Like protocol extensions, you can also constrain extensions of generic types. For instance, you can constrain an extension to only generic types where the type parameter implements a protocol:

```
extension Preference where T: Decodable {
  mutating func save(from json: Data) throws {
    let decoder = JSONDecoder()
    self.value = try decoder.decode(T.self, from: json)
  }
}
```

In the code above, save will only exist on `Preferences` where the type parameter is `Decodable`.

You don't need to constrain the extension — you can also constrain a single method:

```
extension Preference {
  mutating func save(from json: Data) throws where T: Decodable
  {
    let decoder = JSONDecoder()
    self.value = try decoder.decode(T.self, from: json)
  }
}
```

This code does the same thing as the code block you just saw. But it constrains the method itself instead of the whole extension.

Extending PATs works the same way. You'll see an example of that when you get to the practical section of this chapter.

Self and meta-types

"What is the self?" is a philosophical question. More important for this chapter is explaining what self is as well as what Self and T.self are. These are much easier to answer than the philosophical question. Although this section might not relate directly to generics, it has a lot to do with the type system itself. And understanding the different *selves* and ways to use types in Swift will help you better understand generics.

As you already know, self is usually a reference to the object whose scope you're currently in. If you use self inside an instance method of a User struct, self will be that instance of that struct. So far, that's pretty straightforward. However, when you're in a class method of a class, self can't be a reference to an instance because *there is no instance*: You're in the class *itself*.

```
class Networker {
  class func whoAmI() {
    print(self)
  }
}

Networker.whoAmI() // "Networker"
```

In class and static methods, self has the value of the current type, not an instance. It makes sense when you think about it: Static and class methods exist on the type, not an instance.

However, all values in Swift need to have a type, including the self above. After all, you need to be able to store it in variables and return it from functions. What would be the type that holds self in class and static methods, that you now know holds *a type*? The answer is Networker.Type: a type encompassing all Networker subtypes! Just like Int holds all integer values, Int.Type holds all Int *type* values. These types that hold other types are called **meta-types**. It kind of makes your head spin, right?

```
class WebsocketNetworker: Networker {
  class func whoAmI() -> Networker.Type {
    return self
  }
}
```

```
  }

let type: Networker.Type = WebsocketNetworker.whoAmI()
print(type)
```

In the example above, you declare a meta-type variable called `type`. The meta-type can hold not only the `Networker` type itself but also all of its subclasses, such as `WebsocketNetworker`. In the case of protocols, a meta-type of a protocol (`YourProtocol.Type`) can hold the protocol type as well as all concrete types conforming to that protocol.

To use a type itself as a value, such as to pass it to a function or store it in a variable, you need to use `Type.self`:

```
let networkerType: Networker.Type = Networker.self
```

You have to do this for practical reasons. Usually, type names are used to declare the type of a variable or function parameter. When they're not used for declaring types, they're used implicitly as initializers. Using `.self` makes it clearer that you need the type as a value rather than as the type of something else and that you are not calling an initializer.

Finally, there is `Self` with a capital "S". Thankfully, this one is less convoluted than all this meta-talk. `Self` is always an alias to the *concrete* type of the scope it appears in. Concrete is emphasized because `Self` will always be a concrete type, even if it's used inside a protocol method.

```
extension Request {
  func whoAmI() {
    print(Self.self)
  }
}

TextRequest().whoAmI() // "TextRequest"
```

`Self` is useful when you want to return *the current concrete type* from a protocol method or use it as an initializer inside a static method when creating factory methods.

That's enough theory. It's time to fire up Xcode and get into using generics.

Creating a generic networking library

Open the starter project provided in this chapter's materials in Xcode. This project is almost the same one that you wrote in the previous chapter. If you haven't already, read the previous chapter to get familiar with the project. It's a tiny raywenderlich.com client app that uses your networking library powered by protocols.

In this chapter, you'll expand that library to use generics to provide an even nicer API for your users.

Making Networker generic

You'll start by adding a generic function in **Networker.swift** that can download a `Decodable` type and decode it. Add the following function prototype to `Networking`:

```
func fetch<T: Decodable>(url: URL) -> AnyPublisher<T, Error>
```

`fetch(url:)` is a generic function with one generic type parameter called `T`. You declare that `T` is a type that must conform to `Decodable`. Once you declare `T` as a type parameter, you can use it elsewhere in the type signature — like as the return value, for instance.

Next, implement the method inside `Networker`:

```
func fetch<T: Decodable>(url: URL) -> AnyPublisher<T, Error> {
  URLSession.shared.dataTaskPublisher(for: url)
    .map { $0.data }
    .decode(type: T.self, decoder: JSONDecoder())
    .eraseToAnyPublisher()
}
```

Because you have access to the generic type parameter T, you can use it in the function's body to decode the received data into T. Swift will replace T with whatever concrete type the function is called with. Because you declared that T conforms to Decodable, the compiler is happy with your code. If someone tries to call this function with a non-Decodable type like UIImage, the compiler will throw an error.

Using PATs

Using the generic function is good when you have quick one-off requests. But it would help to be able to create reusable requests you can fire from anywhere in your code. To do this, you'll turn Request into a protocol with an associated type. Open **Request.swift** and add the following two lines to the protocol:

```
associatedtype Output
func decode(_ data: Data) throws -> Output
```

The Output type tells the user what this request is supposed to fetch. It can be an Article, [Articles], User, etc. The decode(_:) function is responsible for converting the data received from URLSession into the output type.

Next, add a default implementation of decode(_:) to the bottom of the file:

```
extension Request where Output: Decodable {
  func decode(_ data: Data) throws -> Output {
    let decoder = JSONDecoder()
    return try decoder.decode(Output.self, from: data)
  }
}
```

When you create a Request implementation whose type conforms to Decodable, you'll get this implementation for free. It will try to use a JSON decoder to return the Output type.

Because the raywenderlich.com API provides a JSON response that doesn't necessarily match the models defined in your project, you won't be able to use this default implementation. You'll provide your own in **ArticleRequest.swift**.

Add a new method to the struct:

```
func decode(_ data: Data) throws -> [Article] {
  let decoder = JSONDecoder()
  let articlesCollection = try decoder.decode(Articles.self,
from: data)
  return articlesCollection.data.map { $0.article }
}
```

You first decode the received data into `Articles`, a helper struct that matches the API's response. You then convert that to an array of `Article` and return it. Notice you haven't specified that `Output` is `[Article]`. Because you used it as the return type of `decode(_:)`, Swift can infer the type of `Output` without you saying so.

Next, you'll also implement `decode(_:)` for images. Open **ImageRequest.swift** and add an enum *inside* the struct:

```
enum Error: Swift.Error {
  case invalidData
}
```

You create a custom enum to represent different kinds of errors that can occur while decoding the image. In this case, you'll use only one error, but you can expand this in your own code to be more descriptive. By conforming to Swift's `Error` type, you get the ability to use this enum as the error type of a Combine publisher or to use it with the `throw` keyword.

Finally, implement `decode(_:)` in the struct:

```
func decode(_ data: Data) throws -> UIImage {
  guard let image = UIImage(data: data) else {
    throw Error.invalidData
  }
  return image
}
```

You try to convert the data to `UIImage`. If it doesn't work, you throw the error you just declared.

Type constraints

Now that you've made changes to `Request`, it's time to use those changes in **Networker.swift**. You might have noticed a weird compiler error: "Protocol `Request` can be used only as a generic constraint because it has `Self` or associated type requirements".

Earlier, I mentioned that protocols with associated types are not types themselves, though they may act like types. Instead, they're type constraints.

Change the declaration of fetch(_:) in Networking to the following:

```
func fetch<R: Request>(_ request: R) -> AnyPublisher<R.Output,
Error>
```

You convert fetch(_:) to a generic function over the type R, representing any request. You know that it's a request since you declare that the type must conform to Request. You then return a publisher using the Request's associated Output type. Here, you're no longer using Request as a concrete type. Instead, you're using it as a constraint on R, so the compiler error goes away.

Next, change fetch(_:) in Networker to match the new protocol requirement:

```
func fetch<R: Request>(_ request: R) -> AnyPublisher<R.Output,
Error> {
  var urlRequest = URLRequest(url: request.url)
  urlRequest.httpMethod = request.method.rawValue
  urlRequest.allHTTPHeaderFields = delegate?.headers(for: self)

  var publisher = URLSession.shared
    .dataTaskPublisher(for: urlRequest)
    .compactMap { $0.data }
    .eraseToAnyPublisher()

  if let delegate = delegate {
    publisher = delegate.networking(self, transformPublisher:
publisher)
  }

  return publisher.tryMap(request.decode).eraseToAnyPublisher()
}
```

The function stayed mostly the same except for a couple of key changes. First, you changed the declaration to make it a generic function. Second, you added a line at the end that tries to call the Request's decode(_:) function to return the Output associated type.

Now that you've made all these changes, you can finally use the networker as intended. Open **ArticlesViewModel.swift**.

First, delete the .tryMap([Article].init) line from fetchArticles. Because Request does this for you, you no longer need the line. Further, because ArticleRequest declares [Article] as its Output type, Swift knows to publish [Article] values from the publisher, so the type system is happy.

Next, inside `fetchImage`, replace the whole `fetch(_:)` call chain with the following:

```
let request = ImageRequest(url: article.image)
networker.fetch(request)
  .sink(receiveCompletion: { completion in
    switch completion {
    case .failure(let error): print(error)
    default: break
    }
  }, receiveValue: { [weak self] image in
    self?.articles[articleIndex].downloadedImage = image
  })
  .store(in: &cancellables)
```

Again, there's no need to convert anything to `UIImage` because `ImageRequest` does that for you. Instead, you grab the image when it arrives or print out an error if it doesn't.

Build and run the project.

You should see a list of raywenderlich.com articles together with their images. Congratulations, you just made a working networking library using generics! Don't rest on your laurels, though. You can still improve the library further by adding caching using generics.

Adding caching with type erasure

In the previous chapter, you added a check in your view model that checked whether an image was already downloaded because the `fetchImage` function is called every time a row appears on the screen. This is an ad-hoc way to achieve caching. You can make this behavior more reusable by adding a generic cache class to your project.

Create a new Swift file called **RequestCache.swift** and add the following to the file:

```
class RequestCache<Value> {
  private var store: [Request: Value] = [:]
}
```

You create a new generic class that stores request responses in an in-memory cache inside a plain Swift dictionary. You'll store the responses keyed by the request that fetched them so you can always easily tie a request to its response.

You might notice a compiler error. The error is the same one you saw earlier: "Protocol Request can only be used as a generic constraint because it has Self or associated type requirements". Earlier, you fixed this error by *not* using the Request type directly instead of using it as a constraint.

But in this case, that's not possible. You can't constrain the keys of a dictionary – they all need to be the same concrete type. In cases where you need to use a protocol with an associated type as a concrete type, you need to employ **type erasure**. You can think of PATs as generic protocols. And type erasure, as its name suggests, is a way to convert that generic protocol into a concrete type by *removing* type information.

Head to **Request.swift** and add a new struct to the bottom of the file:

```
struct AnyRequest: Hashable {
  let url: URL
  let method: HTTPMethod
}
```

This struct is what enables type erasure. You can convert any Request, regardless of its associated type, to an instance of AnyRequest. AnyRequest is just a plain Swift struct without any generics. So, naturally, you've lost type information along the way. You can't use AnyRequest to make your code more type-safe. But sometimes you can get away with discarding type information, allowing you to write your code more easily.

Now, you can go back to **RequestCache.swift** and use the type-erased struct instead of Request in store's declaration:

```
private var store: [AnyRequest: Value] = [:]
```

You're not the only one using type erasure in this way. Plenty of Apple's APIs use the same pattern, such as Combine's AnyCancellable or AnyPublisher. AnySequence, AnyIterator and AnyCollection can help you create your own sequences and collections more easily. SwiftUI's AnyView allows you to store different types of views in the same data structure. These are just a few examples to show you that type erasure is a common pattern in Swift. Because the pattern is common, getting familiar with it will help you understand existing APIs as well as create new APIs in the future.

Fetching and saving a response

You can now continue writing your class. You'll add two methods to the class, one to fetch a stored response and another to save a response. Add a new method below the property you just declared:

```
func response<R: Request>(for request: R) -> Value?
  where R.Output == Value {
  let erasedRequest = AnyRequest(url: request.url, method:
request.method)
  return store[erasedRequest]
}
```

This function will get called when someone wants to retrieve an already stored response for a given request. The function's prototype might look a bit complicated, so breaking it down will help. First, you declare a generic parameter R that must conform to Request. You then receive a parameter of that same type and return an instance of Value, the generic type parameter of the RequestCache class. Finally, you specify that R's associated Output type must be the same type as the class's type parameter.

The last bit of the function's prototype verifies that no one will accidentally call the function with the wrong request. If the cache stores images (RequestCache<UIImage>), only Requests that fetch images can be retrieved (R.Output == UIImage). If you try to call the method with a mismatched Request, you'll get a compiler error:

```
let cache = RequestCache<String>()
let request = ArticleRequest()
cache.response(for: request)
  Instance method 'response(for:)' requires the types 'String' and
  '[Article]' be equivalent
```

However, keep in mind that this is *still* a generic function, so multiple `Request` types can be retrieved as long as their output type matches the type of the stored values. For instance, you can use both `AvatarThumbnailRequest` and `ImageRequest` to call this method on a `RequestCache<UIImage>` instance.

Inside the method, you use type erasure by constructing an `AnyRequest` from the provided request, which you can use to retrieve a value from the dictionary.

Next, add a method to save a new response for a request:

```
func saveResponse<R: Request>(_ response: Value, for request: R)
  where R.Output == Value {
  let erasedRequest = AnyRequest(url: request.url, method:
request.method)
    store[erasedRequest] = response
}
```

Once again, you add a `where` clause to the function's signature to verify that the request type matches, disallowing accidental wrong entries. As you did in `response(for:)`, you use type erasure to store a new response in the dictionary.

Now that you have a generic cache, you can create a cache to store all your downloaded images. Open **Networking.swift** and add a new property to `Networker`:

```
private let imageCache = RequestCache<UIImage>()
```

You'll use this instance to store the image request responses.

Next, add a new (unfinished) method to the class:

```
func fetchWithCache<R: Request>(_ request: R)
  -> AnyPublisher<R.Output, Error> where R.Output == UIImage {
  if let response = imageCache.response(for: request) {
    return Just<R.Output>(response)
      .setFailureType(to: Error.self)
      .eraseToAnyPublisher()
  }
}
```

You'll finish up the method in a bit.

You create a new generic method that receives a request and returns a publisher just like `fetch(_:)`. But this method uses the cache to retrieve responses if they're already stored or store new responses if they aren't. The function's prototype declares that this method can be used only by requests whose `Output` type is `UIImage` because you currently only cache `UIImage` instances.

Inside the method, you first check if a response is already cached. If it is, you return a publisher that emits the cached value using `Just`.

Finish the method with the following code at the bottom:

```
return fetch(request)
  .handleEvents(receiveOutput: {
    self.imageCache.saveResponse($0, for: request)
  })
  .eraseToAnyPublisher()
```

If there is no cached response, you use `fetch(_:)` to return a new publisher. You also subscribe to the publisher's output event so you can store the response in the cache.

Next, add your new method to `Networking`:

```
func fetchWithCache<R: Request>(_ request: R)
  -> AnyPublisher<R.Output, Error> where R.Output == UIImage
```

Now that you have your new caching method in `Networker`, it's time to use it from the view model. Open **ArticlesViewModel.swift** and change `fetchImage` to the following:

```
func fetchImage(for article: Article) {
  guard let articleIndex = articles.firstIndex(
    where: { $0.id == article.id }) else {
    return
  }

  let request = ImageRequest(url: article.image)
  networker.fetchWithCache(request)
    .sink(receiveCompletion: { error in
      print(error)
    }, receiveValue: { image in
      self.articles[articleIndex].downloadedImage = image
    })
    .store(in: &cancellables)
}
```

You no longer need to perform any checks here. `Networker` takes care of all caching, letting the view model focus on preparing the view's data and not worry about storing requests.

Build and run the project. It should work just like before, except now you have a much nicer API.

Key points

- Methods, structs, enums and classes all can become generic by adding **type parameters** inside angle brackets!

- Protocols can be generic as well through use of **protocols with associated types**.

- `self` has the value of the current type in static methods and computed properties, and the type of `self` in those cases is a **meta-type**.

- `Self` always has the value of the current concrete type.

- You can use extensions with **generic constraints**, using the `where` keyword to extend generic types when their type parameters satisfy specific requirements.

- You can also specialize methods themselves by using the `where` keyword.

- Use **type erasure** to use generics and PATs as regular types.

Where to go from here?

Now that you're more familiar with generics, you can explore the many generic types inside Swift itself. For instance:

- `Array` (https://bit.ly/3tzPr9V) is a generic struct.

- `Collection` (https://bit.ly/39WVNbJ) is a PAT.

- `AnyHashable` (https://bit.ly/3p4rwMw) is an example of how Swift uses type erasure.

If you want even more introduction to generics, look at the Swift Generics (Expanded) (https://apple.co/3cNKeW7) WWDC 2018 session.

If you want more behind the scenes information on how generics are implemented and laid out in memory, check out the Understanding Swift Performance (https://apple.co/2YTlQtT) WWDC 2016 session.

Section II: Standard Library

This sections covers the base layer of writing Swift programs: Numerics, Ranges, Strings, Sequences, Collections, Codable and the less obvious, but very important topic - Unsafe.

As you'd expect from an advanced book, we don't only explain these topics, but also investigate how they're built, how they're represented, and how to use them effectively.

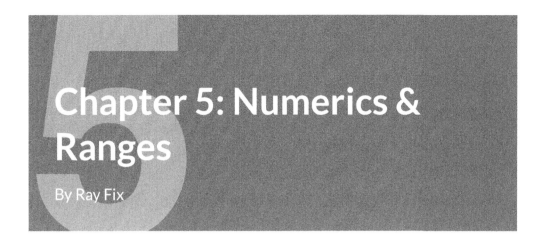

Chapter 5: Numerics & Ranges

By Ray Fix

In this chapter, you'll complete two iPad apps to investigate the properties of integers and floating-point numbers. The first of these apps is **BitViewer**, which lets you look at bit-level representations and operations. The second app is **Mandelbrot**, which allows you to test Apple's new Swift numerics package. The app lets you visualize the precision of different floating-point types. Finally, you'll use a playground to explore how Swift implements ranges and strides. Throughout the chapter, you'll flex your generic programming muscles and write code that works with a family of types.

This chapter might feel a little academic because it deals with the low-level machine representation of numbers. A little knowledge in this area will give you extra confidence and the ability to deal with low-level issues if they ever come up. For example, if you deal with file formats directly, or find yourself worrying about numerical range and accuracy, these topics will come in useful. Swift numerics is also an excellent case study for using protocols and generics that you looked at in previous chapters.

Representing numbers

Computers are number-crunching machines made of switching transistors. Consider the base-10 number 123.75. You can represent it as 1, 2, 3, 7 and 5 if you multiply each digit by an appropriate weight:

$$10^2 \quad 10^1 \quad 10^0 \quad 10^{-1} \quad 10^{-2}$$

1	2	3.	7	5

$$100 \quad 10 \quad 1 \quad 0.1 \quad 0.01$$

$$100 + 20 + 3 + 0.7 + 0.05 = 123.75$$

The decimal representation of 123.75

The diagram shows how the number is composed. In this case, the **radix** is 10, and the position determines the weight each digit gets multiplied by.

Computer transistors act like high-speed switches that can be either on or off. What would it look like if you had only two states (0 and 1) to represent a number instead of 10? 123.75 would look like this:

$$2^6 \quad 2^5 \quad 2^4 \quad 2^3 \quad 2^2 \quad 2^1 \quad 2^0 \quad 2^{-1} \quad 2^{-2}$$

1	1	1	1	0	1	1.	1	1

$$64 \quad 32 \quad 16 \quad 8 \quad 4 \quad 2 \quad 1 \quad 0.5 \quad 0.25$$

$$64 + 32 + 16 + 8 + 0 + 2 + 1 + 0.5 + 0.25$$

$$= 123.75$$

The binary representation of 123.75

The radix here is two. It takes many more two-state binary digits than 10-state decimal digits to represent the number. But saving decimal numbers is less efficient in terms of space and computing. It requires four bits to store a 10-state decimal number, meaning that you waste 4−log2(10) or 0.678 bits for each digit you store.

The first bit (in the 64 position) has a special name. It's called the **most significant bit** or MSB. That's because it has the most significant effect on the overall value. The last bit (in the 0.25 position) is called the **least significant bit** or LSB. It has the smallest effect on the overall value.

You can see that number systems rely on exponents. If you need a refresher on those, you might get a quick review over at the Khan Academy. https://bit.ly/3k0Tsin.

Integers

The first personal computers could deal with only 1 byte — 8 bits — at a time (numbers from 0 to 255). You needed to juggle these small values around to produce anything larger. Over the years, the size of the information computers could handle repeatedly doubled — to 16 bits, 32 bits and now 64 bits on the latest Intel and Apple processors.

Swift supports all the standard integer sizes, including Int8, UInt8, Int16, UInt16, Int32, UInt32, Int64 and UInt64. These bit widths are necessary for systems-level programming and often have native, specialized hardware support as well.

Here's a table showing each type and the range of values it supports:

Type	Bits	Min	Max
Int8	8	-128	127
UInt8	8	0	255
Int16	16	-32768	32767
UInt16	16	0	65535
Int32	32	-2147483648	2147483647
UInt32	32	0	4294967295
Int64	64	-9223372036854775808	9223372036854775807
UInt64	64	0	18446744073709551615

Integer Type Ranges

In your day-to-day programming, you'll want to use Int, which is 32 bits on older 32-bit hardware and 64 bits on 64-bit hardware. Because the limits are so large, you rarely need to worry about overflow. It's treated as so unlikely that Swift will halt your program if you happen to exceed the limit. This safety feature makes a large class of bugs obvious. But if you're using an unsafe language, such as C, your program will continue to run, producing unexpected results that can be ruthlessly hard to debug.

Protocol oriented integers

Swift's integer types are `struct`-based values that wrap an LLVM numeric built-in type. Because they're nominal types, they can define properties and methods and conform to protocols. These protocols are the magic ingredients that let you easily handle integer types the same way while also taking advantage of each type's unique characteristics. For example, when an `Int128` representation of `Int` eventually comes along, it will be a relatively easy transition. The protocol hierarchy for integers looks like this:

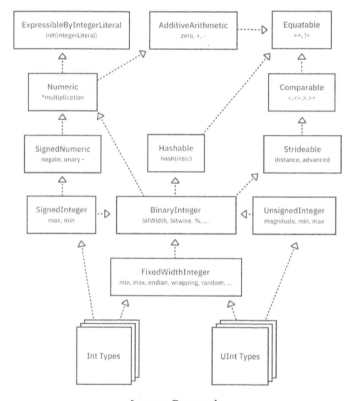

Integer Protocols

`Int` and `UInt` types adopt the `FixedWidthInteger` protocol and the `SignedInteger` and `UnsignedInteger`, respectively. That gives them a ton of shared functionality and codifies their **two's complement** representation, which you'll learn about shortly.

But there's more. Integers losslessly convert to and from `String` types thanks to additional protocols and methods.

The protocol relationships look like this:

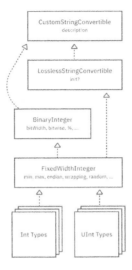

Integer String Protocols

Getting started with BitViewer

To get hands-on experience with the integers, open the **BitViewer** project in the **projects/starter** folder for this chapter. When you run, using either a device or simulator, rotate into landscape and tap on the show sidebar item in the upper-left, you'll see a screen like this:

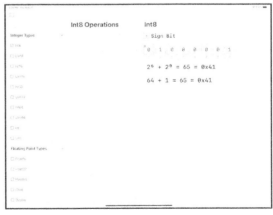

BitViewer Starter App

Select a numeric type. For this section, focus on the integer types. You can see a binary representation of a number and tap on the bits to toggle them. Scroll horizontally through all the bits or check the checkbox to stack them vertically into bytes. In a moment, you'll add code to operate generically on all the integer types.

Understanding two's complement

Using **BitViewer**, you can poke at the bits to see how the values change. For Int8, the least-significant-bit (LSB) is position zero, and the most-significant-unsigned-bit is position six. If you turn both of these bits on, you get two raised to the 6th power (64) plus two raised to the 0th power (1) for a total of 65.

Position seven is special: It's the sign bit. You might guess that flipping this bit would make the value -65. These days, all modern hardware uses two's complement representation, where the sign bit adds in the largest negative value. In this case, negative two raised to the 7th power (-128) added to 65 results in -63. As a diagram, it looks like this:

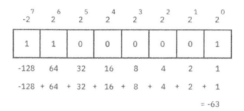

Two's Complement Example

The fantastic thing about two's complement is that every bit pattern has a unique value (only one 0 and not +0 and -0). Also, addition and subtraction use the same hardware circuit — namely, subtraction is just the addition of a negative number. That silicon space savings cemented two's complement as the representation of choice in all modern hardware.

Negation in two's complement

The unary – operator and negate method change the sign of an integer, but what happens to the bits? To negate a number using two's complement, toggle all the bits and add one. For example, 0b00000010 (2) negated would be 0b11111101 + 1 = 0b11111110 (-2). Now try it yourself with a few numbers in **BitViewer**. Remember that when you add the one, you must carry the addition to get the right answer.

> **Note**: Early computer systems used different strategies to represent negative numbers. The IBM 7090, for example, had a sign bit that just flipped the sign of the number. The PDP-1 used **one's complement**, in which negation was achieved by flipping all the bits. The problem with these systems is that they have two representations of zero. Also, addition and subtraction require different hardware circuits. The advent of two's complement solved these problems.

Exercises

- What are the minimum and maximum representable values of a make-believe Int4 and Int10 type?

- What bit pattern represents -2 using Int4? (Add it to 2 to see if you get zero.)

- List all the protocols shown in this chapter (the above diagrams) that an Int32 supports.

Find the answers to the exercises in the chapter's download materials.

Adding integer operations to BitViewer

Time to add some features to the **BitViewer** app. Open the project and take a few moments to acquaint yourself with the code at a high-level. Here are some key points to notice:

- **Model/ModelStore.swift** contains the model — a list of instances of each integer and floating-point type.

- All the numerics get decomposed into bits and displayed by a BitsView contained in IntegerView or FloatingPointView.

- Each bit has a "semantic" type, such as sign, exponent or significand, displayed differently and defined in **Model/BitSemantic.swift**.

- Many of the abstractions are generic so they work with any integer or floating-point type.

Now, open **Model/NumericOperation.swift** and add this to the file:

```
enum IntegerOperation<IntType: FixedWidthInteger> {
  // 1
  typealias Operation = (IntType) -> IntType
```

```
  // 2
  struct Section {
    let title: String
    let items: [Item]
  }

  // 3
  struct Item {
    let name: String
    let operation: Operation
  }
}
```

IntegerOperation is an **uninhabited type** (an enum with no cases) that cannot be instantiated. It provides a namespace and the generic placeholder IntType that conforms to the FixedWidthInteger protocol. If you recall the integer protocol hierarchy earlier, IntType has most of the functionality of both Int and UInt types. Here are some other vital parts of the snippet:

1. Operation is a function that takes an IntType and returns a modified IntType displayed by the UI.

2. Section has a title and let you group operations logically.

3. Item is a menu selection with a display name and the Operation that gets called when selected.

Next, define a static property menu to hold sections of operations you'll add to later.

```
extension IntegerOperation {
  static var menu: [Section] {
    [
      // Add sections below
    ]
  }
}
```

This menu can be rendered by the SwiftUI interface. To enable it, open **Views/ NumericOperationsView.swift** and uncomment the block of code around line 40:

```
// TODO: - Uncomment after implementing IntegerOperation.
// : etc
```

At this point, you can build and run **BitViewer**. You won't see any changes yet. But when you've completed all of the sections below, it will look like this:

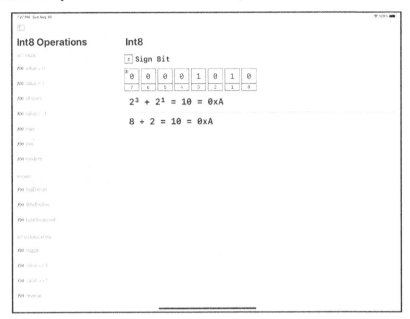

BitViewer Operations

Setting value operations

Back in **Model/NumericOperation.swift**, add the following to the static `menu` property:

```
Section(title: "Set Value", items:
  [
  Item(name: "value = 0") { _ in 0 },
  Item(name: "value = 1") { _ in 1 },
  Item(name: "all ones") { _ in ~IntType.zero },
  Item(name: "value = -1") { _ in -1 },
  Item(name: "max") { _ in IntType.max },
  Item(name: "min") { _ in IntType.min },
  Item(name: "random") { _ in
    IntType.random(in: IntType.min...IntType.max)
  }
]), // To be continued
```

You can build and run the app again. These are all generic methods on `IntType`, which is constrained to `FixedWidthInteger`. So you can select any integer type and run the operation on it to see how the bits change.

The first section's operations rely on the `ExpressibleByIntegerLiteral` to init to 0, 1, and -1. Because it defines a non-failable initializer, if the value falls outside the representable range, it becomes 0. Try this by setting an unsigned type to -1 by tapping the operation.

To set to all ones, use `.zero` from `AdditiveArithmetic` and the bitwise `~` complement operator from `BinaryInteger` to flip all the bits.

`max`, `min` and `random` are supported by `FixedWidthInteger`.

Endian operations

The term **endian** refers to two competing ideologies in "Gulliver's Travels" by Jonathan Swift that clash over whether you should crack the little end or big end of an egg.

In computer number representation, the endian describes whether the smallest or largest byte appears first or last. With little-endian, the smallest (least significant) byte comes first.

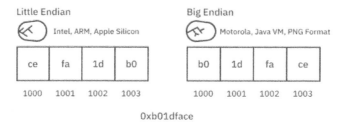

Endian

Add this to the menu property:

```
Section(title: "Endian", items:
[
  Item(name: "bigEndian") { value in value.bigEndian },
  Item(name: "littleEndian") { value in value.littleEndian },
  Item(name: "byteSwapped") { value in value.byteSwapped }
]),
```

Build and run. Because ARM and Intel hardware are little-endian, tapping on the **littleEndian** menu option will do nothing. Tapping on **bigEndian** will swap the bytes. The opposite would be true if you were running on a big-endian machine. The `byteSwapped` accessor always swaps the bytes no matter what platform you're on.

Try out some multi-byte types and make sure they work as you expect.

Even in a hardware ecosystem like Apple's, where everything is little-endian, if you try to decode a file format such as PNG, you'll find yourself needing to deal with both endians. Swift integer types make it easy.

Bit manipulation operations

Still inside `IntegerOperation`'s menu, add some bit manipulation operations:

```
Section(title: "Bit Manipulation", items:
  [
    Item(name: "toggle") { value in ~value },
    Item(name: "value << 1") { value in value << 1 },
    Item(name: "value >> 1") { value in value >> 1 },
    Item(name: "reverse") { print("do later"); return $0 }
]),
```

Build and run.

Thanks to the `BinaryInteger` protocol, Swift integer types have all the basic operations for flipping and masking bits. You already saw the complement operator ~ in the *Set Value* section. Here, it's used to toggle bits.

The operators >> and << can shift bits left and right, respectively. A critical concept here is **sign extension**. The operator >> works differently for unsigned and signed types. If the type is unsigned, >> will always insert a zero into the most-significant-bit. But if it's signed, it will copy the sign bit. Try this with some numbers for yourself.

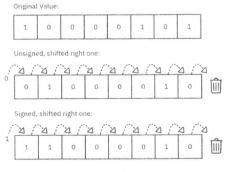

Bit Shifting

The **reverse** operation currently just prints "do later". You'll implement it in a moment to reverse the order of all the bits.

Arithmetic operations

Add these arithmetic operations:

```
Section(title: "Arithmetic", items:
  [
    Item(name: "value + 1") { value in value &+ 1 },
    Item(name: "value - 1") { value in value &- 1 },
    Item(name: "value * 10") { value in value &* 10 },
    Item(name: "value / 10") { value in value / 10 },
    Item(name: "negate") { value in ~value &+ 1 }
  ])
```

While `AdditiveArithmetic` and `Numeric` protocols give you basic addition, subtraction and multiplication, `FixedWidthInteger` introduces the notion of operations that wrap. These look like the familiar operators +, – and * but have an ampersand & prefix. For example, while `UInt8.max + 1` will halt your program, `UInt8.max &+ 1` will wrap it around back to zero. You'll want to use &+ so your program doesn't crash but just wraps around if the user increments beyond the maximum value.

> **Note:** You might think &+ are "fast" operations. They are, but they might also cause an overall slowdown in your program. The reason is that, especially if the operation computes array indices, the compiler can no longer reason about memory safety. As a result, additional checks might end up in your inner loop, causing a substantial performance hit.

`SignedInteger` gives you access to a `negate` method and unary – operator. However, because `IntType` is constrained only to the `FixedWidthInteger` protocol, you need to do it manually. You do it for two's complement by flipping the bits and adding one as you saw previously. Try your custom operation in **BitViewer** and see it work like magic!

Implementing a custom reverse operation

To flex your bit-hacking muscles, make an extension on `FixedWidthInteger` that reverses all the bits.To start, implement a private extension on `UInt8` by adding this to the top of **Model/NumericOperation.swift**:

```
private extension UInt8 {
  mutating func reverseBits() {
    self = (0b11110000 & self) >> 4 | (0b00001111 & self) << 4
    self = (0b11001100 & self) >> 2 | (0b00110011 & self) << 2
    self = (0b10101010 & self) >> 1 | (0b01010101 & self) << 1
  }
}
```

> **Note**: Bit manipulations such as reverse can come in handy when you're doing signal processing or working with low-level hardware such as device drivers. The bit-reverse operation is famously used by the Fast Fourier Transform (FFT) algorithm, which has a wide range of applications.

This code uses the so-called **divide and conquer** approach, which breaks a big problem into sub-problems until the sub-problems become trivial:

- It uses a bitmask and shifting by four to swap nibbles of the byte.

- It swaps the upper half and lower half of the nibble.

- It swaps every other bit.

If you picture each bit as ABCDEFGH, here is how the first line to reverse nibbles works:

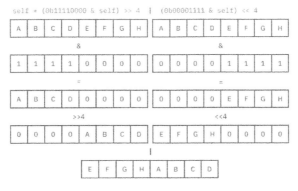

Reverse Line 1

Reversing the upper and lower half of the nibbles and every other bit operates the same way.

Now, inside the same file, add the following to make it work for all integer sizes:

```
extension FixedWidthInteger {
  var bitReversed: Self {
    var reversed = byteSwapped
    withUnsafeMutableBytes(of: &reversed) { buffer in
      buffer.indices.forEach { buffer[$0].reverseBits() }
    }
    return reversed
  }
}
```

You use the endian operation `byteSwapped` to flip around all the bytes and then grab a raw buffer to them. Then, you can call your `reverseBits()` private method to mutate each of the individual bytes.

To hook it into the interface, change the definition of the reverse item in `menu` so it becomes:

```
Item(name: "reverse") { value in value.bitReversed }
```

Improving bitReversed

The above code requires eight iterations to reverse the native 64-bit type. Can you do better and use the full width of the processor? Yes, you can.

First, comment out (or rename) the current definition of `bitReversed` to make room for a new one. Then type:

```
extension FixedWidthInteger {
  var bitReversed: Self {
    precondition(MemoryLayout<Self>.size <=
                  MemoryLayout<UInt64>.size)

    var reversed = UInt64(truncatingIfNeeded: self.byteSwapped)
    reversed = (reversed & 0xf0f0f0f0f0f0f0f0) >> 4 |
               (reversed & 0x0f0f0f0f0f0f0f0f) << 4
    reversed = (reversed & 0xcccccccccccccccc) >> 2 |
               (reversed & 0x3333333333333333) << 2
    reversed = (reversed & 0xaaaaaaaaaaaaaaaa) >> 1 |
               (reversed & 0x5555555555555555) << 1
    return Self(truncatingIfNeeded: reversed)
  }
}
```

It's critical to use an unsigned type to prevent sign extension when you shift the bits. A cryptic looking number such as `0xf0....` is just `0b11110000...` from your first version spelled out eight times in a compact format. The same is true for all the other cryptic looking values.

Finally, the special initializer `FixedWidthInteger.init(truncatingIfNeeded:)` extends small integer widths out to 64 bits. At the end, it chops them off again. The standard integer initializer traps if it can't convert the number. For example, `UInt64(Int(-1))` would halt your program since -1 is unrepresentable. `truncatingIfNeeded` just chops the bits off without an error.

> **Note**: This version only supports a max of 64 bits and halts at runtime otherwise. You might support larger (not yet standard) formats by looping on `words.reversed()` and using the native size `UInt` instead of an explicit `UInt64`.

With this code in place, test it in **BitViewer** and see that it works as you would expect on all the sizes.

Floating-point

Floating-point numbers can represent fractional values. The standard floating-point types include a 64-bit `Double`, a 32-bit `Float` and a relatively new 16-bit `Float16`. There's an Intel-only `Float80` type dating back to when PCs had separate math co-processor chips. Because ARM doesn't support it, you'll only encounter this type on an Intel-based platform, such as an Intel Mac or the iPad simulator running on an Intel Mac.

The floating-point protocols

Just as integers have a hierarchy of protocols to unify their functionality, floating-point numbers conform to protocols that look like this:

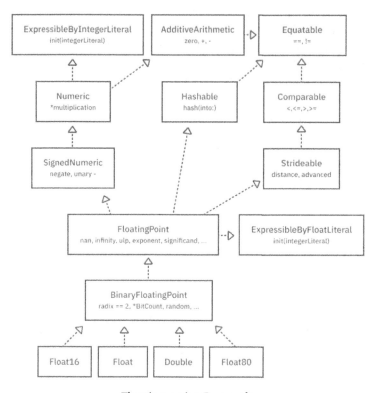

Floating-point Protocols

Some of these protocols, such as SignedNumeric, are the same ones used for integers. The heavy lifting begins in FloatingPoint, which supports most of the hardware-native, IEEE-754 floating-point standard. More functionality is added by BinaryFloatingPoint, which handles the specific case when the radix is two.

Understanding IEEE-754

A 64-bit two's complement integer can range from a colossal -9,223,372,036,854,775,808 (Int64.min) to 9,223,372,036,854,775,807 (Int64.max). But a 64-bit Double can range by an unfathomable ±1.8e+308 (as reported by Double.greatestFiniteMagnitude via the FloatingPoint protocol). Moreover, this same Double can represent numbers as small as 4.9e-324 (as reported by Double.leastNonzeroMagnitude). How is this even possible?

The answer is a thoughtful representation defined by the IEEE-754 standard that leverages the idea of variable precision. It keeps numbers close to zero extremely fine-grained while making huge numbers chunkier.

To explore this, open **BitViewer** again and select a floating-point type. Working with Float16 is the most comfortable because the limits and sizes are relatively small. With Float16, the largest representable finite magnitude is 65504.0 and the smallest non-zero magnitude is 6e-08.

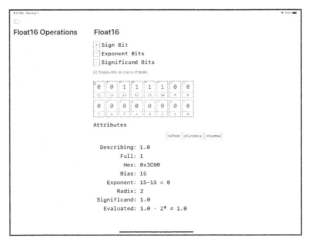

BitViewer Operations

There are three kinds of bits: one sign bit, five exponent bits and 10 significand bits for a total of 16. The equation determines the value of finite numbers:

```
(-1 ^ sign) * significand * (radix ^ exponent)
```

Here are some important points:

- ^ stands for exponentiation.

- For any BinaryFloatingPoint, the radix is two. A radix of two is a very efficient machine representation but can't exactly represent some common numbers such as 0.1.

- The sign flips the number positive or negative. Any number raised to the 0th power is defined to be one (positive). When raised to the first power, the term becomes minus one (negative). Unlike in two's complement, floating-point zero has two representations: -0 and +0.

- The `significand` is derived from the raw significand bits in a particular way described below. The `FloatingPoint` protocol gives you the cooked version of the bits you can use in the above formula.

- The `exponent` is also derived from the bits, and its cooked value can be obtained from the `FloatingPoint` protocol.

The tricky magic lies in how the significand and exponent are computed.

The significand bits determine the actual significand value. To get maximum range in the fewest number of bits, IEEE-754 assumes a phantom, leading ones bit, even though it is not stored in memory. This is known as the **leading bit convention**. It's why the significand bits are set to all zeros to represent the number one. If you turn on bit 9 in the above example, it will add 0.5 (2^-1) and change the overall value to 1.5. Turning on bit 8 will add 0.25 (2^-2) to make 1.75 and so on. Try it out and see.

The exponent computation is equally subtle and clever to produce a maximum range with the fewest bits. The exponent is computed by taking a **bias** value and subtracting the magnitude of the exponent bits. The bias determined by the IEEE-754 standard is:

```
bias = 2 ^ (exponentBitCount -1) - 1
```

In the case of `Float16`, it evaluates as `pow(2, Float16.exponentBitCount-1)` - 1, which is 15. To represent the value 1.0 in the example above, the exponent bits are set to `0b01111` or 15 so that bias - 15 = 0. Because of this, radix ^ 0 = 1.

While experimenting with changing bits, you might have noticed that certain bit patterns are special case values and the computation rules above are ignored. For example, if you turn all the exponent bits on, the number becomes a special **NaN**, which stands for "not a number".

Adding floating-point operations to BitViewer

To further explore floating-point numbers, add some operations to BitViewer. Again, open the source file **Model/NumericOperation.swift** and add this to the bottom:

```swift
enum FloatingPointOperation<FloatType: BinaryFloatingPoint> {
  typealias Operation = (FloatType) -> FloatType

  struct Section {
    let title: String
    let items: [Item]
  }
```

```
    struct Item {
      let name: String
      let operation: Operation
    }

    static var menu: [Section] {
      [
        // Add sections below
      ]
    }
  }
```

This code should look pretty familiar: It's just the floating-point version of what you did with integers. The generic placeholder `FloatType` is constrained to `BinaryFloatingPoint`, which gives you access to a lot of functionality across concrete floating-point types.

To enable the operations in the UI so you can experiment with them, head over to **Views/NumericOperationsView.swift** and uncomment the block of code that begins with:

```
// TODO: — Uncomment after implementing FloatingPointOperation.
// : etc
```

This code displays each operation in a list and calls it when you tap it.

Setting value operations

Back in **Model/NumericOperation.swift**, add this section to the floating-point menu property.

```
Section(title: "Set Value", items:
[
  Item(name: "value = 0") { _ in 0 },
  Item(name: "value = 0.1") { _ in FloatType(0.1) },
  Item(name: "value = 0.2") { _ in FloatType(0.2) },
  Item(name: "value = 0.5") { _ in FloatType(0.5) },
  Item(name: "value = 1") { _ in 1 },
  Item(name: "value = -1") { _ in -1 },
  Item(name: "value = pi") { _ in FloatType.pi },
  Item(name: "value = 100") { _ in 100 }
]),
```

Build and run. Select the `Float16` type. This section of operations primarily uses the protocols `ExpressibleByIntegerLiteral` and `ExpressibleByFloatLiteral` to set the value.

Notice the **Attributes** that describe the value using a set of binary computed properties. `1.0` has `isFinite`, `isCanonical` and `isNormal` set to true. `isFinite` means that it uses the formula you saw previously to compute the value. `isCanonical` implies that the value is in its canonical form.

The same value represented in different ways is known as a **cohort**. Using the *expressible* protocol will ensure you get the canonical representation.

Try some of the other values. In particular, look at `0.1`. With only 16 bits and a radix of two, it is impossible to represent it exactly. Even with a 64-bit `Double`, you can't get it exactly. It would require an infinite number of significand bits to do.

> **Note**: If you're writing apps that deal with currency, you'll probably want to use a numeric type that can represent 0.1 exactly and avoid accounting errors. Although IEEE-754 specifies a radix 10 type that can handle this, it's not yet natively implemented for Swift. However, Swift provides `Decimal`, an **overlay** (wrapper type) on Objective-C's `NSDecimalNumber`.

Subnormals

Values can either be **normal** or **subnormal** or neither in the case of zero. A normal number uses the leading bit convention you saw with `1.0`. A subnormal (also **denormal**) assumes the zero leading bit and supports really small numbers. Subnormal numbers are created by keeping all exponent bits zero and setting one of the significand bits. Try it and see!

> **Note**: Subnormal numbers were a controversial part of the IEEE-754 spec. Although implemented on Intel and newer ARM devices, they aren't implemented on all versions of ARM (ARMv7 and earlier). As a result, you'll find operations on these numbers taking 50-100X the time because everything is implemented in software instead of hardware. These platforms support a **flush-to-zero** control register, which just makes these small values zero.

Set special values operations

Add another section to the floating-point `menu` property:

```
Section(title: "Set Special Values", items:
[
  Item(name: "infinity") { _ in
```

```
      FloatType.infinity
  },
  Item(name: "NaN") { _ in
    FloatType.nan
  },
  Item(name: "Signaling NaN") { _ in
    FloatType.signalingNaN
  },
  Item(name: "greatestFiniteMagnitude") { _ in
    FloatType.greatestFiniteMagnitude
  },
  Item(name: "leastNormalMagnitude") { _ in
    FloatType.leastNormalMagnitude
  },
  Item(name: "leastNonzeroMagnitude") { _ in
    FloatType.leastNonzeroMagnitude
  },
  Item(name: "ulpOfOne") { _ in
    FloatType.ulpOfOne
  }
]),
```

Build and run, and select `Float16`.

As you've already seen, floating-point numbers can represent special values that integers can't. This section of operations sets them so you can look at the bit patterns produced.

Setting all the exponent bits to one represents infinity, and you can make -infinity by setting the sign bit. You can compare this to `greatestFiniteMagnitude` and `leastNormalMagnitude`. For the absolute smallest representable number, you can use the subnormal `leastNonzeroMagnitude`.

Not-a-number comes in two flavors. A **signaling NaN** *may* cause a hardware trap if you operate on it. This behavior is good for stopping as soon as an issue occurs instead of millions or billions of instructions later. Unfortunately, not all hardware (including ARM) supports it, so you can't depend on it. Many hardware platforms will immediately convert a signaling NaN into a quiet one.

You can make a **quiet NaN** by setting all the exponent bits and the most significant significand bit to one.

By setting other significand bits, you can send an error code along with your NaN. This extra information could, in theory, be used to identify the operation that caused the value to become a nan. But this is not done in practice.

> **Aside**: Having such a vast number of error codes representing different NaN codes is considered a significant weakness of IEEE-754. Emerging standards in scientific computing avoid this, but hardware adoption is, as of this writing, not available. Check out Type III Unum - Posit for recent developments in floating-point representations https://en.wikipedia.org/wiki/Unum_(number_format). Might you see support for this in a future version of Apple Silicon? Although it's not in the M1, Swift numerics seem to be mapping a path for this type of evolution.

Stepping and functions operations

The final two sections explore the **ulp** or **unit of least precision** of floating-point numbers. Add them to the menu.

```
Section(title: "Stepping", items:
[
  Item(name: ".nextUp") { $0.nextUp },
  Item(name: ".nextDown") { $0.nextDown },
  Item(name: ".ulp") { $0.ulp },
  Item(name: "add 0.1") { $0 + 0.1 },
  Item(name: "subtract 0.1") { $0 - 0.1 }
]),
Section(title: "Functions", items:
[
  Item(name: ".squareRoot()") { $0.squareRoot() },
  Item(name: "1/value") { 1/$0 }
])
```

Build and run the app. Select Float16.

Many are surprised that the precision of a floating-point number changes depending on its value. The bigger the value is, the less precise it is. Consider the following condition:

```
if value == value + 1 {
  fatalError("Can this happen?")
}
```

The fatalError will happen if the value is large enough. If value is 1e19, for example, adding one doesn't do anything.

On `Float16`, if you select **greatestFiniteMagnitude** and then **ulp**, it will report a value of 32. If you start with `greatestFiniteMagnitude` (65504) and then press **nextDown**, you get 65472, which is 32 away. It gets more extreme with the larger size floating-point value.

The other stepping methods let you experiment with precision. For example, start with zero on a `Float16` and add 0.1 a dozen times. You'll see you're already off by 0.01, which might cause an accountant to go crazy and stay awake at night. Although `BinaryFloatingPoint` types are great for overall range and precision, they're ill-suited to things like currency, for which you should use a `Decimal` type. `Decimal` can represent 0.1 exactly.

Full generic programming with floating-point

With the **BitViewer** app, you saw how you could use `BinaryFloatingPoint` to operate on floating-point types generically. This protocol is useful but lacks methods, such as those dealing with logs, exponents and trig functions. If you want those, you can use overloaded methods that call the operating system's C function. However, calling these functions can't be done generically.

Swift Evolution 0246: Generic Math(s) Functions (https://github.com/apple/swift-evolution/blob/master/proposals/0246-mathable.md), formally accepted by the Swift Core Team in March 2019, fixes this. Unfortunately, because of "source breaking consequences relating to type-checker performance and shadowing rules," it has not *yet* made it into the language proper. However, you can use it by importing the **Numerics** package. Apple thought it was important enough to cover in depth at a WWDC20 session.

Understanding the improved numeric protocols

The Swift Numerics package, which will eventually become part of Swift proper, adds important protocols to the standard library, including: `AlgebraicField`, `ElementaryFunctions`, `RealFunctions` and `Real`. They fit together with the currently shipping protocols like this:

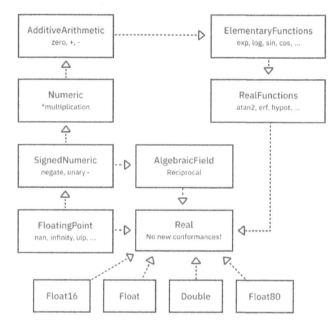

Numeric Protocols

Notice that this improved hierarchy de-emphasizes the importance of radix-two-only `BinaryFloatingPoint`. Instead, it creates a new empty protocol called `Real` that combines all the interesting protocols so you can write generic numeric algorithms like this:

```
func compute<RealType: Real>(input: RealType) -> RealType {
  // ...
}
```

`RealType` is a generic placeholder that can access all the transcendental functions and algebraic operations it needs by conforming to `Real`. That makes it trivial to switch between any floating-point types with relative ease.

The Swift Numerics package also introduces a Complex number type that consists of two floating-point types conforming to Real. It is layout compatible with the complex types found in C and C++, making it possible to play with popular signal processing libraries.

You'll now get some hands-on experience using the numerics package, the Real protocol and the Complex number type by implementing the famous Mandelbrot set. (Don't worry if you've never heard of the Mandelbrot set. You'll be in for a treat.)

Getting started with Mandelbrot

Open the **Mandelbrot** starter project and build and run the app. You'll see that the Swift Numerics package is loaded and built as a dependency.

Xcode lets you easily browse the source of Swift packages in your project. Take a moment to explore the Numerics package, paying particular attention to files under **swift-numerics/Sources/RealModule**. There, you'll see implementations for all the protocols diagrammed above.

The starter app is another SwiftUI app and looks like this in landscape orientation on an iPad:

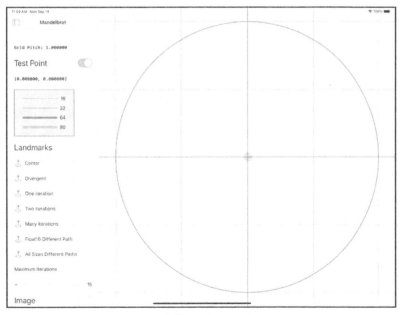

Mandelbrot Starter App

You can drag around the center dot, but it currently doesn't do anything.

Again, you won't focus on the specifics of **SwiftUI**, but you will see how to write floating-point code generically.

For this application, you'll compute millions of values continuously. The starter project sets the debug scheme to release mode to maximize performance. This setting will make specific loops execute faster by an order of magnitude. If you want to enable more reliable debugging, change back to a debug build using the Xcode scheme editor.

What is the Mandelbrot set?

In mathematics, a set is a collection of mathematical objects. The Mandelbrot set is a collection of complex numbers. Sound complex? It isn't. Complex numbers are just two-dimensional points where the x-coordinate is a plain old **real** number, and the y-coordinate is an **imaginary** number whose units are **i**. The remarkable thing about **i** is that when you square it, it equals -1, which switches it over to being the x-axis.

> **Note**: A Complex number is a Swift struct that consists of two values. These real and imaginary components are floating-point values of the same type. Like plain-old numbers, complex numbers support common operations such as sums, differences, products, etc. https://www.khanacademy.org is a great resource for learning about complex numbers if you're interested in the nitty-gritty details beyond what is discussed here.

To find out if a number is contained in the Mandelbrot set, square it repeatedly, and it either blows up (diverges) or does not. Values that don't diverge are in the Mandelbrot set.

Most numbers diverge. For example, take the number 5 and start squaring it. 5, 25, 125, 625, 3125, 15625, … It blows up, so is not in the Mandelbrot set. Take the number 0.1. It equals 0.1, 0.01, 0.001, 0.0001, 0.00001. This number never diverges and is in the set. You simply expand this idea to complex numbers that have two components. Mathematicians have proved that if a complex number gets further away than a radius of two from the origin, it will always diverge. You can use this fact to great effect to determine if a number is in the set or not.

> **Note**: Because sets are binary (either in the set or not in the set), you might wonder why Mandelbrot set drawings appear in psychedelic colors instead of just black and white. The colors come from how fast a given point diverges.

Converting to and from CGPoint

SwiftUI and UIKit depend on Core Graphics for rendering. The red dot that you can drag around in the interface represents a CGPoint with an x and y value consisting of CGFloats.

You'll want to convert CGPoint to a Complex type with real and imaginary parts and back again. The starter project defines a CGFloatConvertable protocol and implements it for all floating-point types to make this easy. You can find the implementation for this in **CGFloatConvertable.swift**.

> **Note**: Float80 is only available on Intel platforms, so it must be conditionalized with #if arch(x86_64). You'll see it only if you run on the iPad simulator on an Intel-based Mac.

Add a test point path

Let the generic programming using Real begin! Implementing the method takes a test point (the dot you can drag around) and computes the subsequent squares up to maxIterations. To do this, open the file **MandelbrotMath.swift** and find points(start:maxIterations:).

Then, replace this function with the following:

```
static func points<RealType: Real>(start: Complex<RealType>,
                                    maxIterations: Int)
  -> [Complex<RealType>] {
  // 1
  var results: [Complex<RealType>] = []
  results.reserveCapacity(maxIterations)

  // 2
  var z = Complex<RealType>.zero
  for _ in 0..<maxIterations {
    z = z * z + start
    defer {
      results.append(z) // 3
    }
  }
```

```
    // 4
    if z.lengthSquared > 4 {
      break
    }
  }
  return results
}
```

This function is generic across any `Real` conforming type. It returns a list of points that can be plotted by Core Graphics. These points are squares — the `start` point for a maximum of `maxIterations` times. Here are some key observations:

1. You don't know how many points will return, but you know it won't be more than `maxIterations`. Pre-allocating the results array will avoid repeated, intermediate allocations.

2. The loop uses the fact that the `Complex` type is an `AlgebraicField`, which can be squared and added. It handles the `real` and `imaginary` parts for you.

3. Using the `defer` block, you can guarantee that a point gets appended on every iteration of the loop, even if there is an early exit via `break`.

4. A point has diverged from the Mandelbrot set if it goes outside radius-two. To avoid calculating the expensive square root, you can use `lengthSquared` and 2^2 (four) as the limit.

Build and run the app. You can now explore specific points in the Mandelbrot set by dragging the dot around. The `MandelbrotView` calls your function with all floating-point types and renders them with different line thicknesses. In most cases, they line up perfectly, but sometimes they don't.

Explore the landmarks

The interface provides a set of named landmarks to try. Tap the landmark name, and the starting dot moves to a preset position.

- **Divergent**: This is outside the radius-two circle, so it stops immediately.

- **One iteration**: This squares the number once and ends up outside the circle for a total of one iteration.

- **Two iterations**: This squares the number, lands inside the circle, then squares it again and winds up outside the circle for a total of two iterations.

- **Many iterations**: This squares the number repeatedly up to Maximum Iterations and stays inside the circle, so it's in the Mandelbrot set.

- **Float16 Different Path**: A complicated path that is different for `Float16`. At about 25 iterations (which you can control with the slider), all the different types diverge.

- **All Sizes Different Paths**: This point appears to converge. But at about 100 iterations, all the different floating-point types take off in different directions. `Float16` stays converged while the other 32-, 64-, and 80-bit floats diverge and go their separate ways.

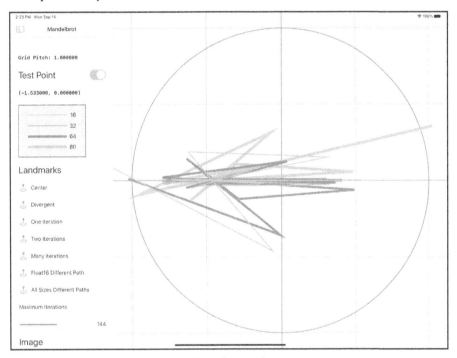

Unstable Paths

You might wonder what would happen if you tested *every single point* in the complex plane and used a different color depending on the number of iterations it took to diverge outside the radius-two circle. Would it look super cool? Yes, it would. You'll implement that now.

Implement Mandelbrot image generation

Time to turn your floating-point generic programming to 11. You'll want to do just what you did above. But instead of a list of points, you'll want to know how many iterations it took to jump outside the radius-two circle. You could use the same method and call .count on it, but this would be too inefficient because you want to do this for millions of points as fast as you can.

In the MandelbrotMath namespace, add the following static function:

```
@inlinable static
func iterations<RealType: Real>(start: Complex<RealType>,
                                max: Int) -> Int {
  var z = Complex<RealType>.zero
  var iteration = 0
  while z.lengthSquared <= 4 && iteration < max {
    z = z * z + start
    iteration += 1
  }
  return iteration
}
```

The @inlinable attribute means that you suggest that the compiler inject the body of this function at the call site, so you don't pay the cost of a function call.

This function computes the number of iterations required for a given start point very efficiently without requiring any heap allocations as the previous point function did for the array.

Next, find this method in **MandelbrotMath.swift**:

```
static func makeImage<RealType: Real & CGFloatConvertable>(
  for realType: RealType.Type,
  imageSize: CGSize,
  displayToModel: CGAffineTransform,
  maxIterations: Int,
  palette: PixelPalette
) -> CGImage? {
  // TODO: implement (2)
  nil
}
```

This method takes a specific RealType (e.g. Float, Double, Float16) and computes an entire image with dimension imageSize, where each pixel is a test point.

`displayToModel` is an **affine transform** that specifies how to go from the display coordinates (where the origin is the upper-left corner) to mathematical coordinates where the origin starts at the center of the view and follows the **right-hand-rule** with the y-axis going upward.

The `palette` is a lookup table that goes from the number of iterations for a particular point and maps to a 32-bit, red-green-blue-alpha pixel.

The starter project contains a pixel and bitmap abstraction to make image generation easy. This abstraction can be found in **Bitmap.swift** and is generic across pixel types.

Start by replacing the above function with:

```
static func makeImage<RealType: Real & CGFloatConvertable>(
  for realType: RealType.Type,
  imageSize: CGSize,
  displayToModel: CGAffineTransform,
  maxIterations: Int,
  palette: PixelPalette
) -> CGImage? {
  let width = Int(imageSize.width)
  let height = Int(imageSize.height)

  let scale = displayToModel.a
  let upperLeft = CGPoint.zero.applying(displayToModel)

  // Continued below
  return nil
}
```

This function truncates the width and height of the image and stores them as an integer in `width` and `height`.

It then takes the `displayToModel` transform, which can transform the display into math model points and grabs the scale stored in the "a" variable of the matrix. This operation is valid because there isn't rotation or skew and the x-scale and y-scale are equivalent.

`upperLeft` takes the display point `(0,0)` and pushes it through the transform to find a position in the complex plane.

Next, replace the `return nil` statement with the following:

```
let bitmap = Bitmap<ColorPixel>(width: width, height: height) {
  width, height, buffer in
    for y in 0 ..< height {
      for x in 0 ..< width {
```

```
        let position = Complex(
          RealType(upperLeft.x + CGFloat(x) * scale),
          RealType(upperLeft.y - CGFloat(y) * scale))
        let iterations =
          MandelbrotMath.iterations(start: position,
                                    max: maxIterations)
          buffer[x + y * width] =
            palette.values[iterations % palette.values.count]
        }
      }
    }
  return bitmap.cgImage
```

This code uses the `Bitmap` abstraction to create a `CGImage` with the specified `width` and `height`. A `CGPoint` initializes the `Complex` type to use as a starting point. Then, it calls the inlined `iterations` function defined above to determine the number of iterations for a particular test point. Finally, it pokes a color value looked up from the `palette` into the pixel location. The `cgImage` accessor initializes an image from these pixels.

With this code in place, rerun the app to explore the Mandelbrot set in detail. Tap the image switch to show the image. You can pan and zoom the image to reveal this fractal world's infinite complexity.

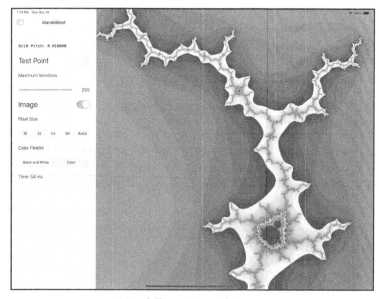

Mandelbrot Zoomed Image

Infinite patterns and complexity. All from squaring a number.

Precision and performance

The **Float Size** control lets you pick which generic version gets called. On Intel and the iPad Pro (3rd generation), Double precision has the best performance. Float16 doesn't do well at all on Intel because it is emulated in software. Surprisingly, it doesn't do that great on an actual device, either — all the conversions between CGFloat and Float16 result in lower performance.

Float16 renders well at low zoom factors, but you can see that it breaks down quickly as you zoom in. You start seeing blocky artifacts like this:

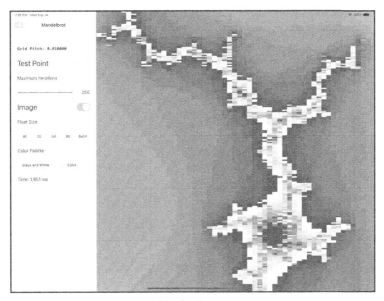

Blocky Image

Float80 is also surprisingly slow on modern Intel machines. This lower performance results from emulating the computations in microcode on the CPU and because it takes time to marshal between the Core Graphics CGFloat size.

If you experiment with the other types, you'll see that same blockiness eventually with all the floating-point types the closer you zoom. The more precision the type has, the deeper you can go without quantization errors.

Improving performance with SIMD

Can you make the rendering loop run faster and remain in pure Swift? Yes, you can.

All modern CPUs support **single-instruction-multiple-data** (SIMD) computation.

For example, instead of doing 16 additions one by one, the processor can group one set of 16 numbers with another set of 16 numbers and perform all 16 additions at once, in parallel. One clock tick. This performance requires some tricky shuffling of the data, and, in some cases, the compiler automatically does it for you. This optimization is known as **auto-vectorization** and is an active area of compiler research.

To help the compiler, Swift provides SIMD types for integers and floating-point numbers. If you group numbers using a SIMD type, the compiler can perform auto-vectorization much more reliably.

Swift supports SIMD2, SIMD4, SIMD8, SIMD16, SIMD32, SIMD64 types. Each of these contains Scalar types that are an integer or floating-point number. SIMD8 is said to contain eight scalar **lanes**.

Now, use SIMD8 to speed up the Mandelbrot image calculation by performing eight test point calculations in parallel.

Once again, open the file **MandelbrotMath.swift** and find the function:

```
static func makeImageSIMD8_Float64(
  imageSize: CGSize,
  displayToModel: CGAffineTransform,
  maxIterations: Int,
  palette: PixelPalette
) -> CGImage? {
  // TODO: implement (3)
  nil
}
```

Replace it with:

```
static func makeImageSIMD8_Float64(
  imageSize: CGSize,
  displayToModel: CGAffineTransform,
  maxIterations: Int,
  palette: PixelPalette
) -> CGImage? {
  typealias SIMDX = SIMD8
  typealias ScalarFloat = Float64
  typealias ScalarInt = Int64
  // Continued below
}
```

This code defines some type aliases you can use to play around with different sizes. ScalarFloat and ScalarInt must have the same width in bits because that is what modern hardware requires. If you accidentally make them different sizes, the program won't type check.

Next, add this code to the method:

```
let width = Int(imageSize.width)
let height = Int(imageSize.height)

let scale = ScalarFloat(displayToModel.a)
let upperLeft = CGPoint.zero.applying(displayToModel)
let left = ScalarFloat(upperLeft.x)
let upper = ScalarFloat(upperLeft.y)
// Continued below
```

This code looks similar to the previous non-SIMD version. But because you can't use `Complex` in a SIMD type, you need to perform the operations explicitly in the loop.

Next, add some useful constants to the method:

```
let fours = SIMDX(repeating: ScalarFloat(4))
let twos = SIMDX(repeating: ScalarFloat(2))
let ones = SIMDX<ScalarInt>.one
let zeros = SIMDX<ScalarInt>.zero
// Continued below
```

These constants appear in the inner loop. Each is eight lanes wide (as determined by SIMDX, which aliases to SIMD8).

Now, use the bitmap initializer:

```
let bitmap = Bitmap<ColorPixel>(width: width, height: height) {
  width, height, buffer in
    // 1
    let scalarCount = SIMDX<Int64>.scalarCount
    // 2
    var realZ: SIMDX<ScalarFloat>
    var imaginaryZ: SIMDX<ScalarFloat>
    var counts: SIMDX<ScalarInt>
    // 3
    let initialMask = fours .> fours // all false
    var stopIncrementMask = initialMask
    // 4
    let ramp = SIMDX((0..<scalarCount).map {
      left + ScalarFloat($0) * scale })
    // 5
    for y in 0 ..< height {
       // Continue adding code here
    }
  }
  return bitmap.cgImage
```

That code creates the bitmap and returns it as an image. Here are the details:

1. `scalarCount` is set to eight because SIMDX aliases SIMD8.

2. `realZ` and `imaginaryZ` are eight lanes of floating-point numbers to keep track of how these eight test points evolve. `counts` are eight lanes of the number of iterations for each test point.

3. The `initialMask` and `stopIncrementMask` control the `counts` that increment in the inner loop. If none of the counts increment, the loop will exit early. Here, you see the operator `.>`. This operation performs a > operation for each of the lanes independently.

4. `ramp` is used to determine the real value starting point of the complex number efficiently below.

5. `y` loops row-by-row, creating the image.

Now, add this into to the y row loop:

```
let imaginary = SIMDX(repeating: upper - ScalarFloat(y) * scale)

for x in 0 ..< width / scalarCount {
  let real = SIMDX(repeating: ScalarFloat(x * scalarCount) *
scale) + ramp
  realZ = .zero
  imaginaryZ = .zero
  counts = .zero
  stopIncrementMask = initialMask

  // Continue adding code here
}
// Process remainder
```

This code computes the starting `imaginary` component used for the whole row of pixels. Then, you process each of the width pixels in chunks of eight. The answers accumulate in `realZ` and `imaginaryZ`, while the iterations accumulate in `counts`.

Next, continue adding this code:

```
// 1
for _ in 0..<maxIterations {
  // 2
  let realZ2 = realZ * realZ
  let imaginaryZ2 = imaginaryZ * imaginaryZ
  let realImaginaryTimesTwo = twos * realZ * imaginaryZ
  realZ = realZ2 - imaginaryZ2 + real
  imaginaryZ = realImaginaryTimesTwo + imaginary
```

```
// 3
let newMask = (realZ2 + imaginaryZ2) .>= fours

// 4
stopIncrementMask .|= newMask

// 5
let incrementer = ones.replacing(with: zeros,
                           where: stopIncrementMask)
if incrementer == SIMDX<ScalarInt>.zero {
  break
}

// 6
counts &+= incrementer
}

// 7
let paletteSize = palette.values.count
for index in 0 ..< scalarCount {
  buffer[x * scalarCount + index + y * width] =
    palette.values[Int(counts[index]) % paletteSize]
}
```

This code does the following:

1. For the eight values, you compute up to the maximum number of iterations.

2. This is the algebra used to compute the square of a complex number spelled out. Recall $(a+b)(a+b) = a^2+2ab+b^2$. Because b is imaginary, squaring it makes it a real number. The `Complex` type handled this for you before, and now you're doing it manually.

3. You check if any of the test points sits outside the radius-two circle. If it is, the mask is true for that lane.

4. You accumulate this mask so that if none of the lanes are incrementing, the loop can exit early.

5. You take a list of eight ones and replace them with zero if that lane has stopped incrementing. This masking is how you avoid doing an if/else computation, which kills parallel performance. If every `count` has stopped incrementing (`incrementer` is all zeros), you cut out early.

6. The incrementer, which is eight lanes of ones and zeros, accumulate into the `counts`.

7. Finally, you need to look up the color for each of the iteration counts in the `palette` and write it into memory.

At this point, the algorithm is done. To make it work for any width (not just multiples of eight), you can add this code to process the remainder:

```
let remainder = width % scalarCount
let lastIndex = width / scalarCount * scalarCount
for index in (0 ..< remainder) {
  let start = Complex(
    left + ScalarFloat(lastIndex + index) * scale,
    upper - ScalarFloat(y) * scale)
  var z = Complex<ScalarFloat>.zero
  var iteration = 0
  while z.lengthSquared <= 4 && iteration < maxIterations {
    z = z * z + start
    iteration += 1
  }
  buffer[lastIndex + index + y * width] =
    palette.values[iteration % palette.values.count]
}
```

The above code is the non-SIMD algorithm. If you had a display width that was not divisible by eight, this code would handle a couple of leftover pixels.

Your SIMD implementation is now complete. You can run the app and now use the 8x64 float type. For fewer iterations, you won't see much of a speedup. However, if you boost the number of iterations to 255, you start seeing enormous performance wins. For example, with max iterations set to 255 and a high zoom factor, Float64 takes 750 ms while the SIMD8<Float64> implementation is 332 ms.

Where are the limits?

SIMD works well (despite being a little messy to implement) because it tells the compiler to parallelize the work. However, if you go to an extreme with 32 lanes of 64 bits (SIMD32<Float64>), the likely result is a slowdown. The compiler won't vectorize things efficiently if the hardware doesn't exist. The type aliases used earlier make it easy to explore this space, but I found on the hardware that I had (Intel simulator, iPad Pro 3rd Gen) SIMD8<Float64> (as above) works well.

> **Note:** To go even faster than what the CPU can provide, you could take the rendering algorithm and port it to the GPU. This involves writing the algorithm as a shader in OpenGL or Metal.

Ranges

Now, turn your attention to another important aspect of Swift numeric types that you've been using all along — ranges. Earlier, you saw that integers and floating-point types conform to the Comparable protocol. This conformance is crucial for supporting operations on ranges of numbers.

Like numeric types themselves, it would be reasonable to guess that ranges are a concept built into the compiler. But, as with many core features in Swift, they're just part of the ever extensible, standard library.

It turns out that a Range is a generic struct with a lower and upper of type Bound that conforms to Comparable. For example, in an empty playground (or the one provided in the starter folder), type this:

```
enum Number: Comparable {
    case zero, one, two, three, four
}
```

With this simple definition, it is possible to form a range:

```
let longForm =
    Range<Number>(uncheckedBounds: (lower: .one, upper: .three))
```

The ..< operator makes it feel like a built-in language feature and is equivalent:

```
let shortForm = Number.one ..< .three
shortForm == longForm    // true
```

A key quality of a range is that it doesn't include the upper bound. You can see that by running this:

```
shortForm.contains(.zero)    // false
shortForm.contains(.one)     // true
shortForm.contains(.two)     // true
shortForm.contains(.three)   // false
```

If you need to include the upper bound, there is another range type called ClosedRange. Try this:

```
let longFormClosed =
    ClosedRange<Number>(uncheckedBounds: (lower: .one,
upper: .three))

let shortFormClosed = Number.one ... .three
```

```
longFormClosed == shortFormClosed   // true

shortFormClosed.contains(.zero)    // false
shortFormClosed.contains(.one)     // true
shortFormClosed.contains(.two)     // true
shortFormClosed.contains(.three)   // true
```

But those aren't all the range types, of course. You can also create partial ranges using prefix and postfix operators. Add this:

```
let r1 = ...Number.three      // PartialRangeThrough<Number>
let r2 = ..<Number.three      // PartialRangeUpTo<Number>
let r3 = Number.zero...        // PartialRangeFrom<Number>
```

As you see, there are many ways to specify a range.

Looping over a range

You might wonder if you can use these ranges in a for loop, such as:

```
for i in 1 ..< 3 {
  print(i)
}
```

For Number, not quite. This capability is conditional on Strideable conformance. You might remember that the Swift numeric types are all Strideable. Additionally, the Strideable associated type Stride must conform to SignedInteger.

To see this, make Number adopt Strideable. First, overwrite the definition to this:

```
enum Number: Int, Comparable {
  static func < (lhs: Number, rhs: Number) -> Bool {
    lhs.rawValue < rhs.rawValue
  }

  case zero, one, two, three, four
}
```

Next, add the conformance:

```
extension Number: Strideable {
  public func distance(to other: Number) -> Int {
    other.rawValue - rawValue
  }
  public func advanced(by n: Int) -> Number {
    Number(rawValue: (rawValue + n) % 4)!
  }
}
```

```
    public typealias Stride = Int
}
```

Importantly, the `Stride` type is set to an `Int`, which is a `SignedInteger`. Using `Int` makes your `Number` type a `CountableRange` which is a typealias defined by the system:

```
typealias CountableRange<Bound> = Range<Bound>
    where Bound: Strideable, Bound.Stride: SignedInteger
```

So now, you can do this:

```
for i in Number.one ..< .three {
    print(i)
}
```

It will print one and two to the debug console.

Striding backward and at non-unit intervals

Ranges always require the lower and upper bounds to be ordered. What if you want to count backward?

A common way to do this is to treat the range like a collection and use the `reversed()` algorithm like so:

```
for i in (Number.one ..< .three).reversed() {
    print(i)
}
```

However, when you conform to `Strideable`, you can use the standard library `stride` functions even if your type is not a `CountableRange`. Try this:

```
for i in stride(from: Number.two, to: .zero, by: -1) {
    print(i)
}

for i in stride(from: Number.two, through: .one, by: -1) {
    print(i)
}
```

You can also see the usage of `stride` with `CGFloat` in the **Mandelbrot** App. In the file **GraphingView.swift**, strides of horizontal and vertical lines are created as part of the `GridLines` shape to give the appearance of scaling graph paper.

Range expressions

If you're writing a function that takes a range as an input, you might wonder which of the five flavors to use. A good option is to use the RangeExpression protocol to conform to all range types. Diagrammed, it looks like this:

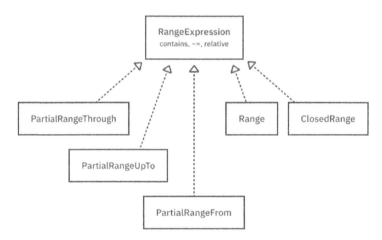

Range Expression

You can take advantage of this protocol by making your function abstracted across range type. For example, if you write this:

```
func find<R: RangeExpression>(value: R.Bound, in range: R)
  -> Bool {
  range.contains(value)
}
```

It lets you use any form of range, like so:

```
find(value: Number.one, in: Number.zero ... .two) // true
find(value: Number.one, in: ...Number.two)        // true
find(value: Number.one, in: ..<Number.three)      // true
```

Making the function generic keeps your API much more flexible than if the user had to remember to use a specific range operator such as ..< or .... Now, they all just work.

Key points

You've seen how Swift builds numeric types and ranges from the ground up using protocols and generics. Here are some key points to take away:

• Swift describes the integer types through a composition of protocols.

• As you move down the protocol hierarchy to `FixedWidthInteger`, you get more and more functionality that you can use generically.

• Integers are represented using two's complement binary.

• To negate a number in two's complement, you flip the bits and add one.

• Signed integers sign extend a value as it shifts right. Unsigned integers don't.

• Swift traps your program if you overflow. But you can shut this safety feature off by using operators that begin with & or special truncating initializers.

• Endian refers to the ordering of bytes in memory. Little-endian is the most common on modern Apple platforms.

• Swift supports IEEE-754 binary floating-point types and uses protocols to describe them.

• Floating-point numbers can be finite, infinite, and nan.

• `BinaryFloatingPoint` conforming types have a radix of two.

• If you're working with currencies, consider using the `Decimal` type, which uses a radix equal to 10.

• Some floating-point types and features are not supported by hardware. (Intel processors emulate `Float16`. `Float80` is not supported on ARM.)

• The Swift Numerics package hasn't been merged into the standard library yet. However, it allows for full generic programming, using the `Real` protocol.

• Swift Numerics provides a `Complex` number type.

• The SIMD types let you group data so the compiler can vectorize them. Using SIMD can significantly increase speed but also adds complexity.

• There are a wide variety of range types defined by the Swift standard library.

• `RangeExpression` can be used to unify the different range types.

Where to go from here?

Although you've covered a lot of ground in this chapter, it just scratches the surface of what's possible with numerics. You can explore some of the corners of IEEE-754 by reading the Wikipedia article at:

https://en.wikipedia.org/wiki/IEEE_754

The Swift Numerics package is one of the more exciting recent developments in Swift. It will bring many powerful features, such as approximate equality, additional number types, generalized tensors and more. For the latest information, check out the forum at:

https://forums.swift.org/c/related-projects/swift-numerics/56

Finally, you've also looked at generic ranges, which can be used as sequences or collections, or to slice existing collections. You'll explore the details of these types in the next chapter.

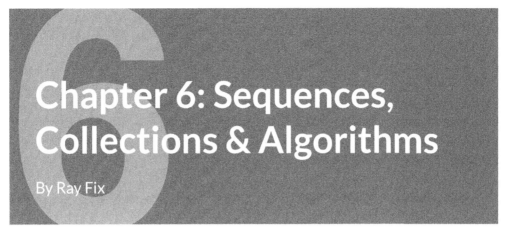

Chapter 6: Sequences, Collections & Algorithms
By Ray Fix

Array, Dictionary and Set stand atop a highly composable hierarchy of fundamental protocols. These protocols, which include Sequence and Collection among others, capture the essence of these types. The Swift standard library design serves as a case study in Swift generics and protocol-oriented programming that you can learn from and leverage.

The concepts these protocols express are general enough that they appear where you might not expect. For example, the ranges and strides you looked at in the last chapter are sequences and collections, just like arrays are. Although a Range type doesn't need to allocate memory for elements like an Array does, it shares many of the same capabilities and characteristics. In this chapter, you'll learn about Sequence, Collection and other related protocols and see how to use them to write generic algorithms that operate across type families.

A family of protocols

By defining primitive notions of a sequence of values, a collection of values and other collection characteristics using protocols, you can write high-performance, generic algorithms. This lets the compiler deal with the specifics of the memory layout that concrete types use to adopt them.

In other languages, the number of implementations for data structures and their algorithms can face what is known as "the M by N problem". Without a language feature like generics and protocols, the number of implementations for M data structures and N algorithms is the simple product of the two.

Non-generic, non protocol-orientated results in N+M implementations

M N	first	sorted	dropped	chunked(by:)
Set	Custom code	Custom code	Custom code	Custom code
Array	Custom code	Custom code	Custom code	Custom code
Dictionary	Custom code	Custom code	Custom code	Custom code
QuadTree	Custom code	Custom code	Custom code	Custom code

M by N implementations

Imagine having to maintain all this code. The above graphic shows just four collection types and four algorithms for a total of sixteen implementations. The truth is that Swift has tons of concrete sequence and collection types such as CollectionOfOne, JoinedSequence, DropWhileSequence and many more.

Thanks to protocols and generics, the number of implementations is only M + N. And that means you never repeat yourself.

Generic, protocol-orientated results in only N+M implementations

first	sorted	dropped	chunked(by:)
Generic code	Generic code	Generic code	Generic code

Set	Array	Dictionary	QuadTree

M plus N implementations

In this world, any type that conforms to the required protocols gets all the algorithm implementations generated on-demand for free. The compiler uses the **protocol witness table** of protocol declaration to implement function definitions. It can also create specializations for particular concrete types as an optimization. Although there's programmer complexity cost in knowing about these fundamental protocol types, this knowledge pays for itself handily, as you'll see.

Sequences and collections

To take full advantage of the system, you need to become familiar with the protocols involved with sequences and collections. Here's what the hierarchy looks like:

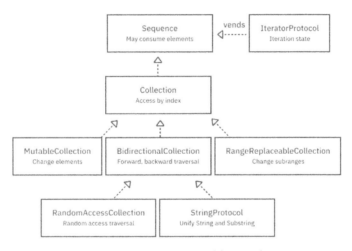

Sequence types protocol hierarchy

The hierarchy includes:

- **Sequence** - This is the most primitive type in the hierarchy that lets you iterate through a list of values. It makes no guarantee about being able to revisit an item. Although a conforming type could be a collection like an array, it could also be a stream of data from a network socket or a sequence of random numbers that never repeat. A type adopting Sequence can be immutable but must vend an associated mutable type that conforms to IteratorProtocol.

- **IteratorProtocol** - This behind-the-scenes protocol knows how to get the next element and returns nil when it's done. It's possible to use an iterator type directly, but usually, the compiler creates one for you when you use a for-statement.

- **Collection** - All collections are sequences, but `Collection` adds a guarantee that you can revisit items using an index type. If you have an index, you can look up an element in constant time **O(1)**. When you implement your collections, it can be tempting to break this guarantee. But doing so breaks the complexity guarantees of the algorithms you inherit. Try not to do this. If you must break the complexity guarantee, make it clear in the documentation of the API.

- **MutableCollection** - This refines collections that let you mutate elements through an index. The mutation is all about poking individual elements. Importantly, it does not imply the ability to add and remove elements.

- **BidirectionalCollection** - This spices up a collection to allow you to traverse it both forward and backward by advancing the index appropriately.

- **RangeReplaceableCollection** - These collections let you modify whole subranges at a time. This conformance lets you delete, insert and append elements.

- **RandomAccessCollection** - This allows a collection to traverse elements in any order in constant time. It lets you update the index and measure distances between indices in constant time.

- **StringProtocol** - This is a bidirectional collection used for `String` and `Substring`. You'll explore `String` in more detail in the next chapter.

This list might feel pretty theoretical, so it's time to get some hands-on practice with some simple, concrete examples.

Iterators and sequences

Create a custom type that counts down to zero when you loop over it with a `for` statement. Open the **Countdown** starter playground for this chapter and add the following:

```
struct CountdownIterator: IteratorProtocol {
  var count: Int
  mutating func next() -> Int? {
    guard count >= 0 else {   // 1
      return nil
    }
    defer { count -= 1 }      // 2
    return count
  }
}
```

As you can see, defining an iterator is easy. You need to implement a mutating `next()` method that updates the state and returns the next element. This code:

1. Keeps going as long as the `count` state is greater than or equal to zero. Otherwise, it terminates the iteration by returning `nil`.

2. Decrements the count *after* returning the current value. Changing a value after returning it is a common use of the `defer` statement.

Now, create the actual `Countdown` sequence type that vends `CountdownIterator`:

```
struct Countdown: Sequence {
  let start: Int
  func makeIterator() -> CountdownIterator {
    CountdownIterator(count: start)
  }
}
```

All this type does is return the iterator above. Now, try it out by adding:

```
for value in Countdown(start: 5) {
  print(value)
}
```

Running the playground counts down from five to zero. Under the hood, the compiler instantiates an iterator for `Countdown` and calls `next()` repeatedly until it returns `nil`. The behind-the-scenes iterator instance is what keeps track of the loop's state.

> **Note:** In case you missed it, there are a lot of type inference and generic constraints in action here. Sequence types have associated types for the iterators (`Iterator`) they create and the elements (`Element`) they return. A generic constraint guarantees that `Sequence.Element` is the same type as `Sequence.Iterator.Element`. It's also possible to hide the iterator's implementation from clients by returning `some IteratorProtocol` from `makeIterator()` instead of a specific type.

Admittedly, the code above is contrived and academic. Still, it's good to get experience building sequences from the ground up like this so you can appreciate the other tools at your disposal in the Swift standard library. This exercise also reveals how the state and its mutation are kept in iterator instances while the sequence remains immutable.

StrideThrough and StrideTo

The previous section might have seemed like a lot of code for the job. Yes, there are simpler ways of accomplishing the countdown task. For example, you could have used a simple `StrideThrough` type, which you create by calling the `stride` function you saw in the last chapter. Add this to the playground:

```
print("---")
for value in stride(from: 5, through: 0, by: -1) {
  print(value)
}
print("---")
for value in stride(from: 5, to: -1, by: -1) {
  print(value)
}
```

Both `StrideThrough` and `StrideTo` conform to `Sequence` and result from `stride(from:through:)` and `stride(from:to:)`, respectively. When you run the playground, you'll see two more countdowns from five to zero. The argument `through:` includes value in the stride, while the argument `to:` goes up to but doesn't include it.

UnfoldFirstSequence and UnfoldSequence

The Swift standard library functions `sequence(first:next:)` and `sequence(state:next:)` let you define custom sequences without needing to define a new sequence type (and iterator). Try it out by adding this to the end of your playground:

```
let countDownFrom5 = sequence(first: 5) { value in
  value-1 >= 0 ? value-1 : nil
}
print("---")
for value in countDownFrom5 {
  print(value)
}
```

Running the playground, you once again see numbers counting down from five to zero in the console. The function `sequence(first:next:)` returns the type `UnfoldFirstSequence`. You need an initial value and a closure taking the current value and returning the element or `nil` when done. Notice this sequence can never be empty because you specify the first element.

Next, add this variant to the end of the playground:

```
let countDownFrom5State = sequence(state: 5) { (state: inout
Int) -> Int? in
  defer { state -= 1 }
  return state >= 0 ? state : nil
}
print("---")
for value in countDownFrom5State {
  print(value)
}
```

Running the playground once again counts down from five to zero. This overload of the `sequence()` function takes an initial state and a closure that lets you mutate that state with an `inout` variable. The value returned from the closure is the `Optional<Element>` type of the sequence. This sequence is represented by `UnfoldSequence` and is more flexible than the first overload because it treats the state and the elements returned independently.

> **Note**: The name "unfold" is a functional programming term that is the opposite of `fold`. Swift uses a common alternate terminology `reduce` instead of `fold`. You might even argue that the standard library authors should have used a name like `Unreduced` instead of `UnfoldSequence`. In practice, you don't need to worry about the name of these types because they're seldom declared explicitly and often hidden behind type erasure. You'll learn more about reduce and friends in Chapter 10: "Higher-Order Functions".

Type erasure with AnySequence

To tame complexity, you'll often want to hide type details of a sequence from users (and yourself). It would be ideal to return an opaque return type, such as `some Sequence`, from your function. However, opaque return types don't currently let you constrain associated types, such as the `Element`, so unfortunately this doesn't work. But there's still a way. Hide these unimportant type details and keep your interface clean with the type erasure `AnySequence`.

Add this handy helper method for `AnySequence` to your playground:

```
extension Sequence {
  func eraseToAnySequence() -> AnySequence<Element> {
    AnySequence(self)
  }
}
```

This code adds an extension to Sequence that erases concrete sequences to AnySequence. It's in the same spirit as when the **Combine** framework type erases publishers, which you might have seen before.

Use the extension helper by adding:

```
let seq = countDownFrom5State.eraseToAnySequence()
print("---")
for value in seq {
  print(value)
}
print(type(of: countDownFrom5State))
print(type(of: seq))
```

Run it to see that the type of seq is AnySequence<Int> instead of the underlying countDownFrom5State, an UnfoldSequence<Int, Int>. It's helpful to type-erase method parameters and return AnySequence so you're not locked into a specific kind of sequence.

Although it hides implementation complexity, there's a minor penalty to this extra indirection. For example, if you wrap an Array in AnySequence (or AnyCollection), you'll no longer be able to access the contiguous storage buffer of the array. This lack of access occurs because, once again, protocols generally make no assumptions about the memory layout of the concrete types that adopt them.

Implementing Sequence with AnySequence and AnyIterator

In the example above, you defined a sequence and then type-erased it, but AnySequence also gives you an initializer to do both in one go. Add this:

```
let anotherCountdown5 = AnySequence<Int> { () ->
AnyIterator<Int> in
  var count = 5
  return AnyIterator<Int> {
    defer { count -= 1}
    return count >= 0 ? count : nil
  }
}
print("---")
for value in anotherCountdown5 {
  print(value)
}
```

When you run the playground, you see another countdown from five. This AnySequence takes a closure that makes an iterator. You could make that type explicitly or use AnyIterator which type erases iterators. This version of the initializer lets you define the next() method inline.

The examples above demonstrate the many ways the Swift standard library lets you create a sequence. In the next section, you'll graduate from counting down from five. First, though, try a few exercises to see if you've got the concepts down.

Exercises

Answers to exercises, as always, are in the final download materials. For best results, don't peek — try it yourself first.

1. Turn the array `["a", "tale", "of", "two", "cities"]` into a type-erased sequence.

2. Write an extension on `Sequence` called `countingDown()` that returns an array of tuples of remaining count and elements. For example, the array from question one returns: `[(4, "cities"), (3, "two"), (2, "of"), (1, "tale"), (0, "a")]`. **Hint**: Existing sequence algorithms `enumerated()` and `reversed()` might help you do the job with minimal code.

3. Create a function `primes(to value: Int) -> AnySequence<Int>` that creates a sequence of the prime numbers up to and possibly including `value`. Brute force prime finding is fine. For example, `primes(through: 32)` will return `[2, 3, 5, 7, 11, 13, 17, 19, 23, 29, 31]`.

Collections

Collections build on top of sequences and feature an additional guarantee that you can revisit elements. To visit an element, all you need is an index that can access an element in constant time **O(1)**. This complexity guarantee is important because many other algorithms rely on this base level of performance to guarantee their own performance.

A FizzBuzz collection

Like sequences, an excellent way to learn about collections is to create a simple one yourself. Looking at all the protocol requirements of `Collection` makes creating one seem a daunting task. However, because most of the API has good default protocol implementations, it's pretty straightforward. In some ways, it's easier to create a collection than to create a sequence from scratch. What's more, because `Collection` **is-a** Sequence, you get all the sequence functionality for free. You'll use **FizzBuzz** to see this in action.

FizzBuzz is a classic exercise in which you print out numbers from 1 to 100. However, if the number is evenly divisible by three, you print "Fizz," and if the number is evenly divisible by five, you print "Buzz". If the number is evenly divisible by both three and five, you print "FizzBuzz". The twist is that instead of just printing the numbers, you'll create a custom collection type of numbers, fizzes, buzzes and fizzbuzzes.

Start by opening the **FizzBuzz** starter playground and adding:

```
struct FizzBuzz: Collection {
  typealias Index = Int

  var startIndex: Index { 1 }
  var endIndex: Index { 101 }
  func index(after i: Index) -> Index { i + 1 }

  // .... subscript with index ....

}
```

This code defines the `FizzBuzz` collection. You first decide what the associated type for `Index` will be and define the start and end index. It isn't necessary to define `Index` here with `typealias`, but doing so clarifies the code. The `endIndex` is defined to be **one past** the valid range. The function `index(after:)` defines how to advance your index. In this case, the implementation is trivial and just adds one.

Next, replace the comment with a working subscript operator:

```
subscript (index: Index) -> String {
  precondition(indices.contains(index), "out of 1-100")
  switch (index.isMultiple(of: 3), index.isMultiple(of: 5)) {
  case (false, false):
    return String(index)
  case (true, false):
    return "Fizz"
  case (false, true):
    return "Buzz"
  case (true, true):
    return "FizzBuzz"
  }
}
```

This code uses Swift pattern matching to implement the actual FizzBuzz logic. The `switch` tuple expression generates the appropriate element for a given index.

That's it. The default protocol implementations do the rest of the work of making a full-blown collection type. You can test your new collection with:

```
let fizzBuzz = FizzBuzz()
for value in fizzBuzz {
  print(value, terminator: " ")
}
print()
```

Run the playground and watch it go. Again, under the hood, the compiler is creating a `FizzBuzz` iterator and calling `next()` on it repeatedly until the loop terminates. But there's more. You can use all the collection algorithms Swift has to offer. For example, you can print the position of all the "FizzBuzz" occurrences using `enumerated()` and `reduce(into:)` by adding this to your playground:

```
let fizzBuzzPositions =
  fizzBuzz.enumerated().reduce(into: []) { list, item in
    if item.element == "FizzBuzz" {
      list.append(item.offset + fizzBuzz.startIndex)
    }
  }

print(fizzBuzzPositions)
```

Running the playground outputs `[15, 30, 45, 60, 75, 90]`. The `enumerated()` method produces a tuple of offsets and elements. You need to make sure you add the `startIndex` to the offset to get a valid position.

BidirectionalCollection

Because you only implemented `Collection` conformance, the standard library algorithms only know how to walk *forward* through your collection. To see this, add some debug printing to your previous implementation of `index(after:)`:

```
func index(after i: Index) -> Index {
  print("Calling \(#function) with \(i)")
  return i + 1
}
```

Comment out your previous test code and add the following:

```
print(fizzBuzz.dropLast(40).count)
```

As you might have expected, this drops the last 40 elements and prints the number 60, the remaining count of elements. You might be surprised to see `after(index:)` being called 220 times.

The first 100 calls are finding the last element in the collection from the beginning. The subsequent 60 calls are to find the first index of the range to be dropped. The final 60 calls are to count the remaining 60 elements.

You can reduce the number of calls by making `FizzBuzz` a `BidirectionalCollection` — one that can be traversed both forward and backward. Add this to the playground:

```swift
extension FizzBuzz: BidirectionalCollection {
  func index(before i: Index) -> Index {
    print("Calling \(#function) with \(i)")
    return i - 1
  }
}
```

This code lets you go to an index before the current one with the trivial implementation `i - 1`.

When you run the playground, you get the same answer as before: 60. But you'll see that `index(before:)` gets called only 40 times as it scans backward to find the first item to drop. And then `index(after:)` gets called 60 times to count the remaining elements. The algorithm adapted to take advantage of the bidirectional traversal capability.

RandomAccessCollection

You can eliminate *all* the extra traversing calls by making `FizzBuzz` a random access collection. Add this to your playground:

```swift
extension FizzBuzz: RandomAccessCollection {
}
```

Now, when you run `print(fizzBuzz.dropLast(40).count)`, the functions `index(before:)` and `index(after:)` aren't called at all. In general, when you make a collection a `RandomAccessCollection`, you need to implement a function called `index(_:offsetBy:)`. However, in this case, because you chose an `Int` to be your index type and because integers are `Strideable` and `Comparable`, you get the implementation for free. In fact, with `RandomAccessCollection` conformance and a strideable index, the library does all the work and you can delete your implementations for `index(before:)` and `index(after:)`. Everything still works without them.

Next, it's time to explore making collections modifiable with a slightly beefier example.

MutableCollection

Because FizzBuzz is not mutable by definition, change gears with another example. Mutable collections allow you to change elements with a subscript setter. MutableCollection implies that items can be swapped and reordered. This operation doesn't imply a change in the size of the collection.

This example features not only mutability but also a custom, non-integer index type. You'll implement Conway's Life, a two-dimensional, cellular automata simulation, using a custom collection.

The rules of Conway's Life

As a so-called "zero-player" game, the rules of Conway's Life are simple:

- **Starvation**: Any cell with fewer than two neighbors dies.

- **Equilibrium**: Any cell with two or three neighbors lives.

- **Overpopulation**: Any cell with more than three neighbors dies.

- **Birth**: Any empty cell with exactly three neighbors is born.

Once the app is complete, it will look like this:

Conway's Life app screenshot

You can draw cells and then start and stop the simulation, watching the cells evolve until they reach a stable point and the simulation automatically stops.

Open the starter project, **ConwaysLife**, and take a moment to familiarize yourself with the files.

Here's a quick rundown to help get you acquainted.

- **AppMain.swift**: This is the standard app definition and @main entry point.

- **ContentView.swift**: This creates and owns simulation model type. It presents a LifeView that displays and lets you interact with the model.

- **Bitmap.swift**: You might remember this type from the **Mandelbrot** project. It represents a 2-D set of pixels. This version generalizes it more by removing the PixelProtocol requirement from the Pixel placeholder type, letting you use it more generally as a 2-D grid of anything. You still have the power of the PixelProtocol and the ability to generate a CGImage using the conditional conformance defined in this file.

- **Bitmap+Collection.swift**: This is where you'll define mutable, random access collection conformance for bitmaps.

- **LifeSimulation.swift**: This is where you'll define the business logic of the game.

- **LifeView.swift**: This is the SwiftUI definition of your user interface that uses your LifeSimulation model.

- **RingMemory.swift**: This is a utility class that remembers the last **n** items. This memory can identify previous cell patterns and stop the simulation automatically when it sees one.

Make Bitmap a collection

Open the file **Bitmap+Collection.swift** and add the following:

```swift
extension Bitmap: RandomAccessCollection, MutableCollection {
  @usableFromInline
  struct Index: Comparable {
    @inlinable static func < (lhs: Index, rhs: Index) -> Bool {
      (lhs.row, lhs.column) < (rhs.row, lhs.column)
    }
    var row, column: Int
  }

  // More to come...
}
```

You make **Bitmap** adopt RandomAccessCollection and MutableCollection. First, you need an Index type. Unlike the previous FizzBuzz example, this type isn't a single Int but two integers that keep track of the row and column.

You need to define what it means for your Bitmap index to be Comparable. A reasonable choice is to make traversal happen in raster-scan order. Using a tuple comparison implements a multi-value comparison. Raster-scan is **row-major**, meaning the row is the most significant value. Only if the rows of the left-hand side (lhs) and right-hand side (rhs) are equal does the column break the tie to determine which is greater.

This type is marked @usableFromInline, with the method marked @inlinable to hint to the compiler that you want these methods to be fast at the potential cost of some additional code size. You'll see @inlinable repeated in the methods below.

Next, add this code below "More to come...":

```
@inlinable var startIndex: Index {
  Index(row: 0, column: 0)
}

@inlinable var endIndex: Index {
  Index(row: height, column: 0)
}

@inlinable func index(after i: Index) -> Index {
  i.column < width-1 ?
  Index(row: i.row, column: i.column+1) :
  Index(row: i.row+1, column: 0)
}

// More to come...
```

Minus the subscript operator that you'll define in a moment, this code provides the basic definition for a Collection type. Of note is the definition for index(after:). To know when to jump down to the next row, you need to know the width of the collection. Needing to know information outside of the index is why advancing the index is the responsibility of the collection and not the index itself. (You might imagine a more complex data structure such as a tree needing to know the collection's internal details to advance.)

> **Note**: Indexes belong to a given collection. However, if you copy your collection, any indexes must work in both the original *and* the copy. Mutating operations such as changing the size of the collection may invalidate an index. You should document these operations. Giving indices value semantics makes them much easier to reason about.

Next, continue adding this code:

```
@inlinable func index(before i: Index) -> Index {
  i.column > 0 ?
    Index(row: i.row,   column: i.column-1) :
    Index(row: i.row-1, column: width-1)
}

// More to come...
```

This fulfills the index requirements for `BidirectionalCollection`. Next, add:

```
@inlinable
func index(_ i: Index, offsetBy distance: Int) -> Index {
  Index(row: i.row + distance / width,
        column: i.column + distance % width)
}

@inlinable
func distance(from start: Index, to end: Index) -> Int {
  (end.row * width + end.column)
    - (start.row * width + start.column)
}

// More to come...
```

These fulfill the index requirements for `RandomAccessCollection`. Because your index moves in raster-scan order, division and modulo arithmetic determine how to jump by arbitrary distances.

Next, add:

```
@inlinable
func index(of i: Index, rowOffset: Int, columnOffset: Int) ->
Index {
  Index(row: i.row + rowOffset, column: i.column + columnOffset)
}

// More to come...
```

This indexing method isn't part of the collection protocol. It's just a convenient method you can use to look at neighboring pixels.

Finally, add:

```
@inlinable func contains(index: Index) -> Bool {
  (0..<width).contains(index.column) &&
  (0..<height).contains(index.row)
}

@inlinable subscript(position: Index) -> Pixel {

  get {
    precondition(contains(index: position),
               "out of bounds index \(position)")
    return pixels[position.row * width + position.column]
  }

  set {
    precondition(contains(index: position),
               "out of bounds index \(position)")
    pixels[position.row * width + position.column] = newValue
  }
}
```

The subscript method makes `Bitmap` a `RandomAccessCollection`, and the setter makes it a `MutableCollection`.

Defining `contains(index:)` isn't required, but it's a good utility and safety measure for this type.

Creating the simulation

Implement the simulation using the `Bitmap` collection. Open **LifeSimulation.swift**. The model object has three published properties — `isRunning`, `generation` and `cells` — that redraw the user interface every time they change. Add this statement to the end of `LifeSimulation`'s initializer:

```
Timer.publish(every: 0.1, on: .main, in: .common)
  .autoconnect()
  .sink { [weak self] _ in
    self?.evolve()
  }
  .store(in: &subscriptions)
```

This code creates a subscription to a **Combine** timer publisher and stores it in `subscriptions`. Every tenth of a second, the publisher will call `evolve()`.

Before implementing `evolve()`, create a helper method that counts the number of neighbors around a given cell. Add the following to `LifeSimulation`:

```
func neighborCount(around index: Bitmap<Bool>.Index) -> Int {
  var count = 0
  for rowOffset in -1...1 {
    for columnOffset in -1...1 {
      guard rowOffset != 0 || columnOffset != 0 else {
        continue
      }
      let probe = cells.index(of: index, rowOffset: rowOffset,
                              columnOffset: columnOffset)
      count += cells.contains(index: probe) ?
        (cells[probe] ? 1 : 0) : 0
    }
  }
  return count
}
```

This function uses an imperative style. It uses the index-creating method and the `contains` helper method you defined earlier. If an index position goes outside the bounds of the `Bitmap` collection, it counts as zero. (This choice is a little bit arbitrary. You could have made it wrap around.)

Next, implement the `evolve()` method. It should look like this:

```
func evolve() {
  guard isRunning else {
    return
  }
  generation += 1
  let neighbors = cells.indices.map(neighborCount(around:))

  // The core rules of Life.
  zip(cells.indices, neighbors).forEach { index, count in
    switch (cells[index], count) {
    case (true, 0...1):
      cells[index] = false // death by starvation
    case (true, 2...3):
      cells[index] = true  // live on
    case (true, 4...):
      cells[index] = false // death by overcrowding
    case (false, 3):
      cells[index] = true  // birth
    default:
      break // no change
    }
  }

  // automatically stop the simulation if stability is reached
  if previous.contains(cells) {
```

```
      isRunning = false
    }
    previous.add(cells)
  }
```

The guard immediately exits if the simulation is not running. If it is, the generation increments and finds the neighbor counts for all the cell positions. cells.indices.map(neighborCount(around:)) produces a sequence of all cell positions and maps it into neighborCount(around:). Next, the core rules of the game are applied. The zip algorithm creates a sequence of tuples of indices with neighbor counts, and the switch statement mutates the collection according to the rules of Life. Finally, previous is used to check if the pattern is a repeat and stops the simulation if it is.

Next, implement the cellImage property getter that creates an image. It should look like this:

```
  var cellImage: UIImage {
    let pixels = cells.map { $0 ? Self.live : Self.none }
    guard let image = Bitmap(pixels: pixels, width: cells.width)
                      .cgImage else {
      fatalError("could not create a core graphics image")
    }
    return UIImage(cgImage: image)
  }
```

This code maps a bitmap of booleans to a bitmap of color pixels it can display. Because you guarantee a valid pixel type, creating the bitmap won't fail and you can just fatalError if it does.

Finally, implement the method that lets you draw cells on the board. Replace the method setLive(row:column:) with the following:

```
  func setLive(row: Int, column: Int) {
    let position = Bitmap<Bool>.Index(row: row, column: column)
    if cells.contains(index: position) {
      cells[position] = true
      previous.reset() // reset automatic stop detection
    }
  }
```

The code here is straightforward. Get the position and set it to true. You don't want to look for previous cell patterns that would stop the simulation, so it's an excellent place to reset the history of patterns seen.

Build and run. Draw some cells in the gray rectangle and see how they simulate.

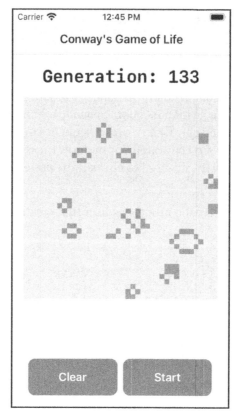

Conway's Life app screenshot

> **Note**: Conway's Game of Life is **Turing complete**. That means that any computation you can make in Swift (or any other Turing complete language) can be made by drawing cells and simulating on a sufficiently large grid in Life. If you're interested in learning more about Life and its amazing creator, John Conway, check out this video: https://www.youtube.com/watch?v=Kk2MH9O4pXY and prepare to have your mind blown.

RangeReplaceableCollection and others

Range replaceable collections allow you to add and remove values from a collection. Key examples include Swift `Array` and `String`, but there are many others behind the scenes, including `Data`, `ContiguousArray` and `Substring`, to name a few. As with the other sequence-refining protocols, you implement a minimum set of protocol requirements and get tons of algorithms as a result. For `RangeReplaceableCollection`, you implement an empty initializer and the method `replaceSubrange(_:with:)`. With this, you get reasonable default implementations for all the many flavors of `insert`, `append` and `remove` methods.

> **Note**: Why not implement `RangeReplaceableCollection` conformance for your `Bitmap` type in Life? If you think about it a little, you'll realize it doesn't make much sense. For example, if you delete a single pixel, what should happen? Should it remove an entire column of pixels? An entire row? It would be far better to create a novel abstraction such as `GridCollection` that deals with row and column operations explicitly and forms generic algorithms from those.

Subsequences and slices

It's common to want to deal with a subset of a sequence or collection. The `Collection` protocol defines a default associated type this way:

```
associatedtype SubSequence: Collection = Slice<Self> where  // 1
        Self.Element == Self.SubSequence.Element,            // 2
        Self.SubSequence == Self.SubSequence.SubSequence     // 3
```

Consider each line:

1. The subsequence type of a collection is itself a collection defaulting to the standard library type `Slice`.

2. The elements of the subsequence are the same as the collection.

3. The subsequence (a collection), in turn, has a subsequence that's the same as the original subsequence. The definition is recursive, so it's the same collection type for subsequences all the way down.

To see this in action, go back to your `FizzBuzz` playground and comment out the debugging print statements so the console isn't too noisy.

Then, add the following to the end:

```
let slice = fizzBuzz[20...30]
slice.startIndex
slice.endIndex
slice.count
for item in slice.enumerated() {
  print("\(item.offset):\(item.element)", terminator: " ")
}
```

Take a moment to appreciate that, without any extra code, you can create a subsequence in the FizzBuzz using a range of indices. The sliced collection, instead of starting from 1 as in the original collection, starts from 20. The end index is 31, for a total of 11 elements. You call enumerated() to loop through the elements in the slice.

You can slice into a slice. Try it with this code:

```
let sliceOfSlice = slice[22...24]
sliceOfSlice.startIndex                     // value of 22
sliceOfSlice[sliceOfSlice.startIndex]
```

Again, the start index matches the numbering in the original collection. Also, just as the generic constraint said, slice and sliceOfSlice are both of type Slice<FizzBuzz>.

Memory management

Slices don't allocate new memory but reference the memory of the original collection. This reference means they're cheap **O(1)** to create because they don't copy elements and can be used to construct efficient, generic algorithms.

But because a Slice references the original collection, even a tiny slice will extend the original collection's lifetime. If you want to disconnect from the original collection so it can deallocate when it goes out of scope, you can explicitly make a copy with the appropriate initializer. To see this in action, add this to your playground:

```
let numbers = Array(0..<100)
let upperHalf = numbers[(numbers.count/2)...]
let newNumbers = Array(upperHalf)
```

The numbers array is initialized from a Range<Int> collection of zero to one hundred. The instance upperHalf is a subsequence of numbers whose startIndex begins with 50. newNumbers allocates and copies into new storage with a startIndex of 0. As such, newNumbers is independent of the original numbers array.

> **Note**: Conceptually the same as a Slice, upperHalf is actually of type ArraySlice, which adds more array-like behavior to the default type Slice. Plain-old Slice *doesn't cut it* when you want your slices to behave more like the original collection they came from or want to build in special index invalidation rules when the underlying collection mutates. Another example of a collection with a special slice type is String. Slices of a string are a type called Substring. This type, along with String, conforms to the StringProtocol, making the two work almost the same.

The world of lazy evaluation

Collections use slice types to control the timing of allocations and copies into new collections. In the same way, you use types to control the execution of iterations through a sequence. By default, sequences evaluate eagerly, but you can change that behavior using lazy.

Consider the following problem. *Find the first three, even non-Fizz, Buzz, FizzBuzz numbers in the FizzBuzz collection.* Solve it by adding this code:

```
let firstThree = FizzBuzz()
  .compactMap(Int.init)
  .filter { $0.isMultiple(of: 2) }
  .prefix(3)

print(firstThree)
```

This code creates a FizzBuzz collection by iterating through all 100 strings and compacts to an array of 53 integers. It then filters that array by creating a new array of 27 even integers. Finally, it picks off the first three values of [2, 4, 8].

Because you want only the first three numbers, it's much more efficient to evaluate this chain of computation lazily. You can stop after you find three instead of finding everything and throwing away all but the first three. You can do that by accessing the lazy property on sequences like so:

```
let firstThreeLazy = FizzBuzz()
  .lazy
```

```
    .compactMap(Int.init)
    .filter { $0.isMultiple(of: 2) }
    .prefix(3)

print(Array(firstThreeLazy))
```

The lazy property returns a type called LazySequence<FizzBuzz> that implements special lazy versions of map, filter, reduce, compactMap and so forth. These implementations take the function or closure you pass into them and only execute on-demand. In the case above, compactMap executes Int.init only eight times and isMultiple(of:) eight times to find the three values. No intermediate temporary arrays need allocation as when the chain executes eagerly.

Note: If you print(firstThreeLazy) without eagerly initializing it as an Array, it will print the unevaluated type of the lazy expression. Wow. That's some type! Just as with Slice types, you should generally not use lazy types at API boundaries or, at least, type erase them.

Generic algorithms

The Swift standard library contains a bevy of algorithms that automatically apply to sequences and collections that meet the appropriate requirements. For example, first, forEach, map, reduce, sort and zip are standard library algorithms.

It's time for you to get some practice creating your own custom algorithm. Chunk the elements in a sequence in the FizzBuzz playground, and add the following:

```
let values: [Int] = [1, 3, 4, 1, 3, 4, 7, 5]

extension Array {
  func chunks(ofCount chunkCount: Int) -> [[Element]] {
    var result: [[Element]] = []
    for index in stride(from: 0, to: count, by: chunkCount) {
      let lastIndex = Swift.min(count, index + chunkCount)
      result.append(Array(self[index ..< lastIndex]))
    }
    return result
  }
}

values.chunks(ofCount: 3)
```

This extension on `Array` breaks elements into chunks of a given count. The last chunk might be smaller than the requested count depending on how many items are in the array. It uses a stride sequence starting from zero up to `count` to initialize smaller arrays repeatedly.

Although this code works, it's not particularly generic or efficient. If, for example, you sliced the array and tried to get the chunks of that, it wouldn't compile because `ArraySlice` isn't an `Array`. It certainly won't work with a collection like `FizzBuzz`. Also, each chunk requires a separate heap allocation and may require reallocations, depending on the size of the array being split into chunks. You can do better. Comment out the previous version and its call site and add this:

```
extension Collection {
  func chunks(ofCount chunkCount: Int) -> [SubSequence] {
    var result: [SubSequence] = []
    result.reserveCapacity(count / chunkCount
                           + (count % chunkCount).signum())
    var idx = startIndex
    while idx < endIndex {
      let lastIndex = index(idx, offsetBy: chunkCount,
                            limitedBy: endIndex) ?? endIndex
      result.append(self[idx ..< lastIndex])
      idx = lastIndex
    }
    return result
  }
}
```

Because you're extending `Collection`, it can be used with many more types than just arrays. It returns an array of `SubSequence`, which might be `Slices` or `ArraySlices` or `SubStrings`, depending on the type. You can't assume a zero-based index like before, so you need to use `startIndex`. Finally, using `reserveCapacity()`, you ensure that there's exactly one allocation instead of many.

Go ahead and test it by adding these:

```
values.chunks(ofCount: 3)
Array(FizzBuzz().chunks(ofCount: 5).last!)
"Hello world".chunks(ofCount: 2)
```

Generic algorithms are powerful and reusable and promote clarity. Using algorithms like this instead of raw loops generally will make your code easier to read and maintain.

Key points

The Swift standard library's sequence and collection protocols fully leverage the generic system to make a consistent and predictable (and incredible) programming model. Here are some key points to take away:

- Sequences, the most primitive type in the sequence hierarchy, guarantee only that you can visit a list of elements once.

- Sequences can be immutable but vend mutable iterators that keep track of your iteration state.

- Iterators can be used directly, but the Swift compiler usually generates and maintains them for you. The compiler makes one every time you write a `for` loop.

- Collections are sequences that can visit elements using an index any number of times.

- Collections are relatively easy to define thanks to default protocol implementations.

- An additional handful of protocols, such as `RangeReplaceableCollection`, further refine a collection's capabilities.

- Algorithms take advantage of the traversal capabilities of a collection to operate more efficiently.

- There are many ways to create custom sequences that range from hand-coding the iterator and sequence type to using standard library utility methods to do the job in much less code.

- `stride` functions create `Stride` types that are `Sequences`.

- `sequence` functions create `UnfoldSequence`, which expands (unfolds) some state into a sequence of values.

- `AnySequence` lets you type-erase the underlying sequence type.

- `AnySequence` and `AnyIterator` have initializers that take closures that compose together to create custom sequences succinctly.

- Collection types have an `index` type you define.

- You achieve conformance to `BidirectionalCollection` by adding an `index(before:)` method.

- `RandomAccessCollection` requirements are automatically fulfilled if you use a `Strideable` and `Comparable` type, such as an `Int`.

- `MutableCollection` mutates the collection without invalidating indices in most cases.

- `SubSequence` is the name of the associated type in `Sequence` and `Collection` that gets a subset of elements.

- `Slice` is the default type that collections use to implement `SubSequence`.

- Using a `Slice` doesn't copy the underlying collection but references into it and extends its lifetime.

- Generally, avoid using subsequences for high-level APIs because even a tiny slice can keep alive a huge underlying collection.

- `String` uses `Substring` and `Array` uses `ArraySlice` instead of the vanilla `Slice` to make working with these subsequences more like the original collection.

- There's a whole set of `LazySequence` types that prevent eager evaluation and can prevent unnecessary computation, speeding your code.

- The Swift standard library uses protocols and generics to define generic algorithms. It's easy to define your own.

- By defining an algorithm in terms of the protocols it requires, you make it usable in more places than if you rely on a concrete type such as `Array`.

Where to go from here?

The more you write code, the more you start seeing algorithms. There's a spectacular WWDC talk by Dave Abrahams, called Embracing Algorithms (https://apple.co/2NHyCcG), that you should watch if you haven't already. In it, he makes a compelling case that you look hard at all your `for` loops and try to replace them with named algorithms.

The talk foreshadows the Swift Algorithms (https://bit.ly/3uiogkn) project focused on sequence and collection algorithms. This GitHub repository contains an implementation of `chunks(ofCount:)`. Although your implementation in this chapter returned an array of subsequences that requires a heap allocation, the Swift Algorithm version returns a custom collection requiring no heap allocations. This optimization makes it significantly faster and enables lazy chunking. Although the implementation there is much lengthier and more involved than the ones presented here, you now should have all the knowledge you need to read and understand the clever things the authors have done.

Even more recently, Apple announced the Swift Collections (https://github.com/apple/swift-collections) project. Like Swift Algorithms and Swift Numerics, Swift collection is intended as a proving ground for general purpose data structures that may eventually make their way into the standard library.

Finally, there are a ton of algorithm resources at raywenderlich.com, including a beginning tutorial (https://bit.ly/3pAly68) about getting started with the Swift Algorithm project to an entire book (https://bit.ly/3pHCszE) on classical data structures and algorithms inspired by the Swift Algorithm Club (https://bit.ly/2MQHkjs) open-source project.

Chapter 7: Strings

By Ehab Amer

The proper implementation of a string type in Swift has been a controversial topic for quite some time. The design is a delicate balance between Unicode correctness, encoding agnosticism, ease-of-use and high-performance. Almost every major release of Swift has refined the String type to the awesome design we have today. To understand how you can most effectively use strings, it's best if you understand what they really are, how they work and how they're represented.

In this chapter, you'll learn:

- The binary representation of characters, and how it developed over the years

- The human representation of a string

- What a grapheme cluster is

- How Swift works with UTF encodings, and how low-level details of UTF affect `String`'s performance

- Ordering of strings in different locales

- What string folding is and how you can best search in strings

- What a substring is and how it relates to memory

- Custom String interpolation and how you can use it to initialize a custom object from a string or convert it to a string

Binary representations

Character representation has changed so much over the years, starting from **ASCII** (American Standard Code for Information Interchange), which represents English numbers and characters using up to seven bits.

128 Ç	143 Å	158 ₧	172 ¼	186 ║	200 ╚	214 ╓	228 Σ	242 ≥
129 ü	144 É	159 ƒ	173 ¡	187 ╗	201 ╔	215 ╫	229 σ	243 ≤
130 é	145 æ	160 á	174 «	188 ╝	202 ╩	216 ╪	230 µ	244 ⌠
131 â	146 Æ	161 í	175 »	189 ╜	203 ╦	217 ┘	231 τ	245 ⌡
132 ä	147 ô	162 ó	176 ░	190 ╛	204 ╠	218 ┌	232 Φ	246 ÷
133 à	148 ö	163 ú	177 ▒	191 ┐	205 =	219 █	233 Θ	247 ≈
134 å	149 ò	164 ñ	178 ▓	192 └	206 ╬	220 ▄	234 Ω	248 °
135 ç	150 û	165 Ñ	179 │	193 ┴	207 ╧	221 ▌	235 δ	249 ·
136 ê	151 ù	166 ª	180 ┤	194 ┬	208 ╨	222 ▐	236 ∞	250 ·
137 ë	152 ÿ	167 º	181 ╡	195 ├	209 ╤	223 ▀	237 φ	251 √
138 è	153 Ö	168 ¿	182 ╢	196 ─	210 ╥	224 α	238 ε	252 ⁿ
139 ï	154 Ü	169 ⌐	183 ╖	197 ┼	211 ╙	225 ß	239 ∩	253 ²
140 î	155 ¢	170 ¬	184 ╕	198 ╞	212 ╘	226 Γ	240 ≡	254 ■
141 ì	156 £	171 ½	185 ╣	199 ╟	213 ╒	227 π	241 ±	255
142 Ä	157 ¥							

Then, Extended ASCII came along, which used the remaining 128 values representable by a single byte.

000 (nul)	016 ► (dle)	032 sp	048 0	064 @	080 P	096 `	112 p
001 ☺ (soh)	017 ◄ (dc1)	033 !	049 1	065 A	081 Q	097 a	113 q
002 ☻ (stx)	018 ↕ (dc2)	034 "	050 2	066 B	082 R	098 b	114 r
003 ♥ (etx)	019 ‼ (dc3)	035 #	051 3	067 C	083 S	099 c	115 s
004 ♦ (eot)	020 ¶ (dc4)	036 $	052 4	068 D	084 T	100 d	116 t
005 ♣ (enq)	021 § (nak)	037 %	053 5	069 E	085 U	101 e	117 u
006 ♠ (ack)	022 ▬ (syn)	038 &	054 6	070 F	086 V	102 f	118 v
007 • (bel)	023 ↨ (etb)	039 '	055 7	071 G	087 W	103 g	119 w
008 ◘ (bs)	024 ↑ (can)	040 (	056 8	072 H	088 X	104 h	120 x
009 (tab)	025 ↓ (em)	041)	057 9	073 I	089 Y	105 i	121 y
010 (lf)	026 → (eof)	042 *	058 :	074 J	090 Z	106 j	122 z
011 ♂ (vt)	027 ← (esc)	043 +	059 ;	075 K	091 [	107 k	123 {
012 ♀ (np)	028 ∟ (fs)	044 ,	060 <	076 L	092 \	108 l	124	
013 (cr)	029 ↔ (gs)	045 -	061 =	077 M	093]	109 m	125 }
014 ♫ (so)	030 ▲ (rs)	046 .	062 >	078 N	094 ^	110 n	126 ~
015 ☼ (si)	031 ▼ (us)	047 /	063 ?	079 O	095 _	111 o	127 ⌂

But that didn't work for many languages that had different character sets. So another standard came out, called **ANSI**. Which is also the name of the entity that created this standard. American National Standards Institute.

Unlike ASCII, ANSI's not a single character set. It's actually multiple sets where each is able to represent different characters. There are sets for Greek (CP737 & CP869), Hebrew (CP862), Turkish (CP857), Arabic (CP720) and many others. Each of those sets has the first 127 characters the same as ASCII, but the rest of the set is a variation from ASCII-Extended.

Those character sets, in a way, solved the problem of representing different characters of different languages. But another problem came up! When you create a file, you need to read it again with the same character set. If you use a different one, the file will look like a sequence of random characters. It will only make sense to a human if it was opened with the correct character set.

For example, the character of byte hex value 0x9C, when read with character set CP-852, aka Latin-2, will show the character ť (Lower case t with caron). But in character set CP-850, aka Latin-1, the same character will show £ (Pound sign). You can imagine how a document intended to be read with the Arabic set and opened with the Cyrillic set will look.

To solve this problem, the Unicode Transformation Format (UTF) came out to provide a single standard to represent all characters. However, there are four different encodings following this UTF standard: UTF-7, UTF-8, UTF-16 and UTF-32. Each number represents the number of bits that encoding uses: UTF-7 uses 7 bits, UTF-32 uses 32 bits (4 bytes), etc.

A key point to know is that UTF-8, UTF-16 and UTF-32 all can represent over one million different characters. It is clear that the latter of the group has a large range. As for the first, it's not limited to 8 bits only — it can expand over 4 bytes. To cover all possible values in the UTF standard requires 21 bits.

UTF-8 binary representation

Each character in UTF-8 varies in size from 1 byte to 4 bytes. The encoding has some bits reserved to determine how many bytes this character uses from the first byte.

A byte with its most significant bit having 0 value is, on its own, a character. The character is 1 byte.

A byte with its three most significant bits having 110 value, along with the following byte, represent a character. The character is 2 bytes.

A byte with its four most significant bits having 1110 value, along with the two following bytes, represent a character. The character is 3 bytes.

A byte with its five most significant bits having 11110 value, along with the three following bytes, represent a character. The character is 4 bytes.

Any byte with its two most significant bits having 10 value is a byte that is part of a character (following byte). It doesn't provide enough information on its own without the leading byte.

The number of bits available to store the value for UTF-8 is calculated as follows:

- 1 byte: 8 bits - 1 reserved = 7 available bits

- 2 bytes: 16 bits - 5 reserved = 11 available bits

- 3 bytes: 24 bits - 8 reserved = 16 available bits

- 4 bytes: 32 bits - 11 reserved = 21 available bits

UTF-16 binary representation

UTF-16 is another variable-length encoding format. A character can be 2 bytes or 4 bytes. Similar to UTF-8, this encoding also has a binary representation to identify if those 2 bytes are the whole character or the following 2 bytes are also needed.

If the 2 bytes start with 0xD8 (110110 in binary), those two bytes complete a character. This character is 4 bytes in size.

The following 2 bytes will start with 0xDC (110111 in binary). This makes for 4-byte values, with 12 bits reserved and 20 bits to define the value.

With those reserved values, characters can't be represented with values in the range between 0xD800 to 0xDFFF, because doing so would confuse their values with length extensions.

UTF-32 binary representation

It's obvious how UTF-32 works. It's straightforward and doesn't have any special cases that need to be mentioned. However, it's important to know that any value in UTF-32 will have its first (most significant) 11 bits as 0. UTF possible values cover only 21 bits, and those 11 bits are never used.

It's worth noting that UTF-16 and UTF-32 aren't backward compatible with ASCII, but UTF-8 is. That means a file saved with ASCII encoding can still be read with UTF-8 encoding, but can't in the other two encodings.

Human representation

Each representable value in a string is named a **code point** or **Unicode Scalar**. Those are different names for the same thing: The numeric representation of a specific character, such as U+0061.

Each number is represented by a different drawing, which is called **Character Glyph**. UTF, with all its variations, has the same mapping for each Unicode scalar to a glyph. The standards differ only in how the machine represents that scalar value.

For example, the Unicode scalar U+0061 represents the letter a (Latin lowercase letter "a"), and U+00E9 represents é (Latin lowercase letter "e" with acute).

Fonts are a pallet of glyphs that have a different drawing. Each glyph/letter is drawn in a different style, but in the end, they all have maps to a binary representation. A font affects only the rendering; it changes nothing in the stored information.

Grapheme cluster

Knowing how UTF-8 and UTF-16 work to represent variable sizes, you can imagine that knowing the length of a string isn't as straightforward as it is for ASCII and ANSI representations. For the latter, an array of 100 bytes is simply 100 characters. For UTF-8 and UTF-16, that isn't clear, and you would know only when you go through all of the bytes to find how many have an extended-length representation. For UTF-32, this isn't an issue. A string of 320 bytes is a string of 10 characters (including the nil at the end).

To make it a little more complicated, say you have 4 bytes for a UTF-16 string, and there are no extended lengths. You would think that this means you have a string of length two. The answer is: *not necessarily!*

Take the character U+00E9 é (Latin lowercase letter "e" with acute) as an example. It can be represented like that or by two Unicode scalar values of the standard letter e U+0065 (Latin lowercase letter "e") followed by U+0301 (combining acute accent).

Open a new playground project and try the following:

```
import Foundation

let eAcute = "\u{E9}"
let combinedEAcute = "\u{65}\u{301}"
```

Those are the two representations, and they both represent é:

```
eAcute.count // 1
combinedEAcute.count // 1
```

In Swift, both of those strings have a length of 1, although they have different binary sizes. Also, those strings are equal:

```
eAcute == combinedEAcute // true
```

When different Unicode sequences form the same result, those results are said to have **canonical equivalence**. Swift equality checks the canonical equivalence of the content and not the absolute equality of the content.

Try the same with Objective-C types:

```
let eAcute_objC: NSString = "\u{E9}"
let combinedEAcute_objC: NSString = "\u{65}\u{301}"

eAcute_objC.length // 1
combinedEAcute_objC.length // 2

eAcute_objC == combinedEAcute_objC // false
```

Objective-C String didn't read any of that. It simply compared the contents of the bytes. It didn't check its contents and didn't figure out that both represent the same thing.

A character in Swift doesn't represent a byte as in Objective-C. It represents a **grapheme cluster**, which can be one or more scalar values combined to represent a single glyph.

If you keep two characters separate that normally would form a grapheme cluster if merged together, they'll both be treated as normal characters. It's only when you merge them that they become a different character:

```
let acute = "\u{301}"
let smallE = "\u{65}"

acute.count // 1
smallE.count // 1

let combinedEAcute2 = smallE + acute

combinedEAcute2.count // 1
```

Now that you understand how characters are represented in zeros and ones, let's see how Swift works with them and how all those "under the hood" details affect how you can work with strings.

UTF in Swift

Until Swift 4.2, Swift used UTF-16 as the preferred encoding. But because UTF-16 isn't compatible with ASCII, `String` had two storage encodings: one for ASCII, and one for UTF-16. Swift 5 and later versions use only UTF-8 storage encoding.

UTF-8 is the most common server-side encoding: Over 95% of the internet uses it. You might think for a moment that the internet isn't only English and UTF-16 is the more logical choice because less extended byte values will be used. But most of a webpage is HTML, and HTML can be completely represented in ASCII. This makes the usage of UTF-8 for internet content a better choice for size and transfer speed. That said, the change to UTF-8 storage encoding made any communication between Swift and a server straightforward, because they use the same encoding and therefore require no conversion.

Collection protocol conformance

`String` conforms to the two collection protocols: `BidirectionalCollection` and `RangeReplaceableCollection`:

```
var sampleString = "Lōrem ipsum dōlōr sīt ãmet"

sampleString.last
// temã tīs rōlōd muspī merōL
let reversedString = String(sampleString.reversed())
```

```
if let rangeToReplace = sampleString.range(of: "Lorem") {
  // Lorem ipsum dolor sit amet
  sampleString.replaceSubrange(rangeToReplace,
      with: "Lorem")
}
```

You can traverse a Swift String in either direction, and you can also replace a range of values. But it doesn't conform to RandomAccessCollection.

```
sampleString[2]    ⊗ 'subscript(_:)' is unavailable: cannot subscript String with an Int, use a String.Index instead.
```

You could extend String with subscript(_:) so you can easily access characters by their index:

```
extension String {
  subscript(position: Int) -> Self.Element {
    get {
      let characters = Array(self)
      return characters[position]
    }
    set(newValue) {
      let startIndex = self.index(self.startIndex,
        offsetBy: position)
      let endIndex = self.index(self.startIndex,
        offsetBy: position + 1)
      let range = startIndex..<endIndex
      replaceSubrange(range, with: [newValue])
    }
  }
}
```

Then the following code will work:

```
sampleString[2] // r
sampleString[2] = "R"

sampleString // LoRem ipsum dolor sit amet
```

In the code above, there doesn't seem to be a problem. Try the following code:

```
for i in 0..<sampleString.count {
  sampleString[i].uppercased()
}
```

With a quick look, you would think this code has a complexity of O(n), but that is incorrect. In the `subscript(_:)` implementation, you converted the string to an array to get the index you want. That itself is an O(n) operation, giving the loop you added a complexity of O(n^2).

You can't reach the **n**th character directly without passing by the n-1 characters first. A character — aka grapheme cluster — can be a long sequence of Unicode scalars, making the operation of reaching the **n**th character one of O(n), not O(1), thus not meeting the requirement of `RandomAccessCollection`.

Although the extension you created simplifies and shortens your code, it also affects the performance:

```
for element in sampleString {
  element.uppercased()
}
```

This code is the same. It didn't use the subscript approach and traverses the collection once. Using the subscript approach will often seem appealing, but that approach causes you to do many more operations than you think. Thus, understanding how the `String` class works, as well as what `Character` is and how Swift treats it, can make a huge difference in how you approach challenges and implement solutions.

String ordering

You're already well acquainted with string comparison. The default sorting in a string ignores localization preference.

String comparison is always consistent, as it should be. However, for different locales, it should be different.

For example, the ordering of Ö is different than Z between German and Swedish:

```
let OwithDiaersis = "Ö"
let zee = "Z"

OwithDiaersis > zee // true

// German 🇩🇪
OwithDiaersis.compare(
  zee,
  locale: Locale(identifier: "DE")) == .orderedAscending // true

// Sweden 🇸🇪
```

```
OwithDiaersis.compare(
  zee,
  locale: Locale(identifier: "SE")) == .orderedAscending //
false
```

When you're ordering text for internal use in the system, the locale must not affect it. But if you're ordering it to show it to the user, you must be aware of the differences.

Also, there is a notorious problem that arises when strings have numbers. A string with value "11" should be higher than a string of value "2". But this isn't the case unless it is a comparison that is considering the locale:

```
"11".localizedCompare("2") == .orderedAscending // true

"11".localizedStandardCompare("2") == .orderedAscending // false
```

String folding

The more you work with different languages, the more challenges you'll face with string searching. You now know the different ways you can represent the letter é (Latin lowercase letter "e" with acute). But the word "Café" doesn't match "Cafe":

```
"Café" == "Cafe" // false
```

And checking if it contains the letter e (Latin lowercase letter "e") will return false:

```
"Café".contains("e") // false
```

Using diacritics on a character transforms it into a different character. Although it originates from the same, comparing it to the original will fail — almost the same idea behind different cases:

```
"Café" == "café" // false
"Café".contains("c") // false
```

When you want to compare strings and ignore casing, you convert the original string and keyword to the same casing, upper or lower. This is called **String Folding**, where you remove distinctions on the strings to make them suitable for comparison.

In the case of diacritics, you want to remove all of the marks and return all of the characters to their original letter to simplify comparison. To continue with our example, this would return Café, or any other diacritic variation of it, to Cafe.

Consider the following example:

```
let originalString = "Hello World!"
originalString.contains("Hello") // false
```

`originalString` contains a combining character for each letter in the string `Hello World!`. That makes it very hard to search for any words. Luckily, `String` provides a mechanism for folding so you can specify what distinctions you want to remove. Cases, diacritics, or both:

```
let foldedString = originalString.folding(
    options: [.caseInsensitive, .diacriticInsensitive],
    locale: .current)
foldedString.contains("hello") // true
```

The options parameter in `folding(options:locale:)` gives you that control. In this example, it removed both cases and diacritics. The resulting string is `hello world!`

Another, shorter way to do the same is by using `localizedStandardContains(_:)`:

```
originalString.localizedStandardContains("hello") // true
```

This method does the same. It performs a case- and diacritic-insensitive, locale-aware comparison. Without **folding** the string to remove the diacritics, you'll have a very hard time searching for text, or you'll give the user a very unpleasant experience.

String and Substring in memory

Another tricky point related to performance in `String` is `Substring`. Just as how `String` conforms to `StringProtocol`, so does `Substring`.

As you can see from its name, a substring is a part of a string. And it is a very fast and optimized datatype when you're breaking down a large string. However, there is a key point that you should be aware of, especially when working with large strings:

```
func doSomething() -> Substring {
    let largeString = "Lorem ipsum dolor sit amet"
    let index = largeString.firstIndex(of: " ") ??
largeString.endIndex
    return largeString[..<index]
}
```

The code above returns the first word of a large string.

What you expect with a quick look is that you worked with the large string, finished using it, and returned only the small part of the string you need:

```
let subString = doSomething() // Lorem
subString.base // "Lorem ipsum dolor sit amet"
```

You still have the large string loaded in memory. Substring shares memory with the original string. If you're working with a large string and need a lot of smaller strings from it, *while still using the large string,* there will be no additional memory cost. But if you want to just break it and remove the large string from memory, then you need to create a new string object from your substring right away:

```
let newString = String(subString)
```

If you don't, the original string will stay in memory for much longer without your awareness.

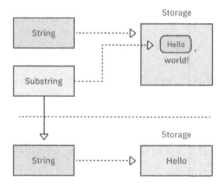

That was a lot of info about String. The next part will cover a very interesting perk from Swift that you've been using frequently. You'll know how it works under the hood and builds on top of it.

Custom string interpolation

String interpolation is a powerful tool for creating strings. But it's not narrowed to the creation of strings. Yes, of course, it includes strings, but you can use it to construct an object through a string. Yes, I know it's confusing.

Consider the following type:

```
struct Book {
    var name: String
```

```
    var authors: [String]
    var fpe: String
}
```

Wouldn't it be super cool if you could define a new instance from Book with a string like "Expert Swift by: Ehab Amer,Marin Bencevic,Ray Fix,Shai Mishali"?

Swift allows you to define any type by a string literal by conforming to the protocol ExpressibleByStringLiteral, and implementing init(stringLiteral value: String).

Add this extension:

```
extension Book: ExpressibleByStringLiteral {
  public init(stringLiteral value: String) {
    let parts = value.components(separatedBy: " by: ")
    let bookName = parts.first ?? ""
    let authorNames = parts.last?.components(separatedBy:
",") ?? []
    self.name = bookName
    self.authors = authorNames
    self.fpe = ""
  }
}
```

You break down the string into two parts with the " by: " separator: The first part is the book name, and the second part is the author names, comma-separated. Ignore the "fpe" (final pass editor) for now, but you'll use this property later.

The string defining the book should be **[Book name]** + **by:** + **Author1,Author2,Author3,....**:

```
var book: Book = """
Expert Swift by: Ehab Amer,Marin Bencevic,\
Ray Fix,Shai Mishali
"""

book.name // Expert Swift
book.authors.first // Ehab Amer
```

This is a very human-friendly way to construct your object, but if anything changed in this format, unexpected data will be saved in the object!

```
var invalidBook: Book = """
Book name is `Expert Swift`. \
Written by: Ehab Amer, Marin Bencevic, \
Ray Fix & Shai Mishali
"""
```

```
invalidBook.name // Book name is `Expert Swift`. Written
invalidBook.authors.last // Ray Fix & Shai Mishali
```

Now, the name contains invalid information, and the last author is actually two of them together. You can fix this by improving the implementation of init(stringLiteral value: String), but will you ever be able to expect all possible inputs to make sure that the string will be parsed properly?

There is another way you can construct Book: using string interpolation. To do this, you define a string that has clear, explicit mention of the book name and the array of authors:

```
extension Book: ExpressibleByStringInterpolation { // 1
  struct StringInterpolation: StringInterpolationProtocol { // 2
    var name: String // 3
    var authors: [String]
    var fpe: String

    init(literalCapacity: Int, interpolationCount: Int) { // 4
      name = ""
      authors = []
      fpe = ""
    }

    mutating func appendLiteral(_ literal: String) { // 5
      // Do something with the literals?
    }

    mutating func appendInterpolation(_ name: String) { // 6
      self.name = name
    }

    mutating func appendInterpolation(
      authors list: [String]) { // 7
      authors = list
    }
  }

  init(stringInterpolation: StringInterpolation) { // 8
    self.authors = stringInterpolation.authors
    self.name = stringInterpolation.name
    self.fpe = stringInterpolation.fpe
  }
}
```

1. To use custom interpolation to define a `Book`, you need it to conform to `ExpressibleByStringInterpolation`.

2. This requires defining a struct with the name `StringInterpolation` that conforms to `StringInterpolationProtocol`. The visibility of this struct is only from within the `Book` type.

3. The new struct must carry properties to store the values that will be provided in the string. For this example, `name` and `authors` will do. You can also have any properties you may need. Ignore `fpe` for now.

4. The string will contain literal strings and interpolations. This initializer is the first that gets called. It provides the counts of every character in the literal and the number of interpolations present.

5. This gets called for literals in the string. For this example, do nothing with them. This method declaration identified the generic type for the literal as `String`.

6. This added an interpolation with a string that defines the name of the book. Interpolation should look like `"\(String)"`

7. This added an interpolation signature that looks like `"\(authors: [String])"`. This is a labeled interpolation for the authors list.

8. You define a new initializer with a parameter of type `StringInterpolation`, which is the same struct you defined.

Now you can create an instance of `Book` like this:

```
var interpolatedBook: Book = """
The awesome team of authors \(authors:
  ["Ehab Amer", "Marin Bencevic", "Ray Fix", "Shai Mishali"]) \
wrote this great book. Titled \("Expert Swift")
"""
```

The book was defined with a lot more description. Even the list of authors came before the name of the book. But because each interpolation has its form, either through a label and/or data-type, there was no mixup.

What actually happened behind the scenes is as follows:

```
let stringInterpolation = StringInterpolation(
  literalCapacity: 59,
  interpolationCount: 2)

stringInterpolation.appendLiteral("he awesome team of authors ")
```

```
stringInterpolation.appendInterpolation(
  authors: ["Ehab Amer",
            "Marin Bencevic",
            "Ray Fix",
            "Shai Mishali"])

stringInterpolation
  .appendLiteral(" wrote this great book. Titled ")

stringInterpolation
  .appendInterpolation("Expert Swift")

Book(stringInterpolation: stringInterpolation)
```

`init(literalCapacity: Int, interpolationCount: Int)` is called with the number of total character literals and the number of interpolations.

Then, for each literal sequence, `appendLiteral(_:)` is called. After that, for each interpolation, its appropriate method is called. Finally, the initializer is called with the interpolation object.

Notice that each interpolation was translated to a method. `\(_:)` was translated to `appendLiteral(_:)`, and `\(authors:)` was translated to `appendLiteral(authors:)`.

Remember the `fpe` that you didn't use? So far, you focused only on the title and authors of the book. But at the point of creating the interpolation object, you had no use for this property and left it empty.

Add an extension to `StringInterpolation` defined inside `Book`:

```
extension Book.StringInterpolation {
  mutating func appendInterpolation(fpe name: String) {
    fpe = name
  }
}
```

Then, define a new book with this interpolation:

```
var interpolatedBookWithFPE: Book = """
\("Expert Swift") had an amazing \
final pass editor \(fpe: "Eli Ganim")
"""
```

This created a new instance of a book and used the interpolation you identified in the extension to set `fpe`. You can define as many additional interpolation formats as you wish:

```
extension Book.StringInterpolation {
  mutating func appendInterpolation(bookName name: String) {
    self.name = name
  }

  mutating func appendInterpolation(anAuthor name: String) {
    self.authors.append(name)
  }
}
```

This added an alternative way to define the name of the book and a way to add authors one by one:

```
var interpolatedBook2: Book = """
\(anAuthor: "Ray Fix") & \(anAuthor: "Shai Mishali") \
were authors in \(bookName: "Expert Swift")
"""
```

The type `String` is no different from `Book`. You have already been using its `StringInterpolation` subtype for some time with your standard interpolations, such as including a number in a string:

```
var num = 1234
var string = "The number is: \(num)"
```

Just as you added a new interpolation for `fpe` on `Book`, you can do the same on `String` to interpolate `Book`.

Try to include the first book instance into a string:

```
var string = "\(book)"
// Book(name: "Expert Swift", authors: ["Ehab Amer", "Marin
Bencevic", "Ray Fix", "Shai Mishali"], fpe: "")
```

The string doesn't have a friendly representation of the book. But you can control that. Add an extension to `StringInterpolation` inside `String`:

```
extension String.StringInterpolation {
  mutating func appendInterpolation(_ book: Book) {
    appendLiteral("The Book \"")
    appendLiteral(book.name)
    appendLiteral("\"")

    if !book.authors.isEmpty {
```

```
    appendLiteral(" Authored by: ")
      for author in book.authors {
        if author == book.authors.first {
          appendLiteral(author)
        } else {
          if author == book.authors.last {
            appendLiteral(", & ")
            appendLiteral(author)
            appendLiteral(".")
          } else {
            appendLiteral(", ")
            appendLiteral(author)
          }
        }
      }
    }

    if !book.fpe.isEmpty {
      appendLiteral(" Final Pass Edited by: ")
      appendLiteral(book.fpe)
    }
  }
}
```

Add the fpe to `interpolatedBook` object you defined earlier, and convert it to a string:

```
interpolatedBook.fpe = "Eli Ganim"
var string2 = "\(interpolatedBook)"
// The Book "Expert Swift" Authored by: Ehab Amer, Marin
Bencevic, Ray Fix, & Shai Mishali. Final Pass Edited by: Eli
Ganim
```

Now, this is a much more friendly way to describe a book.

In the extension, you had full control over how the fields were printed, their order and what user-friendly text to precede and/or follow each property.

The reason appendLiteral(_:) was heavily used here is that you don't know the internal implementation of String.StringInterpolation, and you don't know what temporary fields it has to store the information. But it's not like Book.StringInterpolation. The literals are stored just like interpolations and in order, so you can safely convert an interpolation to a series of literals. In the end, it is only **one** string. Not **multiple** fields like in Book.

Key points

- ASCII was the first standard for storing characters, and it evolved to UTF to represent all the possible characters in one single standard.

- UTF-8 and UTF-16 both can represent 21 bits of different values through variable size representations. A UTF-8 character can take up to 4 bytes.

- UTF-16 and UTF-32 aren't backward compatible with ASCII.

- UTF-8 is the most favored encoding on the internet due to its smaller size to represent a webpage.

- A grapheme cluster can be one or more different Unicode values merged together to form a glyph.

- A character in Swift is a grapheme cluster, not a Unicode value. And the same cluster can be represented in different ways. This is called canonical equivalence.

- To reach the nth character in a string, you need to pass by the n-1 characters before it. It is **not** an O(1) operation.

- The order of strings can vary based on the locale.

- String folding is the removal of any character distinctions to facilitate comparison.

- `Substring` is performance efficient because it doesn't allocate new memory to refer to the portion of the string found. However, this means that the original string is still present in memory.

- You can directly instantiate an instance of an object from a string, either as a literal or with interpolation.

- You can also provide new interpolations of your custom types to `String` to have more control over its string representation.

Chapter 8: Codable

By Shai Mishali

When developing your app, you'll often deal with a myriad of data models and various external pieces of data that you'll want to represent as data models in your app.

To solve this problem, you'll often use a technique called **serialization**, where you create an external representation of your data models in one of many consumable formats supported by multiple platforms. The most popular of the bunch by far is **JSON (Javascript Object Notation)**.

The need for data serialization in Apple's platforms is so common that they solved it all the way back in Xcode 3.0, with the introduction of NSCoding, which lets you describe how to encode and decode your data.

Unfortunately NSCoding, while an incredible abstraction at the time, suffers from many issues and a lack of modern touch that fits the Swift world — such as automatically synthesized encoding and decoding, support for value types and more. Enter Codable.

What is Codable?

Codable is a type alias combining two protocols: Encodable and Decodable. These let you define how objects are **encoded** and **decoded** to and from an external data representation, such as JSON.

The great thing about Codable is that it's mostly agnostic toward the format it encodes to and decodes from. It uses an additional set of abstractions called Encoder and Decoder to achieve this separation.

These abstractions own the specific intimate knowledge of how to encode and decode in and out of their specific data formats. For example, a JSONEncoder would know how to encode a given data model into a JSON response, while a PropertyListDecoder would know exactly how to take a plist file and decode it into a given data model.

This abstraction means that your objects only have to conform to Codable or either of its parts once, and can be encoded to and decoded from many different formats using various encoders and decoders.

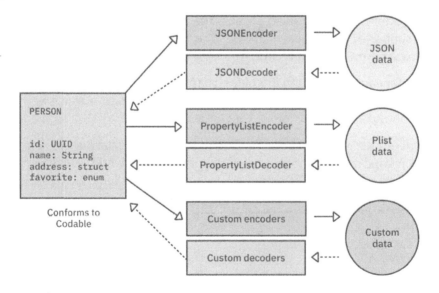

What you'll learn, and what you won't

Because this is an advanced book, you'll quickly browse through the basic Codable knowledge, mostly focusing on the advanced materials down the dark corners of Codable.

Since JSON represents the vast majority of Codable use cases, you'll focus on using JSONEncoder and JSONDecoder, with the majority of this chapter focusing on the Decodable portion of the equation.

Specifically, you'll work on three real-life API responses and write the appropriate Decodable and Encodable conformances for them, teaching you everything you need to tackle the weirdest of responses.

Brushing up on the basics

When decoding or encoding a data structure, you often get to use Codable with literally no boilerplate.

Given the following JSON:

```
{
  "name": "Shai Mishali",
  "twitter": "@freak4pc",
  "github": "https://github.com/freak4pc",
  "birthday": "October 4th, 1987"
}
```

And the following Person struct:

```
struct Person {
  let name: String
  let twitter: String
  let github: URL
  let birthday: Date
}
```

All you'd have to do to make Person compatible with its JSON structure is simply conform it to Codable, like so:

```
struct Person: Codable {
  ...
}
```

And use the appropriate encoder or decoder:

```
// Decode
let decoder = JSONDecoder()
let person = try decoder.decode(Person.self, from: jsonData)

// Encode
let encoder = JSONEncoder()
let jsonData = try encoder.encode(person)
```

Swift will know to match the keys in your JSON to the ones in your Person struct, and will even know how to automatically convert the String date and URL to Swift's Date and URL!

You'll learn more about how Swift knows to do this automatically for you later in this chapter.

With this quick refresher behind you, it's time to work on some APIs!

API #1: Ray's Books

Getting started

Open the starter playground found in **projects/starter** and look at the Navigation pane on the left:

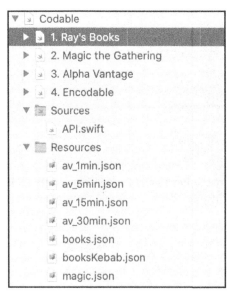

You'll notice a few things:

- The playground comprises several pages, each representing a different API.

- The **Sources** folder includes an API helper you'll use throughout this chapter.

- The **Resources** folder includes JSON files containing the responses you'll interact with in this chapter.

Open **books.json** and note the response's JSON structure:

```
[
  {
    "id": "comb",
    "name": "Combine: Asynchronous Programming with Swift",
    "store_link": "https://store.raywenderlich.com/...",
    "authors": [
        "Scott Gardner",
        "Shai Mishali",
        "Forent Pillet",
        "Marin Todorov"
    ],
    "image_blob": "..."
  }
]
```

This file provides an array of books from the raywenderlich.com book catalog.

Basic decoding

Open the page **1. Ray's Books**. The easiest path to decoding the response is to start with properties you get "for free" from Swift.

Add the following code to your playground:

```swift
struct Book: Decodable {
  let id: String
  let name: String
  let authors: [String]
}
```

Above your new struct, add the following piece of code to try it out:

```swift
let data = API.getData(for: .rwBooks)
let decoder = JSONDecoder()

do {
  let books = try decoder.decode([Book].self, from: data)
  print("— Example of: Books —")
```

```
    print(books)
  } catch {
    print("Something went wrong: \(error)")
  }
```

Run your playground and you'll see a response similar to the following:

```
— Example of: Books —
__lldb_expr_1.Book(id: "comb", name: "Combine: Asynchronous
Programming with Swift", authors: ["Scott Gardner", "Shai
Mishali", "Forent Pillet", "Marin Todorov"]), ...])]
```

Nice! You've got the basics down. You'll now learn how to decode the other fields, starting with `store_link`.

Key decoding strategies

Add the following property to Book:

```
let storeLink: URL
```

Run your playground. You'll see the following error:

```
— Example of: Books —
keyNotFound(CodingKeys(stringValue: "storeLink", intValue: nil),
... debugDescription: "No value associated with key
CodingKeys(stringValue: \"storeLink\", intValue: nil")
```

As the error outlines, no key called `storeLink` exists in the JSON response. However, there is one called `store_link`!

`Codable`'s automatically synthesized keys use a one-to-one mapping, so the decoder doesn't know it should translate `store_link`, a snake-cased key, to `storeLink`, a camel-cased key.

Fortunately, `JSONDecoder` provides an extremely useful concept called a **key-decoding strategy**, which tells the decoder how it should translate the response keys into Swift's camel-cased keys.

The snake-case option is so common that it's already built into `JSONDecoder`.

Below the following line:

```
let decoder = JSONDecoder()
```

Add this code:

```
decoder.keyDecodingStrategy = .convertFromSnakeCase
```

This tells the JSON decoder to automatically convert snake-cased keys as needed.

Run your playground again, and you'll be good to go:

```
— Example of: Books —
[__lldb_expr_5.Book(... storeLink: https://
store.raywenderlich.com/products/combine-asynchronous-
programming-with-swift), ...]
```

Data decoding strategies

Four keys decoded, and one final key to go — `image_blob`. This key contains a Base 64 representation of image data, so you can easily transport small thumbnails along with your JSON response.

Decoding data using `Decodable` is not as hard as it sounds. It uses a concept similar to a key decoding strategy — a **data decoding strategy**.

With a data decoding strategy, whenever `JSONDecoder` sees a property of type `Data`, it checks with the data decoding strategy to determine how it should translate the JSON data into Swift's `Data` type.

Below the `keyDecodingStrategy` you added earlier, add the following line:

```
decoder.dataDecodingStrategy = .base64
```

Finally, add the following two properties to `Book`:

```
let imageBlob: Data
var image: UIImage? { UIImage(data: imageBlob) }
```

The code above defines Base 64 as the data decoding strategy (which is also the default), an `imageBlob` property to correlate with the `image_blob` key in your JSON response and, finally, wraps everything up with an `image` computed property you can use to see the image itself.

Inside the do block in the example, replace `print(books)` with:

```
for book in books {
  print("\(book.name) (\(book.id))",
```

```
            "by \(book.authors.joined(separator: ", ")).",
            "Get it at: \(book.storeLink)")
    _ = book.image
}
```

Run the playground and you'll see output similar to the following:

```
— Example of: Books —
Combine: Asynchronous Programming with Swift (comb) by Scott
Gardner, Shai Mishali, Forent Pillet, Marin Todorov. Get it at:
https://store.raywenderlich.com/products/combine-asynchronous-
programming-with-swift
...
```

In the gutter area, in the line that says _ = book.image, press the **Show Result** button:

```
do {
  let books = try decoder.decode([Book].self, from: data)    |(id "comb", name "Co... ▣
  for book in books {
    print("\(book.name) (\(book.id)) by                          (5 times)          ▣
        \(book.authors.joined(separator: ", ")). Get it
        at: \(book.storeUrl)")
    _ = book.image                                               (5 times)          ▣
  }
} catch {
```

Then, right-click the resulting image area and choose **Value History**:

Now you can scroll and see all the loaded Base 64 decoded images from your JSON response. Excellent!

You're still not done with the Ray Books API. Before wrapping up, you'll take a small detour to learn a bit more about **Coding keys**.

Understanding coding keys

A `CodingKey` is a simple protocol describing how a key of a specific property is represented. It has two properties: `stringValue`, for string keys such as the ones you've just seen, and an optional `intValue`, for cases when the key is part of an array:

```
public protocol CodingKey {
    var stringValue: String { get }
    var intValue: Int? { get }

    init?(stringValue: String)
    init?(intValue: Int)
}
```

It can be decoded with *either* a numeric key or a string key, but not both.

If you think back to the decoding error you saw earlier, a `CodingKey` with a `stringValue` of `storeLink` wasn't found in the original response until you added the appropriate key decoding strategy.

When your properties match perfectly with those of the JSON response, you don't have to manually create any coding keys. As soon as a single one of them requires a custom key, however, you'll need to define your own coding keys.

A common way to do this is to use an enum with a raw value of `String`. There's no need to copy this into your playground.

```
enum CodingKeys: String, CodingKey {
    case id, name, authors
    case storeLink = "store_link"
    case imageBlob = "image_blob"
}
```

When you explicitly specify the coding keys as shown above, you don't need a key decoding strategy.

Custom key decoding strategies

As mentioned earlier, there's one final challenge for you to tackle in this section: creating your own decoding strategy.

Replace the following line:

```
let data = API.getData(for: .rwBooks)
```

With this one:

```
let data = API.getData(for: .rwBooksKebab)
```

This uses a **kebab-case** version of the Ray's Books API, meaning that `store_link` is now `store-link`, and `image_blob` is now `image-blob`.

Run your playground and you'll find a new error waiting for you:

```
[...] No value associated with key CodingKeys(stringValue:
\"storeLink\", intValue: nil) (\"storeLink\"), converted to
store_link."
```

As the error mentions, the decoder tries to convert `storeLink` to `store_link` but can't find a key that matches it in the JSON response.

Unfortunately, there's no built-in `convertFromKebabCase` decoding strategy, so you'll just have to make your own!

One of the key decoding strategies you can use, the aptly named `.custom`, lets you take full control of the key decoding and conversion.

At the end of the playground, add the following code:

```
extension JSONDecoder.KeyDecodingStrategy {
  static var convertFromKebabCase:
JSONDecoder.KeyDecodingStrategy = .custom({ keys in

  })
}
```

This new static property returns a custom key decoding strategy that takes in an array of `CodingKeys` and returns a single, transformed coding key. Don't worry about the compilation errors for now.

Add the following lines inside your new custom strategy:

```
// 1
let codingKey = keys.last!
let key = codingKey.stringValue

// 2
guard key.contains("-") else { return codingKey }

// 3
let words = key.components(separatedBy: "-")
let camelCased = words[0] +
                 words[1...].map(\.capitalized).joined()
```

```
return ???
```

In this code, you:

1. Get the last coding key in the array. The array of coding keys represents the entire path from the root of the JSON response to the specific key you're working on, so you're only interested in the last one, in this case.

2. If the key doesn't contain a dash, it's definitely not kebab-case, so you return the coding key as-is.

3. If it is kebab-case, you split the key by the dashes and capitalize every word but the first one.

camelCased now contains the *kebab-case-turned-camel-case* key you need. But what should you actually return at the end? A CodingKey!

Unfortunately, you can't just instantiate one because it's a protocol. But you can easily write your own concrete helper type to aid in this task. Add the following piece of code to your playground:

```
struct AnyCodingKey: CodingKey {
  let stringValue: String
  let intValue: Int?

  init?(stringValue: String) {
    self.stringValue = stringValue
    self.intValue = nil
  }

  init?(intValue: Int) {
    self.intValue = intValue
    self.stringValue = "\(intValue)"
  }
}
```

This AnyCodingKey type simply lets you instantiate a CodingKey with either an integer or a string. This exact implementation is actually part of Apple's documentation, but unfortunately, it's not currently part of the standard library.

With your new AnyCodingKey ready, you can finalize your custom key decoding implementation.

Replace return ??? with the following:

```
return AnyCodingKey(stringValue: camelCased)!
```

Finally, replace the following line:

```
decoder.keyDecodingStrategy = .convertFromSnakeCase
```

With this one:

```
decoder.keyDecodingStrategy = .convertFromKebabCase
```

This will tell `JSONDecoder` to use your new custom key decoding strategy.

Run your playground page for the final time and everything should work as it did before. Hooray!

Getting this API to parse beautifully and elegantly with Swift's type system took a bit of work, but look how much you've learned so far. And you're just getting started. Time for the next challenge!

API #2: Magic: The Gathering

Magic: The Gathering was the first modern trading card game and it remains wildly popular among fans of the genre. Various cards have different powers, rarity, types and much more, and span over 20 different card sets.

In this section, you'll work on creating a custom `Decoder` to decode an actual response from https://magicthegathering.io/, an API consolidating data about these cards.

To get started, switch over to the playground page, **2. Magic the Gathering** and look around. The playground already includes some boilerplate code to save time, which gets the API response and decodes it into a basic `struct` where all keys are automatically synthesized.

Run the playground and you'll see that the basics are already up and running:

```
Archangel of Thune #8
Thoughtseize #110
Batterskull #130
Force of Will #28
Krenko, Mob Boss #15
Rishkar's Expertise #123
```

Open **magic.json** in the **Resources** folder to get a glimpse of the somewhat complex data structure you'll work on in this section. When you're ready, move over to the next section.

Decoding the card's mana

Each card has something called a **Mana Cost** — the cost needed to put the card into play. The first card in the JSON response has a manaCost of {3}{W}{W}, which means three of any color (colorless), and two white mana cards.

The response uses a string for this, but it could have a much nicer, typed representation in Swift.

To do this, you'll add two new data types: Card.Mana, which will represent the mana cost, and include an array of Card.Mana.Color — an enum of the various mana color options.

Add the following piece of code to the end of the playground page:

```
extension Card {
  /// Card's Mana
  struct Mana: CustomStringConvertible {
    // 1
    let colors: [Color]

    // 2
    var description: String { colors.map(\.symbol).joined() }
  }
}

extension Card.Mana {
  /// Card's Mana Color
  enum Color {
    // 3
    case colorless(Int)
    case extra
    case white
    case blue
    case black
    case red
    case green

    // 4
    var symbol: String {
      switch self {
      case .white: return "W"
      case .blue: return "U"
      case .black: return "B"
      case .red: return "R"
```

```
      case .green: return "G"
      case .extra: return "X"
      case .colorless(let number): return "\(number)"
      }
    }
  }
}
```

Here's the breakdown of the code above:

1. You define a new `Card.Mana` type, which has an array of `Card.Mana.Color` models.

2. `Mana` also conforms to `CustomStringConvertible` and prints out the color symbols of the mana cost, joined.

3. The `Color` enum contains cases for all individual mana colors, as well as `.colorless`, which has an associated value of the number of colorless mana.

4. Finally, the mana color has a `symbol` computed property to print out the single-character symbol of the mana color.

So far, so good. But how do you actually make `Mana` conform to `Decodable` in a way that processes the source string 5{W}{W}? `Codable` obviously can't know how to translate this information automatically.

This is where a custom `Decodable` conformance proves extremely useful.

First, you'll add an initializer to `Card.Mana.Color` that accepts the mana symbol. You'll use this in the `Decodable` conformance of `Mana` itself.

Add the following initializer to `Card.Mana.Color` enum:

```
init?(symbol: String) {
  if let value = Int(symbol) {
    self = .colorless(value)
    return
  }

  switch symbol.lowercased() {
  case "w":
    self = .white
  case "u":
    self = .blue
  case "b":
    self = .black
  case "r":
    self = .red
  case "g":
```

```
    self = .green
  case "x":
    self = .extra
  default:
    print("UNKNOWN \(symbol)")
    return nil
  }
}
```

This initializer simply accepts the symbol, such as W or 3, and returns the appropriate enum case. If the value is numeric, it returns the `.colorless` case with the associated numeric value.

Before you move on to the next section, you'll want to learn more about one of the foundations of how encoding and decoding are structured in Codable — **containers**.

Understanding containers

If you've ever written a custom Decodable or Encodable initializer, it's quite likely you've worked with a decoding or encoding container, accordingly:

There are three unique types of containers:

• **Keyed Container**: The most common kind of container. In the example above, you decode a dictionary **keyed by** a set of CodingKeys, hence the name.

• **Unkeyed Container**: As its name suggests, you use this to decode structures that don't have string-based coding keys — arrays, for example.

• **Single Value Container**: Use this when decoding a single value into some concrete type. In the example above, you could have a Status enum with a custom decoder that uses a single value container to resolve the decoded value.

These containers can each be **nested**, meaning they can be sub-containers of a different container.

You can think of a container as **a context for your decoding or encoding**.

Looking at the example above, the top keyed container lets you work in the context of the keys id, status, name, family and location, while the inner-most coordinate nested container lets you decode in the context of the longitude and latitude keys.

You'll use both keyed and single-value containers during this chapter.

Custom Decodable conformance for Card.Mana

With the Card.Mana.Color initializer ready to roll, it's time to start taking care of Card.Mana itself. Start by conforming Card.Mana to Decodable by replacing:

```
struct Mana: CustomStringConvertible {
```

With:

```
struct Mana: Decodable, CustomStringConvertible {
```

Then, add Decodable's required initializer:

```
init(from decoder: Decoder) throws {

}
```

Swift automatically synthesizes this initializer for you when it can determine how to properly decode your response. For example, if the coding keys accurately match the response. More often then not, though, you'll want more granular control, as in this case.

Remember that decoding mana works on a simple String and not a dictionary or array. As mentioned above, the solution is to use a **single value container**.

Add the following code inside your new initializer:

```
let container = try decoder.singleValueContainer()
let cost = try container.decode(String.self)
```

You first ask the decoder for a single-value container. You're basically telling the decoder: "Hey there, this type is only dealing with a single value type, not a dictionary or other complex structure."

Because this container works on a single value, it doesn't need coding keys, and you can simply attempt to decode it as the String you're expecting.

Now that you have the raw string, for example "{5}{W}{W}", you can perform the necessary processing to break it down into an array of Colors. Finish your initializer with the following block of code:

```
self.colors = try cost
  .components(separatedBy: "}") // 1
  .dropLast()
  .compactMap { rawCost in
    let symbol = String(rawCost.dropFirst()) // 2

    // 3
    guard !symbol.isEmpty,
          let color = Color(symbol: symbol) else {
      throw DecodingError.dataCorruptedError(
        in: container,
        debugDescription: "Unknown mana symbol \(symbol)")
    }

    // 4
    return color
  }
```

In this code, you:

1. Separate the string by the } sign, getting an array such as ["{5", "{W", "{W", ""]. You then use dropLast() to get rid of the empty string at the end.

2. Strip the first character for each of the array parts, which leaves you with ["5", "W", "W"].

3. Attempt to create a new Mana.Color instance by passing the clean symbol to the initializer you added in the previous section. If the initializer returns nil or the symbol is empty, you throw a DecodingError.dataCorruptedError to notify the consumer of the unexpected result.

4. If you got a valid color, you simply return it.

By the end of this initializer, colors will contain an array of strictly-typed Mana.Color.

You've worked so hard, so how about actually using your Mana object?

Implementing the Mana object

Add the following property to Card:

```
let manaCost: Mana
```

Everything builds successfully, as Mana conforms to Decodable as well, so you don't need to do any extra work.

Finally, in the for loop at the top of the file, modify print to look as follows:

```
print(" ⚜ \(card.name) #\(card.number), \(card.manaCost)")
```

Run the playground, then check the output produced by Mana's conformance of CustomStringConvertible:

```
⚜ Archangel of Thune #8, 3WW
⚜ Thoughtseize #110, B
⚜ Batterskull #130, 5
⚜ Force of Will #28, 3UU
⚜ Krenko, Mob Boss #15, 2RR
⚜ Rishkar's Expertise #123, 4GG
```

Although the produced output is a simple String, your data model is now an actual concrete enum you can work with inside Swift's type system.

Decoding the card's rarity

The card rarity is mostly simple, comprising a fixed set of strings: Common, Mythic Rare, Basic Land etc.

Add the following extension to the bottom of your playground:

```
extension Card {
  enum Rarity: String, CustomStringConvertible, Decodable {
    case common = "Common"
    case uncommon = "Uncommon"
    case rare = "Rare"
    case mythicRare = "Mythic Rare"
    case special = "Special"
    case land = "Basic Land"

    var description: String { rawValue }
```

```
    }
  }
```

In the code above, you create a simple `Rarity` enum with the appropriate cases, which also provides a custom `String` value for each case. This is similar to a single-value container, except that Swift takes care of that boilerplate for you behind the scenes.

Add the following property to `Card`:

```
let rarity: Rarity
```

Also, add `, \(card.rarity)` to the end of the `print` statement at the top to see the result of your new property:

```
🎴 Archangel of Thune #8, 3WW, Mythic Rare
🎴 Thoughtseize #110, B, Rare

...
```

You have three more properties to take care of as part of this section. Unfortunately, they all require `Card` to provide a custom `Decodable` initializer.

To save some time, add the following initializer and `CodingKeys` enum to `Card`:

```
init(from decoder: Decoder) throws {
  let container = try decoder.container(keyedBy:
CodingKeys.self)
  self.id = try container.decode(UUID.self, forKey: .id)
  self.name = try container.decode(String.self, forKey: .name)
  self.manaCost = try container.decode(Mana.self,
                                        forKey: .manaCost)
  self.type = try container.decode(String.self, forKey: .type)
  self.rarity = try container.decode(Rarity.self,
                                      forKey: .rarity)
  self.text = try container.decodeIfPresent(String.self,
                                      forKey: .text) ?? ""
  self.flavor = try container.decodeIfPresent(String.self,
                                      forKey: .flavor)
  self.number = try container.decode(String.self,
                                      forKey: .number)
  self.imageUrl = try container.decodeIfPresent(URL.self,
                                      forKey: .imageUrl)
}

enum CodingKeys: String, CodingKey {
  case id, name, manaCost, type, rarity
  case text, flavor, number, set, setName
```

```
    case power, toughness, rulings, imageUrl
  }
```

The code above is basically the manual implementation of what Swift automatically synthesized for you so far. But as mentioned earlier, you can easily get to cases where your models don't directly correlate to your response. In this case, Codable gives you the ability to take matters into your own hands.

Decoding the card's set and attributes

Cards are released as part of **sets**, which contain a name and a symbol. Each creature card also features power and toughness, which determine how strong the creature's attack is and how much damage it can withstand.

Unfortunately, set, setName, power and toughness are scattered in the JSON response. Wouldn't it be much more aesthetic and "Swifty" to put them in their own structures? Why, of course!

Start by adding the following two structs to the end of your playground:

```
extension Card {
  struct Attributes {
    let power: String
    let toughness: String
  }
}

extension Card {
  struct Set {
    let id: String
    let name: String
  }
}
```

This code defines Card.Attributes, which unifies power and toughness and Card.Set, which unifies set and setName.

In this specific case, you can't simply conform these objects to Decodable, because they don't work on a single property of your original response. You'll want to decode each value as needed and construct these objects by hand to achieve the wanted result.

Start by adding the following two properties to Card:

```
let set: Set
let attributes: Attributes?
```

Next, at the end of your custom `Decodable` initializer, add the following code:

```
// 1
// Set
self.set = Set(id: try container.decode(String.self,
                                         forKey: .set),
            name: try container.decode(String.self,
                                       forKey: .setName))

// 2
// Attributes
if let power = try container.decodeIfPresent(String.self,
                                             forKey: .power),
   let toughness = try container.decodeIfPresent(String.self,
                                                 forKey: .toughness) {
  self.attributes = Attributes(power: power,
                               toughness: toughness)
} else {
  self.attributes = nil
}
```

In the code above, you attempt to create both `Set` and `Attributes`:

1. You initialize `Set` and directly provide the calls to
    `container.decode(_:forKey:)` as arguments to it. If any of the properties are
    missing, the initializer will throw an error, as expected because `Set` is mandatory.

2. `power` and `toughness` are optional, as they only apply to creature cards. You use
    `decodeIfPresent` to try and decode the two values from the container. If they
    exist, you initialize a new instance of `Attributes` from them. Otherwise, you set
    `Attributes` to `nil`.

You now have most of the data from the JSON response decoded into your `Card`
model. Replace the `print` statement inside the `for` loop at the top of your
playground with the following:

```
print(
  " ☀ \(card.name) #\(card.number) is a \(card.rarity)",
  "\(card.type) and needs \(card.manaCost).",
  "It's part of \(card.set.name) (\(card.set.id)).",
  card.attributes.map { "It's attributed as \($0.power)/\
($0.toughness)." } ?? ""
)
```

Here, you simply print out everything about the card in a prettified way and
conditionally print the card's attributes using `Optional`'s map method.

Run the playground and you'll see output like the following:

```
♣ Archangel of Thune #8 is a Mythic Rare Creature — Angel and
needs 3WW. It's part of Iconic Masters (IMA). It's attributed as
3/4.
♣ Thoughtseize #110 is a Rare Sorcery and needs B. It's part of
Iconic Masters (IMA).
...
```

You'll wrap up this section with one final property. How exciting!

Decoding the card's rulings

Each card possesses an array of rulings containing dates and textual rulings about the card throughout its history.

To be honest, though, the ruling dates aren't too interesting. Having a simple array of String rulings instead would be great, in this case.

This calls for one final round of Decodable wrangling.

First, add the following property to Card:

```
let rulings: [String]
```

Now, it's time to add the decoding you need in Card's initializer. You can take one of two approaches:

1. Define a private Ruling struct that conforms to Decodable, only to extract its text.

2. Decode the property directly to a Dictionary and extract only its text key directly.

Although both approaches are entirely valid, you'll use the second option today. Despite this rather lengthy introduction, you'll only need to add the following two lines to the end of the initializer:

```
// Rulings
let rulingDict = try container.decode([[String: String]].self,
                                      forKey: .rulings) // 1
self.rulings = rulingDict.compactMap { $0["text"] } // 2
```

With this code, you:

1. Decode the `rulings` key into a raw array of dictionaries. This correlates directly to the way `rulings` is structured in the API response.

2. Use `compactMap` on the array and try to extract only the `text` of each ruling dictionary.

Rulings are quite verbose, so you'll add a separate `print` statement for them. Inside the `for` loop at the top of the file, add:

```
print("Rulings: \(card.rulings.joined(separator: ", "))")
```

Run the playground, and you'll see the various rulings printed out for each of the cards:

```
🜂 Archangel of Thune #8 is a Mythic Rare Creature — Angel and
needs 3WW. It's part of Iconic Masters (IMA). It's attributed as
3/4.
Rulings: Archangel of Thune's last ability triggers just once
for each life-gaining event, whether it's 1 life from Auriok
Champion or 6 life from Tavern Swindler. [...]
```

Wow, you've gone through a massive decoding session here. Kudos to you! Now, it's finally time to head over to the last `Decodable` challenge for this chapter.

API #3: Alpha Vantage

You'll tackle the most challenging task last.

Sometimes, you get something special to work on. A massive, non-standard response that makes you scratch your head and say: "I have no idea how to decode this thing!"

This section will deal with an API in this very category: **Alpha Vantage**.

Alpha Vantage provides free financial APIs around Stocks, FX, Cryptocurrency etc. The one you'll work with today is the Stocks API.

Open **av_1min.json** in the **Resources** folder and you might notice some of the challenges this response poses:

1. All of the static keys are relatively strange, and some are numbered.

2. The `Time Series` key is actually dynamic, depending on the interval in minutes you ask of the API. It could be `Time Series (1 min)`, `Time Series (5 min)`, or any other key.

3. If that's not enough, each key inside the `Time Series` key is both *dynamic* and a *date*.

Yikes.

This response might be quite painful to deal with on its own, but Swift's strictly typed nature makes this even more challenging. It's nothing you can't deal with, though!

Exploring the starter page

In the navigation pane, open the page **3. Alpha Vantage**. You'll notice there's already some starter code waiting there for you:

1. `getStock(interval:)`: For retrieving information about a stock, along with updates in specific intervals.

2. `Stock`: An empty struct waiting for you to fill it out.

3. A call to `getStock(interval:)` prints out the decoded `Stock`.

Analyzing the response

If you look in **av_1min.json** again, you'll notice the structure looks similar to the following:

```
{
  "Meta Data": {
    "1. Information": "Intraday (1min) open...",
    "2. Symbol": "RAY",
    "3. Last Refreshed": "2020-08-14 20:00:00"
  },
  "Time Series (1min)": {
    "2020-08-14 20:00:00": {
      "1. open": "101.9000",
      "2. high": "102.0000",
      "3. low": "101.9000",
```

```
        "4. close": "102.0000",
        "5. volume": "1807"
    },
    [...]
  }
}
```

Quite a convoluted structure, indeed. In Swift, a consumer would usually prefer to directly access the nested properties without the excessive nesting in the original JSON response.

To start with the basics, add the following two properties to the `Stock struct`:

```
let info: String
let symbol: String
```

Decoding the nested metadata

Because the structure of `Stock` doesn't directly correlate with the JSON response, you'll need a custom decoding initializer. Add the following initializer, along with coding keys for the top level and the `Meta Data` level:

```
init(from decoder: Decoder) throws {
  // 1
  let container = try decoder.container(
    keyedBy: CodingKeys.self
  )
}

// 2
enum CodingKeys: String, CodingKey {
  case metaData = "Meta Data"
  case updates = "Time Series (1min)"
}

// 3
enum MetaKeys: String, CodingKey {
  case info = "1. Information"
  case symbol = "2. Symbol"
  case refreshedAt = "3. Last Refreshed"
}
```

That piece of code causes a compilation error, but don't worry about that for now. It:

1. Creates a top-level container keyed by `CodingKeys`.

2. Defines `CodingKeys` for that top level, which represents the metadata and time series keys.

3. Define `MetaKeys` to represent the individual keys inside the metadata key.

With that done, you can now decode your stock's `info` and `symbol` properties. But how?

If you remember the explanation about containers earlier in this chapter, the answer might already pop into your head — simply use a **nested container**.

Using nested containers

To start, add the following line inside your initializer:

```
let metaContainer = try container.nestedContainer(
    keyedBy: MetaKeys.self,
    forKey: .metaData
)
```

In the following line, you ask the top-level container to give you a new, nested container, which represents the metadata. Basically, you're asking the top container: "Give me a new decoding context for the `.metaData` key that I can decode using the `MetaKeys` coding keys".

Now that you have access to the meta data scope, all that's left is decoding the individual properties. Add the following lines immediately after the previous one:

```
self.info = try metaContainer.decode(String.self, forKey: .info)
self.symbol = try metaContainer.decode(String.self,
                                       forKey: .symbol)
```

You decode the two individual `String` values from their appropriate keys. Notice how the available keys in the `forKey` argument are the ones from `MetaKeys` since that's the decoding container you're working on at the moment.

Swift's type system really helps with getting the right keys for the task.

Run the playground. You'll see output similar to the following:

```
Stock(info: "Intraday (1min) [..]", symbol: "RAY")
```

Great work! With that done, there are still two more pieces of information to decode: the last refresh date and the individual updates for the stock.

Decoding custom date formats

Start by adding the following property to `Stock`:

```
let refreshedAt: Date
```

Then, add the following line at the end of `Stock`'s initializer to decode the date:

```
self.refreshedAt = try metaContainer.decode(
  Date.self,
  forKey: .refreshedAt
)
```

Run the playground, and you'll see the following error:

```
typeMismatch(...debugDescription: "Expected to decode Double but
found a string/data instead."...)
```

By default, decoding to date expects a Unix timestamp as its source. But in Alpha Vantage's API, you have a string date formatted like: `2020-08-14 20:00:00`.

Fortunately, much like `JSONDecoder`'s key-decoding strategy, you can also pick a **date-decoding strategy**. As of the time of writing this chapter, there are six date-decoding strategies in `JSONDecoder`.

Although you might be tempted to reach to the `custom` decoding strategy, like in the case of a key decoding strategy, there's a much more fitting strategy called `formatted` which takes a `DateFormatter` and uses it to decode the `Date`. It's time for you to try this out.

First, you'll create a `DateFormatter`. Above `getStock(interval:)`, in the global scope, add the following code:

```
let dateFormatter: DateFormatter = {
  let df = DateFormatter()
  df.dateFormat = "yyyy-MM-dd HH:mm:ss"
  return df
}()
```

You just created a `DateFormatter` with the appropriate `dateFormat` for Alpha Vantage's JSON response.

> **Note**: I highly recommend https://nsdateformatter.com/ to create the perfect `dateFormat` string without too much hassle.

Now, all you have to do is apply the decoding strategy to your decoder. After creating `JSONDecoder` inside `getStock(interval:)`, add the following line:

```
decoder.dateDecodingStrategy = .formatted(dateFormatter)
```

This will cause `JSONDecoder` to always defer decoding of `Date`s to the underlying `NSDateFormatter`.

Run your playground again and everything should work, with output similar to the following:

```
Stock(info: "Intraday (1min) ...", symbol: "RAY", refreshedAt:
2020-08-14 17:00:00 +0000)
```

Excellent, everything is almost ready to go, but you still have a big challenge ahead — decoding the individual updates in the time series key.

Decoding the individual stock updates

As before, it's best to try and define what you want the data structure to eventually look like in Swift.

In this case, it would be much nicer to have an array of `updates` available directly on `Stock`, instead of needing to dig through a dictionary of dictionaries, like in the original response.

You'll start bottom-up, by defining what an update should look like. Add the following extension to the end of your playground:

```
extension Stock {
  struct Update: Decodable, CustomStringConvertible {
    // 1
    let open: Float
    let high: Float
    let low: Float
    let close: Float
    let volume: Int
    var date = Date.distantPast

    // 2
    enum CodingKeys: String, CodingKey {
```

```
    case open = "1. open"
    case high = "2. high"
    case low = "3. low"
    case close = "4. close"
    case volume = "5. volume"
  }

  init(from decoder: Decoder) throws {
    let container = try decoder.container(keyedBy:
CodingKeys.self)

    // 3
    self.open = try Float(container.decode(String.self,
forKey: .open)).unwrapOrThrow()
    self.high = try Float(container.decode(String.self,
forKey: .high)).unwrapOrThrow()
    self.low = try Float(container.decode(String.self, forKey:
.low)).unwrapOrThrow()
    self.close = try Float(container.decode(String.self,
forKey: .close)).unwrapOrThrow()
    self.volume = try Int(container.decode(String.self,
forKey: .volume)).unwrapOrThrow()
  }

  // 4
  var description: String {
    "\(date)|o:\(open),h:\(high),l:\(low),c:\(close),v:\
(volume)"
  }
 }
}
```

This code represents what each update looks like. It's meant to decode the internal dictionaries inside each dated key in the time series key.

Here's the breakdown:

1. You create properties to match the individual updates in the response. You've also added a date property, which you'll use momentarily.

2. You define the necessary custom coding keys for each of the decoded properties.

3. Because the values in the response are strings, you decode them as such and attempt to cast them to Float or Int, as needed. To verify the casting succeeded, you also use a custom unwrapOrThrow() on Optional, which can be found in **Optional+Ext.swift**.

4. Finally, you provide a human-readable output for the update.

Decoding updates into Stock

Now, to deal with `Stock` itself. Start by adding the following property to it:

```
let updates: [Update]
```

The tricky part is that each update is keyed under an unknown, dynamic key. Not only that, but that key is also the date you wish to associate with each `Update`.

Dynamic keys... um, does that ring any bells? It's time for some `AnyCodingKey` magic!

This specific case is a bit trickier — you don't even know what the dynamic keys you need to create are, so you'll start by getting those.

Inside `Stock`'s initializer, add the following lines:

```
let timesDictionary = try container.decode(
  [String: [String: String]].self,
  forKey: .updates
)

let timeKeys = timesDictionary.keys
  .compactMap(AnyCodingKey.init(stringValue:))
```

Because you don't know the dynamic keys inside the `Time Series (1 min)` key, you simply decode the entire structure as a raw dictionary of dictionaries. You then get only the keys (i.e., the dates) and create new `AnyCodingKeys` from them. Finally, you store them in `timeKeys`.

To use these keys, you'll need to use a nested container once again. Add the following line:

```
let timeContainer = try container.nestedContainer(
  keyedBy: AnyCodingKey.self,
  forKey: .updates
)
```

As before, you create a nested container for the `.updates` coding key, meaning `Time Series (1 min)`. This time, however, note it's keyed by `AnyCodingKey` because there's no finite set of keys like your enum-based coding keys.

Everything is now in place to decode your individual updates. All you have to do is iterate over the new keys you've created, and decode each of them.

Decoding your new keys

Finalize your initializer with this piece of code:

```
// 1
self.updates = try timeKeys
  .reduce(into: [Update]()) { updates, currentKey in
    // 2
    var update = try timeContainer.decode(Update.self,
                                    forKey: currentKey)
    // 3
    update.date = dateFormatter
        .date(from: currentKey.stringValue) ?? update.date
    // 4
    updates.append(update)
  }
  .sorted(by: { $0.date < $1.date }) // 5
```

This might look a bit complicated, but it's easier once you break it down. In the code outlined above, you:

1. Use `reduce(into:)` on the `timeKeys` you created. You start with a seed of an empty array of `Updates`, which you'll fill up as you go.

2. Use the `timeContainer`, the one scoped to the time series key, to decode the individual update found in the `currentKey` key.

3. Use the same `DateFormatter` you created earlier and try to parse the string date into a `Date` object. This is because, as mentioned before, the date of the update is actually the key itself.

4. Append the new update into the `reduced` result array: `updates`.

5. Sort all updates by date, once they are parsed out of a dictionary.

Testing your Stock decoding

To test all of the incredible work you've just done, below `Stock`, replace `print(stock)` with the following:

```
print("\(stock.symbol), \(stock.refreshedAt):",
      "\(stock.info) with \(stock.updates.count) updates")
for update in stock.updates {
  _ = update.open

  print("   >> \(update.date), O/C: \(update.open)/\
(update.close), L/H: \(update.low)/\(update.high), V: \
```

```
    (update.volume)")
    }
```

Here, you simply print out the stock info and each individual update. Run your playground and you'll see output similar to the following:

```
RAY, 2020-08-14 17:00:00 +0000: Intraday (1min) [...] with 100
updates
    >> 2020-08-14 15:02:00 +0000, O/C: 101.81/101.81, L/H:
101.81/101.81, V: 1020
    >> 2020-08-14 13:55:00 +0000, O/C: 101.95/102.09, L/H:
101.95/102.09, V: 1765
    >> ...
```

Click the show result icon next to the line that says `_ = update.open`:

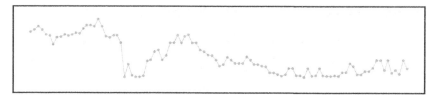

You'll see a nice graph showcasing the opening value updates for the stock:

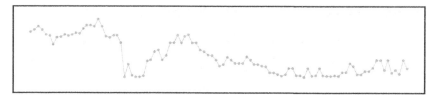

> **Note**: If you can't see the graph, right-click the value area and change the mode to **Graph**.

How cool is that? Through some fiddling, nested containers, and custom raw `AnyCodingKeys`, you massaged this extremely massive and oddly structured JSON response to a strictly typed, easily consumable Swift struct.

You've got all of your decoding logic in place, but there's still something missing. Can you guess what it is? Handling other time intervals!

At the top of the do block, replace the following line:

```
let stock = try getStock(interval: .oneMinute)
```

With this one:

```
let stock = try getStock(interval: .fifteenMinutes)
```

Run the playground, and you'll see an error similar to the following:

```
... No value associated with key CodingKeys(stringValue: \"Time
Series (1min)\", intValue: nil)[...]
```

Whoops! The code you've written always expects the specific key `Time Series (1 min)`, but in this case, the interval is actually 15 minutes.

You could use an `AnyCodingKey` here as well, but how would you know what the API call's interval is from inside your decodable initializer? You have no access to that data in that scope.

Passing information with user-info keys

The question you need to answer is: "How can I pass information down from the external world into my decodable initializer?" That answer is simpler than you'd come to expect.

`Codable` decoders feature a type called `CodingUserInfoKey`. As with the `userInfo` key on notifications and other constructs that let you pass a dictionary of key-value pairs, you can pass down custom information to decoders, keyed by this concrete type.

At the end of your playground, add the following code:

```
extension CodingUserInfoKey {
  static let timeInterval = CodingUserInfoKey(
    rawValue: "timeInterval"
  )!
}
```

Then, in `getStock(interval:)`, below `let decoder = JSONDecoder()`, add the following line:

```
decoder.userInfo = [.timeInterval: interval.rawValue]
```

With these two pieces of code, you define a concrete `CodingUserInfoKey` to represent your time interval. Then, you pass the `JSONDecoder` the requested interval's raw value with that key.

Now that the decoder has all the needed information, you need to modify your
Stock's initializer accordingly. Replace the following line in Stock.init(from:):

```
let container = try decoder.container(
  keyedBy: CodingKeys.self
)
```

With the following code:

```
// 1
guard let time = decoder.userInfo[.timeInterval] as? Int else {
  throw DecodingError.dataCorrupted(
    .init(codingPath: [],
        debugDescription: "Missing time interval")
  )
}

// 2
let metaKey = AnyCodingKey(stringValue: "Meta Data")!
let timesKey = AnyCodingKey(stringValue: "Time Series (\
(time)min)")!

// 3
let container = try decoder.container(
  keyedBy: AnyCodingKey.self
)
```

In this code, you:

1. Access the decoder's user info and try to get the passed time interval. If it doesn't
    exist, you throw an error.

2. Create two AnyCodingKeys representing the metadata and time series key, using
    the dynamic time interval. You switch the metadata key to AnyCodingKeys
    because a container has to be decoded by a single concrete type.

3. Replace the CodingKeys scoped container with one scoped by AnyCodingKey. At
    this point, you can entirely remove the CodingKeys enum if you wish to do so.

To fix the last three compilation errors, you should:

1. Replace forKey: .metaData with forKey: metaKey.

2. Replace the two instances of forKey: .updates with forKey: timesKey.

With that completed, run your playground a final time and you'll see that everything works as expected, with the interval dynamically passing down to the decoder:

```
RAY, 2020-08-14 17:00:00 +0000: Intraday (15min) open, high,
low, close prices and volume with 100 updates
...
```

Feel free to experiment with `getStock(interval:)` and call it with different intervals to confirm it works correctly in all cases.

Encoding

You've spent the majority of this chapter working on decoding because that's where most of the challenges arise in daily work. But you're definitely not going to leave this chapter without at least touching a bit on the other side of the equation: encoding.

In the decoding process, you take an external representation (such as JSON) and decode it into a Swift type. On the other hand, encoding lets you describe how to encode arbitrary Swift types into various external representations.

In this final section, you'll write your own `Encodable` conformance for a Swift struct to explore the various options at your disposal.

Exploring the starter page

Open the **4. Encodable** playground page in the Navigation pane and you'll notice there's already a considerable amount of boilerplate written for you:

1. A `Customer` struct that conforms to `Encodable`.

2. An instance of `Customer`.

3. Code using `JSONEncoder()` to print out the JSON representation resulting from the encoding.

Note that, like `Decodable`, adding the `Encodable` protocol conformance is enough for Swift to automatically synthesize encoding for your struct by using the same keys as its properties.

Also, notice that `JSONEncoder.encode(_:)` returns `Data` and not a `String`. You use `String(data:encoding:)` to make things nice and readable.

Run your playground to see the default output you get from JSONEncoder (abbreviated):

```
{"street":"3828 Piermont
Drive","atmCode":"1132","city":"Albuquerque",...}
```

Encoder customizations

Like JSONDecoder's various customizable properties, JSONEncoder packs quite a punch. The first customization opportunity for you is output formatting. Add the following line immediately after creating your JSONEncoder:

```
encoder.outputFormatting = [.prettyPrinted,
                            .sortedKeys,
                            .withoutEscapingSlashes]
```

Run your playground and you'll see output similar to the following:

```
{
  "accessKey": "S|_|p3rs3cr37",
  "addedOn": 619552896.56153595,
  [...]
  "website": "http://github.com/freak4pc",
  "zip": 87112
}
```

Wow, this already looks quite different. The code you've added customizes how JSONEncoder outputs its data:

- .prettyPrinted: Properly indents and adds new lines to the JSON to make it easier to read.

- .sortedKeys: Sorts the JSON keys alphabetically. Notice how the initial JSON keys look, and how the current output looks. It starts with accessKey and ends with zip.

- .withoutEscapingSlashes: Lets you disable the automatic escaping of slashes. By default, slashes get escaped using a preceding backslash, which might not be needed for presentation purposes, like in the website property in this example.

Encoding strategies

Exactly like Decodable has decoding strategies, Encodable has **encoding strategies**: keyEncodingStrategy, dateEncodingStrategy and dataEncodingStrategy.

Add the following two lines after the previous one to try these out:

```
encoder.keyEncodingStrategy = .convertToSnakeCase
encoder.dateEncodingStrategy = .iso8601
```

Run your playground and you'll see that all your keys have automatically been converted to snake case and that the date is now presented as ISO8601 instead of a regular timestamp.

Before:

```
"addedOn": 619553518.18203104
```

After:

```
"added_on": "2020-08-19T18:12:23Z"
```

Customizing encoding with intermediate types

One thing you might have noticed is that two properties — accessKey and atmCode — contain rather sensitive information. It's a good idea to encrypt this information before encoding the object to JSON.

You could create a custom encoder and manually encode and decode these values as needed, but a more elegant option is to add an intermediate type responsible for this.

Add the following code to the end of your playground page:

```
struct EncryptedCodableString: ExpressibleByStringLiteral,
                               Codable {
  let value: String

  // 1
  let key = SymmetricKey(data:
                          "Expert Swift !!!".data(using: .utf8)!)

  // 2
  init(stringLiteral value: StringLiteralType) {
    self.value = value
  }

  // 3
  init(from decoder: Decoder) throws {
    let container = try decoder.singleValueContainer()
    let combined = try container.decode(Data.self)
    let result = try AES.GCM.open(.init(combined: combined),
```

```
                                        using: key)
    self.value = String(data: result, encoding: .utf8) ?? ""
  }

  // 4
  func encode(to encoder: Encoder) throws {
    var container = encoder.singleValueContainer()
    let data = value.data(using: .utf8)!
    let sealed = try AES.GCM.seal(data, using: key)
    try container.encode(sealed.combined)
  }
}
```

You just defined a new `EncryptedCodableString` responsible for performing encryption and decryption using **CryptoKit**, which was already imported in your playground.

Here's the breakdown:

1. You define a CryptoKit symmetric key, which uses a hard-coded weak key for educational purposes. In production, you should use a strongly hashed key stored securely in your keychain.

2. Your type conforms to `ExpressibleByStringLiteral`, which lets you instantiate it with a raw string literal without explicitly stating its type.

3. To satisfy the `Decodable` conformance, you define a custom decoding initializer and use a single-value container to decode a `String` and then decrypt it with CryptoKit.

4. To satisfy the `Encodable` conformance, you define a custom `encode(to:)` method and use a single-value container to encode the CryptoKit-encrypted version of the underlying `value`.

Great! How can you actually use this?

Simply replace `String` with `EncryptedCodableString` for both `accessKey` and `atmCode`. Then, run your playground page, and you'll see output similar to the following:

```
{
  "access_key" : "6CFbMLD0IojD7MaJwDH[...]iS4cr9i2vu0C2N/Q=",
  "atm_code": "mZjZ17+VM8Nh0e3DwceF8hfT/6gpl0D+n5c/jpNVIws="
  [...]
}
```

Your strings were encrypted specifically when encoded to JSON, and all you had to do was replace the String type with your new type.

This concept has many useful applications: conforming custom property wrappers, custom formats specific to encoding, etc.

Restructuring your output

To wrap up this chapter, you'll learn about one final thing: How to manipulate the structure of the encoded JSON.

You got some free auto-synthesized encoding, but like decoding, it's quite common to want a different output or structure for your consumers than you have in your app.

All you have to do in this case is to add a custom implementation of encode(to:) and manually define the encoding. In this case, it would be nice to encapsulate the user's address information in an address key and their contact info under a contactInfo key.

Before you do this, add the following coding keys to Customer:

```
enum CustomerKeys: String, CodingKey {
  case name, accessKey, atmCode, addedOn, address, contactInfo
}

enum AddressKeys: String, CodingKey {
  case street, city, zip
}

enum ContactInfoKeys: String, CodingKey {
  case homePhone, cellularPhone, email
}
```

Here you define three sets of coding keys: the first for the top level, and two more sets of coding keys specific for the address details and contact info.

It's time to get some encoding going on, isn't it?

Add the following basic implementation for encode(to:) inside Customer:

```
func encode(to encoder: Encoder) throws {
  var customer = encoder.container(keyedBy: CustomerKeys.self)
  try customer.encode(name, forKey: .name)
  try customer.encode(accessKey, forKey: .accessKey)
  try customer.encode(atmCode, forKey: .atmCode)
  try customer.encode(addedOn, forKey: .addedOn)
}
```

You simply ask the encoder for a keyed container based on `CustomerKeys` to build the top-level response. Notice that the `customer` container is mutable so you can write into it.

Run the playground to see what you have so far:

```
{
    "access_key": "AwENrgpbFvL[...]XS57sWpOQ==",
    "added_on": "2020-08-19T18:44:27Z",
    "atm_code": "AwFkTXStHHy[...]FoUOdAGHfjuUwkw==",
    "name": "Shai Mishali"
}
```

Only the keys you've encoded are part of the response. This is great because it means you can customize your response to whatever you see fit for your consumer.

Encoding the customer's information

Next, you'll deal with the customer's address and contact information. Can you guess how? Exactly like decoding, you can use nested containers to create nested structures in your encoding!

Add the following lines to complete your custom encoder:

```
var address = customer.nestedContainer(
  keyedBy: AddressKeys.self,
  forKey: .address
)
try address.encode(street, forKey: .street)
try address.encode(city, forKey: .city)
try address.encode(zip, forKey: .zip)

var contactInfo = customer.nestedContainer(
  keyedBy: ContactInfoKeys.self,
  forKey: .contactInfo
)
try contactInfo.encode(homePhone, forKey: .homePhone)
try contactInfo.encode(cellularPhone, forKey: .cellularPhone)
try contactInfo.encode(email, forKey: .email)
```

These two sections are quite similar. In both, you:

1. Ask the main container, `customer`, for a nested keyed container. The first one is based on `AddressKeys` and the second on `ContactInfoKeys`.

2. Simply encode the appropriate properties from `Customer` into each container. Once you have these nested containers, each represents its own encoding context.

Build and run your playground to see your tailored response:

```
{
  "access_key": "AwE4[...]DFL+m6NOPNw==",
  "added_on": "2020-08-19T18:50:26Z",
  "address": {
    "city": "Albuquerque",
    "street": "3828 Piermont Drive",
    "zip": 87112
  },
  "atm_code": "AwGw[..]Y7w==",
  "contact_info": {
    "cellular_phone": "+972 542-288-482",
    "email": "freak4pc@gmail.com",
    "home_phone": "+1 212-741-4695"
  },
  "name": "Shai Mishali"
}
```

Notice how both address and contact_info represent their appropriate keys and the nested containers you've defined.

This is great! Think about it — you could have a Server-Side Swift app that uses custom encoding to provide a consumer-friendly representation of your data models without compromising your own Swift models.

As an exercise to you, the reader, try writing the Decodable part of Customer to "reverse" the encoding JSONEncoder is doing. You'll be surprised by how similar the Decodable and Encodable implementation will end up looking like.

Key points

You covered a lot in this chapter. Here are some of the key takeaways:

- `Codable` is a mechanism that lets you define how to decode and encode various data representations in and out of your models.

- Swift can do a lot of the heavy lifting for you automatically if your keys match up perfectly with your properties.

- When the automatically synthesized code just doesn't cut it, you have full control to customize decoding, encoding or both.

- You can use key strategies, data strategies, date strategies etc. to further customize how specific encoders and decoders treat specific types of properties or their keys.

- When writing your own custom encoding and decoding, you can use various types of **containers** to gain access to different encoding and decoding contexts.

- If your keys are dynamic or aren't known in advance, you can still leverage `Codable` by using an `AnyCodingKey` type as needed.

Wow, what a chapter this has been! You've learned almost everything there is to know about decoding data and touched a bit on how to encode data and customize the encoding using various container types.

There's still much more to learn and experiment with: abstracting containers for shared structures, leveraging property wrappers with their own `Codable` conformances, writing custom encoders and decoders for custom types, and more, but there are only so many pages in this book.

Now, you're ready for anything this JSON-centric API world has to throw at you!

Chapter 9: Unsafe

By Ehab Amer

Swift is an easy language to learn. It can take care of a lot of things for you and help you keep your code safe and clear to minimize bugs. If you were to compare it to C++, many people would say C++ is harder. Swift takes care of type checking, memory allocation, and many things on your behalf so you can focus on what you want to do in your code, and not how the machine will handle your code. But C++ gives you more power and more control. As we're told in the Spider-Man comics and movies, *"With great power comes great responsibility"*.

By default, Swift is a memory-safe and type-safe language. This means you cannot access uninitialized memory and can only treat an instance as the type it was created. You can't treat a `String` as if it were an `Int` or a `Numeric` and vice-versa. But this doesn't cover completely what the word **safe** means.

For a more general description, Swift validates any input, whether it's valid or invalid, and behaves accordingly. So storing a number in a string property, for example, will fail. Additionally, forcing a value from an optional that doesn't have a value is not a valid behavior. Neither is storing a number that exceeds the maximum allowed value of your variable. All of those are different cases related to safety.

In some cases, you might need your code to be **extremely** optimized, in which case the tiny overhead added by the safety checks from Swift might be too expensive. You might be dealing with a huge stream of real-time data, manipulating large files or other large operations that deal with large data. Or you might even be working with C++ code within your app. In such cases, you want to have full control over your objects, or in other words: **Pointers**.

In this chapter, you'll learn how you can gain this control. You'll learn about:

- The memory layout of types, and what size, alignment and stride are

- How to use typed and untyped pointers

- Binding memory to a type and the rules you must follow to rebind it to another type

- Other unsafe operations in the standard library and overflow arithmetic operations

But before going into those points, you need to understand a few things first.

Definition of unsafe & undefined behaviors

As stated earlier, type safety means that Swift checks any input or operation whether it is valid or not and behaves accordingly. However, there is also a whole other world in Swift that has the keyword unsafe. This gives you more control and moves the responsibility of validation to you, the developer. Swift will trust that you know what you're doing.

Before going deeper into what this keyword means, you must understand how Swift behaves when you violate any of the type safety rules. Some violations are checked at compile time, while others are checked during runtime — and those consistently cause a runtime crash. A rule to remember: Safe code doesn't mean no crashes. It means that if your code received unexpected input, it **will** stop execution. One of the ways it can do that is to throw a fatal error. But with unsafe code, it will use the invalid input, work with it and eventually — maybe — provide an output. Such situations are hard to debug.

This is how the keyword unsafe works. The moment a rule is violated, the behavior of your code is completely unknown. Your code **might** crash, or it might resume. It might give you a wrong value or change the value of another property. How your application will proceed is undefined and can change from one execution to another. It's extremely important to know how your code will behave and what to expect once you start using unsafe so you're careful with it.

The Swift standard library provides pointers for unsafe that are similar in concept to C++ pointers. There is no better way to learn how to use these pointers than to understand how they work.

What is a pointer?

Swift has a linear memory layout, so imagine your app's address space is from 0x0000 to 0xFFFF. The actual address space is represented by 64 bits rather than 16. But to keep it simple here, this chapter will use smaller numbers.

This address space contains the executable of your app, dynamic libraries, assets, etc. A pointer is something that points to a specific address in memory. So say that you created an object at 0x0AC4, and this object was 4 bytes in size. This object's memory space extends from 0x0AC4 to 0x0AC7.

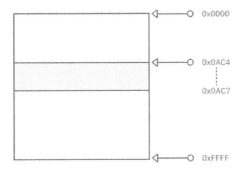

To write in memory, you specify what you want to write at which address. This means that if you want to write the number 9 in the second byte (index 1), you specify in the application to go to address 0x0AC4 + 1, and write 9.

If you happen to write 0x0AC4 + 100, then you might overwrite an existing value and corrupt your app's state. This is clearly out of bounds for your object. But in this case, you're trusted to know what you're doing.

Another possible problem is the object that was in this address location was deleted, but you still have the pointer to this location and used it to store a value. In this case, you'll overwrite an existing object or an undefined behavior will occur. You might not know what will happen, but this will cause a problem.

A pointer is simply the **address** of where your information resides in memory. The size of the object in memory is a different story, which you'll cover shortly.

Now that you think about it, what is the difference between **reference** and **pointer**? A reference can also be described as something that refers to an object in memory, which is the same thing as a pointer.

Pointer vs. reference

In a way, they're quite similar, yet there is quite a difference. Behind the scenes, a reference is a pointer, but pointer operations aren't available to you. When you work with pointers, you take care of the life-cycle of the pointer itself as well as the object it points at. Normally, you define a pointer and then allocate and initialize the object it points at. If you lose that pointer and you didn't clear out this object, you can never reach it again. And if you delete the object and keep the pointer, you'll come across a variety of undefined behaviors if you try to use that pointer again.

So to restate in fewer words, they're similar in concept, but a reference is an abstraction of those operations that the standard library takes care of for you. This is why using pointers gives you more control over objects and data in memory because you're expected to take care of those things yourself. As said before, it gives you more power, but _ "With great power comes great responsibility"_.

Memory layout

To use pointers properly, you must understand how memory itself is organized. Memory layout for value types is quite different than the layout of reference types. This section will start by covering value types.

There are three values you need to understand:

- **Size**: This refers to the number of bytes it takes to store a value of this type. A size of four means this type requires four bytes of storage.

- **Alignment**: For a simple explanation, the address must be divisible by the alignment value. A value of two means this type can't be stored on a pointer of odd value. You'll learn more about this shortly.

- **Stride**: This refers to how many bytes to increment on your pointer to read the next object.

The size influences the other two values, as the alignment and stride can never be smaller. Size has a clear meaning, but the other two require explanation.

Consider a type that has an alignment value of four. This means this type must be stored on an address divisible by four. So why does this matter?

Imagine that the device reads only four bytes at a time. Such a system can read only bytes 0-3, 4-7, 8-11, etc. Imagine now that an object was stored from bytes 2 through 5. To read these bytes from memory, the device would need to read the first set of bytes, then cut out only its second half (2-3), then read the second set, and then, finally, concatenate the first half (4-5) with the previous half to properly construct the object's value. This describes a misaligned value.

Misaligned values severely affect performance. Compilers keep this from happening even if it costs more memory.

For stride, imagine you have an array of items in which each item takes up eight bytes of memory. Here, it makes sense that each time you want to read the next value, you do so by incrementing the pointer by the item size.

But now imagine that the item size is nine. If the compiler depended only on the size to increment the pointer, then there would be misaligned objects. And as you just learned, the compiler actively tries to avoid these.

With an item size of nine, you would need to have a stride of 16. Thus, moving the pointer that accesses the first item by 16 bytes will point to the second item. Those remaining 7 bytes (16 minus 9) are called padding and aren't used at all.

Layout for Swift types

You can determine those values directly through code. For example, for the type Int, you can use the enum MemoryLayout to see those values.

```
MemoryLayout<Int>.size       // returns 8 (on 64-bit)
MemoryLayout<Int>.alignment  // returns 8 (on 64-bit)
MemoryLayout<Int>.stride     // returns 8 (on 64-bit)
```

On a 64-bit system, an Int will have size, alignment and stride with a value of eight.

> **Note**: On a 64-bit system, Int defaults to the Int64 type, which has eight bytes. On a 32-bit system, it defaults to Int32, which has four bytes.

You can check the values of other types, too:

```
MemoryLayout<Int16>.size        // returns 2
MemoryLayout<Int16>.alignment   // returns 2
MemoryLayout<Int16>.stride      // returns 2

MemoryLayout<Bool>.size         // returns 1
MemoryLayout<Bool>.alignment    // returns 1
MemoryLayout<Bool>.stride       // returns 1

MemoryLayout<Float>.size        // returns 4
MemoryLayout<Float>.alignment   // returns 4
MemoryLayout<Float>.stride      // returns 4

MemoryLayout<Double>.size       // returns 8
MemoryLayout<Double>.alignment  // returns 8
MemoryLayout<Double>.stride     // returns 8
```

You could also use type inference to determine the same values:

```
let zero = 0.0
MemoryLayout.size(ofValue: zero) // returns 8
```

In the next section, you'll see how a combination of types affects the memory layout of the struct itself.

Trivial types

You can copy a trivial type bit for bit with no indirection or reference-counting operations. Generally, native Swift types that don't contain strong or weak references or other forms of indirection are trivial, as are imported C++ structs and enums.

In other words, the basic data types such as Int, Float, Double and Bool are all trivial types. Structs or enums that contain those value types and don't contain **any** reference types are also considered trivial types.

Consider the following example:

```
struct IntBoolStruct {
  var intValue: Int
  var boolValue: Bool
}
```

This is a struct that has the first property as an Int and the second property of Bool.

Now, check its memory layout:

```
MemoryLayout<IntBoolStruct>.size        // returns 9
MemoryLayout<IntBoolStruct>.alignment   // returns 8
MemoryLayout<IntBoolStruct>.stride      // returns 16
```

An `Int` has a size of 8, and a `Bool` has a size of 1, so it makes sense the struct has a size of 9.

For the alignment, it makes sense that it is 8 to ensure that `intValue` is not misaligned. As for stride, it has a value of 16 to maintain the alignment and to reserve enough space for the struct. It can't be 9, nor can it be 8.

0	1	2	3	4	5	6	7	8	9	10	11	12	13	14	15

Ordering properties

Now, consider this other example:

```
struct BoolIntStruct {
    var boolValue: Bool
    var intValue: Int
}

MemoryLayout<BoolIntStruct>.size        // returns 16
MemoryLayout<BoolIntStruct>.alignment   // returns 8
MemoryLayout<BoolIntStruct>.stride      // returns 16
```

This struct is almost identical to the previous one except for the order of the properties inside it: The boolean appears before the integer.

The size reported for this type is completely different! Why?

0	1	2	3	4	5	6	7	8	9	10	11	12	13	14	15

For the struct to be aligned, all the properties inside it must also be aligned. To have the boolean property stored before the integer, this means that a seven-bit padding is required right after the boolean to allow the integer to be properly aligned. This causes the padding to be considered in the size of the struct directly. The alignment and the stride values are the same as in `IntBoolStruct`.

Allocating for alignment

The two examples above don't mean that any extra consideration is required for the ordering of the properties. The padding remained the same in the two examples, except only one of them considered it in the size property.

According to Apple's guidelines, if you're allocating memory directly for a pointer, you should allocate bytes equal to the stride, not the size. This will ensure that any consecutive memory allocations are also aligned.

To explain this directly, consider the following struct:

```
struct EmptyStruct {}

MemoryLayout<EmptyStruct>.size        // returns 0
MemoryLayout<EmptyStruct>.alignment   // returns 1
MemoryLayout<EmptyStruct>.stride      // returns 1
```

This struct has no properties at all, so it's logical to have a size of zero bytes. But you can't have a non-existent object in memory. Anything in memory should have a size! Thus, one byte is allocated to the object, and this value is represented in the stride. This is why you should depend on `stride` instead of `size` when you allocate memory yourself.

Reference types

Reference types have a quite different memory layout. When you have a pointer of such a type, you're pointing to a reference of that value and **not** the value itself. Think of it as if you have a pointer on a pointer.

Consider the following types and their memory layout:

```
class IntBoolClass {
  var intValue: Int = 0
  var boolValue: Bool = false
}

MemoryLayout<IntBoolClass>.size        // returns 8
MemoryLayout<IntBoolClass>.alignment   // returns 8
MemoryLayout<IntBoolClass>.stride      // returns 8

class BoolIntClass {
  var boolValue: Bool = false
  var intValue: Int = 0
}
```

```
MemoryLayout<BoolIntClass>.size         // returns 8
MemoryLayout<BoolIntClass>.alignment    // returns 8
MemoryLayout<BoolIntClass>.stride       // returns 8

class EmptyClass {}

MemoryLayout<EmptyClass>.size           // returns 8
MemoryLayout<EmptyClass>.alignment      // returns 8
MemoryLayout<EmptyClass>.stride         // returns 8
```

All three classes have a value of eight for their size, alignment and stride. Regardless of whether the class had properties, the values remained the same.

Pointer types

Swift provides different pointer types. Each provides its own control safety levels or unsafety levels.

- UnsafeRawPointer

- UnsafePointer<Type>

The first is the basic raw pointer that doesn't know any information of the type it is pointing at. It's a basic pointer on a specific byte.

The second is a pointer that knows the type of the object it points at. It's also called a typed pointer.

Raw pointers can't work on reference or non-trivial types. For those, you must use a typed pointer.

If you're working with arrays, there's a set of pointer types that can make things a little easier for you:

- UnsafeRawBufferPointer

- UnsafeBufferPointer<Type>

All those pointers are read-only access. To allow read-and-write access, you need mutable pointers. Any of the above pointer types can be mutable, as seen below:

- UnsafeMutableRawPointer

- UnsafeMutablePointer<Type>

- UnsafeMutableRawBufferPointer

- UnsafeMutableBufferPointer<Type>

This gives you a total of **eight** different pointer types you can use. But still ... what is the need for all those, and what is the real difference?

Raw pointers

To understand raw pointers, consider the following example. Create a playground and add the following code:

```
var int16Value: UInt16 = 0x1122 // 4386
MemoryLayout.size(ofValue: int16Value) // 2
MemoryLayout.stride(ofValue: int16Value) // 2
MemoryLayout.alignment(ofValue: int16Value) // 2
```

This creates an unsigned-Int-16 with the value 4386. Then, as you saw previously, you're checking the values of size, stride and alignment. As expected, the UInt16 has a size of two bytes. How about using a raw pointer to get the value of each byte separately?

Add the following code:

```
let int16bytesPointer = UnsafeMutableRawPointer.allocate(
  byteCount: 2,
  alignment: 2)
defer {
  int16bytesPointer.deallocate()
}
int16bytesPointer.storeBytes(of: 0x1122, as: UInt16.self)
```

This defines a new mutable raw pointer, allocates two bytes for it and specifies that it must have an even alignment (alignment of two). For pointers, you're taking care of everything. You're responsible for allocating the memory and for deallocating it. Don't forget the deallocation part or your code will leak memory. Afterward, you store the hex value **0x1122**, which is equivalent to **4386** as an UInt16. You must specify the type of the value that you'll save in the raw pointer.

> **Note**: If you print the value of int16bytesPointer itself, it will give you the memory address where **4386** is stored. Each time you run your playground, it will give a different address.

Add this line:

```
let firstByte = int16bytesPointer.load(as: UInt8.self)  // 34
(0x22)
```

This loads whatever is the memory address of `int16bytesPointer` and stores it in a new variable of the type you specified. `firstByte` now is of type `UInt8` and has the value of **34**, which has the hex value of **0x22**.

Notice that the first byte is the least significant. This is because your values are stored in little-endian format, as you learned in **Chapter 5: Numerics & Ranges**.

To read the second byte, add the following:

```
let offsetPointer = int16bytesPointer + 1
let secondByte = offsetPointer.load(as: UInt8.self)       // 17
(0x11)
```

The first line creates a new pointer that points to an address one value above what's in `int16bytesPointer`, thus referring to the next byte. The second line is just as you did before, you're loading the contents of this address in a `UInt8` variable. Its value is **0x11**, as expected.

Unsafety of raw pointers

Now, nothing is stopping you from reading more addresses using `int16bytesPointer`. You can read the next address:

```
let offsetPointer2 = int16bytesPointer + 2
let thirdByte = offsetPointer2.load(as: UInt8.self)  //
Undefined
```

Just as before, you're reading the third byte of the stored value, although the stored value itself is only two bytes in size. But because you're manually specifying the address, Swift assumes you know what you're doing and won't stop you.

This will work, but there's no way to guarantee what its result will be. In your playground, this **might** give you a value of zero, but in a real app, you can never know.

To make it worse, you can store a value in an address that isn't yours:

```
offsetPointer2.storeBytes(of: 0x3344, as: UInt16.self)
```

This is a more dangerous operation. You're changing a value you don't own, and Swift won't stop you from doing that.

Another dangerous thing to do is misalignment:

```
let misalignedUInt16 = offsetPointer.load(as: UInt16.self)
```

`offsetPointer` is `int16bytesPointer + 1`. You're reading the value using a type that has an alignment of two from an address in an odd location. Thus, this line will produce an error, and your log will show this message:

```
Fatal error: load from misaligned raw pointer
```

In this example, the line will always crash and there's no way the execution will pass it. But if you use different types with different alignment values, there's a chance the alignments will coincidentally match, and times it won't. For example, if you create the pointer with a type of alignment of four and later try to read it with a type that has an alignment of eight, sometimes it will work and sometimes it won't. This won't give your users a good experience at all.

Raw buffer pointers

Raw buffers provide a way to go through a block of memory as if it were an array of `UInt8`.

In your playground, add the following:

```swift
let size = MemoryLayout<UInt>.size // 8
let alignment = MemoryLayout<UInt>.alignment // 8

let bytesPointer = UnsafeMutableRawPointer.allocate(
  byteCount: size,
  alignment: alignment)
defer {
  bytesPointer.deallocate()
}
bytesPointer.storeBytes(of: 0x0102030405060708, as: UInt.self)
```

As in the previous example, you reserve eight bytes of memory and store a UInt with the value **0x0102030405060708**.

Add these lines afterward:

```swift
let bufferPointer = UnsafeRawBufferPointer(
  start: bytesPointer,
  count: 8)
for (offset, byte) in bufferPointer.enumerated() {
  print("byte \(offset): \(byte)")
}
```

This defines a raw buffer pointer starting from the raw pointer you previously defined. It also sets the length of the buffer to eight, because that's how many bytes you allocated, which equals the size of `UInt`.

The buffer provides an enumeration that you can loop on to go through all the bytes. After you run the playground, the log will show the following:

```
byte 0: 8
byte 1: 7
byte 2: 6
byte 3: 5
byte 4: 4
byte 5: 3
byte 6: 2
byte 7: 1
```

> **Note**: Remember that the bytes are stored in small-endian format.

Buffers provide a way to go through multiple bytes with clear and specific boundaries. `UnsafeRawBufferPointer` accesses the values as `UInt8`. To access them as a different type, you'll need to use typed pointers.

Typed pointers

In the raw pointer examples above, you needed to tell the compiler a value's type every time you read it. This can be very tedious if you're using the same type over and over.

A typed pointer means that the compiler tracks the data type for this pointer and reads the number of bytes matching the type's size to give you a proper value. This means you don't need to specify the type anymore.

Override the contents of your playground with the following:

```swift
let count = 4

let pointer = UnsafeMutablePointer<Int>.allocate(capacity:
count) // 1
pointer.initialize(repeating: 0, count: count) // 2
defer {
  pointer.deinitialize(count: count)
  pointer.deallocate()
}
// 3
pointer.pointee = 10001
pointer.advanced(by: 1).pointee = 10002
(pointer+2).pointee = 10003
pointer.advanced(by: 3).pointee = 10004
```

```
pointer.pointee // 10001
pointer.advanced(by: 1).pointee // 10002
(pointer+1).pointee // 10002
pointer.advanced(by: 2).pointee // 10003
(pointer+3).pointee // 10004
// 4
let bufferPointer = UnsafeBufferPointer(
  start: pointer,
  count: count)
for (offset, value) in bufferPointer.enumerated() {
  print("value \(offset): \(value)")
}
```

This is similar to how you used raw pointers:

1. First, you allocate the number of items you want in memory. Notice that you didn't specify the number of bytes or alignments — you just specified the count. But you also specified the type `Int` to `UnsafeMutablePointer`. That was more than enough for `allocate(:)` to know exactly how to do it.

2. Then, you initialize the buffer with an initial value. This is important to do in general when you work with buffers so you clean up the memory from whatever was previously stored there. And, of course, you want to de-initialize and de-allocate the memory after you finish using it.

6. Looping over the buffer to print all the values that you saved, the log will show:

```
value 0: 10001
value 1: 10002
value 2: 10003
value 3: 10004
```

Once you create a raw pointer, you can bind it to a type by creating a typed pointer and use it normally. Also, you can rebind a typed pointer to a different type. But this might cause you some serious problems if you aren't careful. First, before you learn how to do that, you should understand some rules and concepts that affect rebinding.

Memory binding

Memory binding means specifying an area in memory as a value of a specific type. For example, if you specify the four bytes between 0x0010 and 0x0013 as an `Int32`, this means you bound them to that type. If you just read or write on them once as `Int32`, that doesn't count as binding.

You should understand a few concepts before diving deeply into memory binding:

- Type punning
- Related types
- Strict aliasing
- Layout compatibility

Punning

Type punning is when a part of memory is bound to a type, then you bind it to a different and unrelated type.

Try the following example:

```
let rawPointer = UnsafeMutableRawPointer.allocate(byteCount: 2,
alignment: 2)
defer {
  rawPointer.deallocate()
}

let float16Pointer = rawPointer.bindMemory(to: Float16.self,
capacity: 1)
let uint8Pointer = rawPointer.bindMemory(to: UInt8.self,
capacity: 2)
```

You created a raw pointer of two bytes and then bound it twice with two different typed pointers: a Float16 pointer and another for two UInt8.

```
float16Pointer.pointee = 0xABC0 // 43968

uint8Pointer.pointee // 0x5E = 94
uint8Pointer.advanced(by: 1).pointee // 0x79 = 121
```

You save the hex value of **0xABC0**, which is equivalent to **43968** in the float pointer. When you read the two other values from the UInt8 pointers, you get the hex values of **0x5E** and **0x79**. Two hex values don't resemble anything from the float value at all.

```
uint8Pointer.pointee -= 1

float16Pointer.pointee // 43936
```

> **Note**: You must never use two differently typed pointers to the same memory locations. Doing so will cause unknown and unexpected behavior. This example uses primitive data types to show you a way that minor changes can cause larger, unexpected changes.

When you alter the value of one lower byte of the float, the value of the float gets reduced by a value much more than one. Remember that values are saved in small-endian. That's why the lower byte comes first.

The binary representation of floats differs from integers, as you learned in **Chapter 5: Numerics & Ranges**. Thus, any small changes in the binary representation will cause a more significant change in the value itself.

Although this example may seem harmless, the effects can be much greater with different types. And if you're punning between a value type and a reference type, the consequences will be severe, to say the least.

Related types

In the last example, you bound the float pointer to another unsigned int-8 pointer and read that value as a UInt8. That value was completely unrelated to what was stored for the Float16. Thus, the rebinding here was wrong. So when is the rebinding right?

To rebind from one type to another type safely, both types should be related and layout compatible, and should respect strict aliasing rules. To begin, have a look at the first of those requirements.

To say two types are related, they must match one of the following rules:

- Both types are identical or one is a typealias of the other. Somewhat logical, isn't it?

- One type may be a tuple, a struct or an enum that contains the other type.

- One type may be an existential (a protocol) that conforming types will contain the other type.

- Both types are classes, and one is a subclass of the other.

Layout compatibility

Remember the memory layout explanation at the beginning of this chapter? To say two types are **mutually** layout compatible means they have the same size and alignment or contain the same number of layout compatible types.

Further, types can be layout compatible but not mutually. They're compatible if one aggregate type is layout compatible with a larger type containing the same common types. For example, the tuple (Int,Int) is memory compatible with (Int,Int,Float) because they both have the same common types, but they aren't mutually compatible.

Strict aliasing

If you have two pointers of value types or class types, they both must be related. This means that changing the value of one pointer changes the other pointer in the same way. In such cases, both pointers are aliases to each other.

One reason it's important to ensure the two types are related and not only layout compatible is to make sure that compiler optimizations don't break your code in future versions.

Safe rebinding

Swift provides three different APIs to bind/rebind pointers:

- `bindMemory(to:capacity:)`
- `withMemoryRebound(to:capacity:)`
- `assumingMemoryBound(to:)`

You have already used the first to bind a raw pointer to a typed pointer. What are the other two for?

If you have a typed pointer and you want to temporarily bind it to a different type, `withMemoryRebound(to:capacity:)` is what you need. Add the following in a playground:

```
let count = 3
let size = MemoryLayout<Int16>.size
let stride = MemoryLayout<Int16>.stride
let alignment = MemoryLayout<Int16>.alignment
let byteCount =  count * stride
```

```
let rawPointer = UnsafeMutableRawPointer.allocate(
  byteCount: byteCount,
  alignment: alignment)
defer {
  rawPointer.deallocate()
}

let typedPointer1 = rawPointer.bindMemory(
  to: UInt16.self,
  capacity: count)
```

Here, you allocate memory for three UInt16 objects in a raw pointer. Then, you bind it to a UInt16 typed pointer.

Add this code afterward:

```
typedPointer1.withMemoryRebound(
  to: Bool.self,
  capacity: count * size) {
  (boolPointer: UnsafeMutablePointer<Bool>) in
  print(boolPointer.pointee)
}
```

Next, you temporarily rebind that typed pointer to another one. The other typed pointer's life is only within the closure of withMemoryRebound(to:capacity:).

It's extremely important that you don't access self within this closure or return the newly bound pointer outside this closure. Doing either will cause undefined behaviors.

For the next example, consider having a C++ API that initializes memory with two different objects and returns them as a raw pointer. A Swift imitation for this API would look like this:

```
func initRawAB() -> UnsafeMutableRawPointer {
  let rawPtr = UnsafeMutableRawPointer.allocate(
    byteCount: 2 * MemoryLayout<UInt16>.stride,
    alignment: MemoryLayout<UInt16>.alignment)

  let boundP1 = rawPtr.bindMemory(to: UInt16.self, capacity: 1)
  boundP1.pointee = 101

  let boundP2 = rawPtr.advanced(by: 2).bindMemory(to:
Float16.self, capacity: 1)
  boundP2.pointee = 202.5

  return rawPtr
}
```

This function creates a `UInt16` and a `Float16` and returns both together through a raw pointer. The return type completely erases the types. Add this code to use it:

```
let rawPtr = initRawAB()

let assumedP1 = rawPtr
  .assumingMemoryBound(to: UInt16.self)
assumedP1.pointee // 101

let assumedP2 = rawPtr
  .advanced(by: 2)
  .assumingMemoryBound(to: Float16.self)
assumedP2.pointee // 202.5
```

This did not rebind the memory to those types. It relied on the precondition that the memory is already bound to this type. And, of course, if the memory wasn't already bound to that type, an undefined behavior will occur.

Unsafe operations

As mentioned before, safe code isn't code that doesn't crash. It's code that behaves consistently.

You're used to seeing crashes when you force unwrap a variable with a null value or perform an arithmetic operation with a value that exceeds the boundaries of the data type you're using. Those operations will consistently signal an error.

You can bypass those errors, but that doesn't mean your code will be more stable. Crashes aren't the worst thing you can encounter, as mentioned before. This is a different area for undefined behaviors. They can have their benefits, but you need to be careful when using them.

Unsafe unwrap

Consider the following code:

```
var safeString: String? = nil
print(safeString!)
```

The print statement obviously will cause a crash. But if you're performing a complex operation and are sure an optional property can't be `nil`, you can use `unsafelyUnwrapped`.

```
var unsafeString: String? = nil
print(unsafeString.unsafelyUnwrapped)
```

In debug mode, the print statement will also crash. But if optimization is enabled, like in a release build, this line won't crash. Instead, it will proceed normally with whatever data was already stored in the memory of `unsafeString`.

This is good because while you're developing and working on your code, the compiler will show you mistakes and trap any nils for you. That will prevent you from struggling with undefined behaviors while your project remains a work in progress.

This **MUST NOT** make you overconfident with trivial nil checks and guards, saying: "Hey, I could just use this and skip the whole extra code I write to check for nils". If you do that, I can promise you things will not be better. You won't gain any noticeable performance improvements or even safer code in 99% of your day-to-day situations. Just like pointers, this can over-complicate your life if not used properly.

Unsafe unowned

As you already know, marking a property as unowned in the capture list of a closure means not to increment the reference count of this property while using it as a non-optional. In a way, saying it's unowned somewhat guarantees that this will never be nil when the closure executes. If for any reason it is a nil, your code will crash.

The keyword unowned is short for unowned(`safe`). It has another counterpart unowned(`unsafe`).

This is a dangerous operation that you shouldn't use lightly. Here, you tell the compiler not to track the lifetime of the object at all. If the object is deallocated, the property will be a pointer to an area in memory that was deallocated. This is called a **dangling pointer**.

Dangling pointers are dangerous because you have no idea what they point to. Attempting to read or write from them can produce unexpected results that can include an immediate crash or data loss.

Overflow operations

The last point relates to arithmetic operations. When you do any operation on a number, the compiler makes sure that the data-type you're using can store the value.

`UInt8` has a possible range from 0 to 255. Representing the number 256 requires 9 bits.

Try this in a playground:

```
UInt8.max + 1
```

This line will give you this error:

```
error: arithmetic operation '255 + 1' (on type 'UInt8') results
in an overflow
UInt8.max + 1
```

There's an alternative operand that won't crash. Update the last line to this:

```
UInt8.max &+ 1 // 0
```

The result of this add operation is zero. You must be asking yourself how?

Adding an ampersand — "&" — before an arithmetic operator means that this is an overflow operation. Look at the last example.

The new value from this addition should be 256, but this requires 9 bits, where the most significant bit (the 9th bit) is 1 and all the others are 0.

The overflow operations disregard bits beyond their limits, just like a rollover counter works (aka mechanical counter). If the counter contains only two digits, then the maximum number it can represent is 99. The next number will be zero.

Overflow operators can be extremely confusing and misleading. Large numbers, as they keep growing, will suddenly be in the negative range:

```
Int8.max &+ 1 // -128
Int8.max &* 2 // -2
```

And negative numbers will suddenly jump to large numbers as they keep decreasing:

```
Int8.min &- 1 // 127
```

Key points

- Safe code means the behavior is always expected even if the input is unexpected. Crashing is considered a safe behavior if the input is not allowed as long as this crash is consistent.

- References are pointers in origin. But the standard library handles their allocation, initialization and entire cycle.

- Each type has size, alignment and stride values that control how its memory is allocated. Also, the order of the properties in each type affects those numbers.

- The standard library has different types of unsafe pointers. Each gives a certain level of control, from pointers that access memory as raw bytes to those that know exactly the type of the bytes accessed.

- There are several rules you must follow before you bind or rebind memory to a type.

- Unsafe operations and overflow arithmetic can skip the safety validations on the standard library.

Where to go from here?

- You can learn more about unsafe pointers from the 107 proposal https://github.com/apple/swift-evolution/blob/master/proposals/0107-unsaferawpointer.md.

- And you can learn more details and examples about related types and layout compatible examples here https://github.com/atrick/swift/blob/type-safe-mem-docs/docs/TypeSafeMemory.rst.

Section III: Techniques

The final section of this book covers advanced techniques to super-charge your Swift powers, and use all of what Swift has to offer.

We'll cover topics like Higher order functions, Functional reactive programming, Objective-C interoperability, using Instrumentation, and API design.

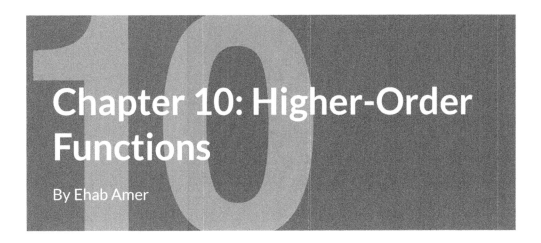

Chapter 10: Higher-Order Functions

By Ehab Amer

A higher-order function takes one or more functions as a parameter. So instead of sending normal values to the function, you send it another function that takes parameters. The normal function is called a first-order function. Too many "functions" there.

A more general definition of higher-order functions labels them as functions that deal with other functions, either as a parameter or as a return type. In this chapter, you'll start with sending a function as a parameter. Then you'll move to having a function return another function.

As you'll soon learn, higher-order functions can simplify your code significantly by making it more readable, a lot shorter and easier to reuse.

A simple text printer

Before going deeply into what higher-order functions are or how Swift makes them fun, consider this example for a text printer.

Create a new playground and add the following:

```
class TextPrinter {
  var formatter: ParagraphFormatterProtocol
  init(formatter: ParagraphFormatterProtocol) {
    self.formatter = formatter
  }

  func printText(_ paragraphs: [String]) {
    for text in paragraphs {
      let formattedText = formatter.formatParagraph(text)
      print(formattedText)
    }
  }
}

protocol ParagraphFormatterProtocol {
  func formatParagraph(_ text: String) -> String
}
```

The code above is for a text printer. All it does is receive an array of strings, run each through a formatter and then print the formatted value. TextPrinter doesn't specify how the formatting operation is done. But it does specify that it needs an object that conforms to ParagraphFormatterProtocol, which will implement this functionality.

Add this new class to your playground:

```
class SimpleFormatter: ParagraphFormatterProtocol {
  func formatParagraph(_ text: String) -> String {
    guard !text.isEmpty else { return text } // 1
    var formattedText =
      text.prefix(1).uppercased() + text.dropFirst() // 2
    if let lastCharacter = formattedText.last,
      !lastCharacter.isPunctuation {
      formattedText += "." // 3
    }
    return formattedText
  }
}
```

This simple formatter conforms to the required protocol, and its format function does the following:

1. Makes sure the provided string is not empty. If it is, then there's nothing to format and the formatter returns the string as-is.

2. Capitalizes the first character

3. Checks whether the last character is punctuation. If it isn't, then it adds a full-stop ".".

Now, use this new class in your playground:

```
let simpleFormatter = SimpleFormatter()
let textPrinter = TextPrinter(formatter: simpleFormatter)

let exampleParagraphs = [
  "basic text example",
  "Another text example!!",
  "one more text example"
]

textPrinter.printText(exampleParagraphs)
```

You created an instance of the simple formatter you just defined and used it to create an object of the printer. The output in the console from the code above should be:

```
Basic text example.
Another text example!!
One more text example.
```

First-order functions

The two main methods here are **first-order functions**. Both `ParagraphFormatterProtocol.formatParagraph(_:)` and `TextPrinter.printText(_:)` take normal values. You didn't go into the higher-order ones yet.

Another way to perform the formatting is by adding a new first-order function to string arrays. Add this new extension at the end of your playground:

```
extension Array where Element == String {
  func printFormatted(formatter: ParagraphFormatterProtocol) {
    let textPrinter = TextPrinter(formatter: formatter)
    textPrinter.printText(self)
```

```
    }
  }
```

This extension adds a method to `Array` only if the type of the stored elements is `String`. So this method won't be available to an array of `Int` or an array of `Any` but only to `String`.

Use it by calling:

```
exampleParagraphs.printFormatted(formatter: simpleFormatter)
```

This will print the same result as before.

There's nothing wrong at all with the implementations above. They deliver the needed operations and offer a clear integration method to provide different formatting operations. But creating a formatter every time or using the same one over and over is not particularly Swifty. What if there were a way to send the formatting operation itself as a parameter instead of packaging it in an object?

Your first higher-order function

Create a new playground and try this in a new way. Extract the formatting function you created in `SimpleFormatter` from the previous example and add it as a function:

```swift
func formatParagraph(_ text: String) -> String {
  guard !text.isEmpty else { return text }
  var formattedText =
    text.prefix(1).uppercased() + text.dropFirst()
  if let lastCharacter = formattedText.last,
    !lastCharacter.isPunctuation {
    formattedText += "."
  }
  return formattedText
}
```

Next, create this new extension:

```swift
extension Array where Element == String {
  func printFormatted(formatter: ((String) -> String)) {
    for string in self {
      let formattedString = formatter(string)
      print(formattedString)
    }
  }
}
```

This extension has the same idea only for [`String`]. But in its method, notice the different type of the parameter. (`(String) -> String`) means that this is not a property. Instead, it's a method that takes a `String` as a parameter and returns a `String`.

In the parentheses, anything that precedes the arrow describes parameters, and what follows the arrow defines a return type.

That method you added in the extension is a **higher-order function**. For it to work, it takes another function as a parameter and not a normal property. You can use it like this:

```
let exampleParagraphs = [
  "basic text example",
  "Another text example!!",
  "one more text example"
]

exampleParagraphs.printFormatted(formatter: formatParagraph(_:))
```

You sent the actual function itself as a parameter. Another way to pass the function as a parameter is like this:

```
let theFunction = formatParagraph
exampleParagraphs.printFormatted(formatter: theFunction)
```

The variable `theFunction` is actually a function and not a normal property. You can see its type as (`(String) -> String`) and can describe it as a reference to a function.

Closures

There's also another form of passing over the function as a parameter that you're familiar with:

```
exampleParagraphs.printFormatted { text in
  guard !text.isEmpty else { return text }
  var formattedText = text.prefix(1).uppercased() +
text.dropFirst()
  if let lastCharacter = formattedText.last,
     !lastCharacter.isPunctuation {
    formattedText += "."
  }
  return formattedText
}
```

In this call, you sent a closure, not a function. Practically, both are the same. This is identical to sending the function reference directly. Another way is to call the function in the closure.

```
exampleParagraphs.printFormatted { formatParagraph($0) }
```

This form is perfect when the function you want to pass in as a parameter to the higher order function doesn't match the parameter signature. An example of this is if the function you're going to call or use has two parameters, but you'll send one of them as a constant, and the other will be from the main operation. Then you can have a format as follows:

```
aHigherOrderFunction { someOperation($0, "a constant") }
```

All those examples will work the same, but they each have a slight difference. Think of a closure as if it's a function that's created only for the current scope. The last two examples used a closure, but the first gave a ready-made function directly to the `printFormatted`.

You can still use functions directly as a parameter, but the signature of `someOperation(::)` will need to change to match what `aHigherOrderFunction()` expects. This change is called **Currying** and is covered in the second half of the chapter.

The Swift standard library has many of those operations that use this concept. Each of them does some operation, but there's a small detail inside it that's left out. Take the `sort` function as an example. There are many sorting algorithms. Some perform better in a small set but not as well in a large one. However, in the end, they all have a comparison between two items that define if the final ordering will be ascending or descending. Which algorithm is used and how it's used aren't relevant when calling the function, except for how the final result is ordered.

A function that returns a function is also considered a higher-order function. The return type is defined by a data-type after the arrow ->. So instead of defining a class or a struct, you can have something like (()->()), which is a function that doesn't take any parameters and doesn't return anything, or as many parameters as you want with any return type you want: ((p1: Type1, p2: Type2, p3: Type3) -> ReturnType).

Higher-order functions in the standard library

Swift brought you a few higher-order functions, which deliver several common operations and have a neat way to call them in your code. Some of those functions are:

- map
- compactMap
- flatMap
- filter
- reduce
- sorted
- split

You'll go through them in more detail now to see an example of their usage.

map

`Array.map(_:)` applies an operation on all the elements of the array, and the result is a new array of the same size. This is a much shorter version of iterating over the elements and adding the new items of an operation to a new array. Try this example in a playground:

```
var numbers = [1, 2, 3, 4, 5, 6, 7, 8, 9, 10]
var newNumbers: [Int] = []

for number in numbers {
  newNumbers.append(number * number)
}

print(newNumbers)
```

This creates a new array that contains the square of each number. An alternative way to do this using `map(_:)` is this:

```
let newNumbers2 = numbers.map { $0 * $0 }
print(newNumbers2)
```

This code is much simpler and shorter than the previous one. This is because it uses the shorthand provided by Swift and all the code reductions possible for a Swift closure. But as you learned above, higher-order functions can receive a function instead of a closure. Try this example:

```
func squareOperation(value: Int) -> Int {
  print("Original Value is: \(value)")
  let newValue = value * value
  print("New Value is: \(newValue)")
  return newValue
}
```

This function squares an Int value and prints its original value and its square value. You can use map(_:) by sending the new function to it like this:

```
let newNumbers3 = numbers.map(squareOperation(value:))
```

compactMap

Array.compactMap(_:) is like the previous one, but the result array doesn't need to be the same size as the original array. This one filters out nil values from the resulting operation. The operation in the parameter has an optional result, but map(_:) didn't allow for that.

A common usage for this method is to transform the items in the array to a different type, knowing that not all the items can be transformed and that you'll get only the elements that were successfully transformed. Consider the following example:

```
func wordsToInt(_ str: String) -> Int? {
  let formatter = NumberFormatter()
  formatter.numberStyle = .spellOut
  return formatter.number(from: str.lowercased()) as? Int
}
```

The function receives a string and finds out if this string is a number represented in letters. For example, the word "one" is the number "1". If it is, then the function returns that number. Otherwise, it returns nil.

```
wordsToInt("Three") // 3
wordsToInt("Four") // 4
wordsToInt("Five") // 5
wordsToInt("Hello") // nil
```

Next, add this function at the end of your playground:

```
func convertToInt(_ value: Any) -> Int? {
  if let value = value as? String {
    return wordsToInt(value)
  } else {
    return value as? Int
  }
}
```

This function receives any value and attempts to convert it to an integer. If it's a string, it passes it over to the previous function that you added. Otherwise, it attempts to cast it to an integer.

```
convertToInt("one") // 1
convertToInt(1.1) // nil
convertToInt(1) // 1
```

The value "1.1" failed to convert because it's a Double. Now, try it with this sample array:

```
let sampleArray: [Any] = [1, 2, 3.0, "Four", "Five", "sixx",
7.1, "Hello", "World", "!"]

let newArray = sampleArray.compactMap(convertToInt(_:)) // [1,
2, 4, 5]
```

So far, it looks good. But while working on the project, you learned the values "3.0" and "7.1" should be converted to integers. The problem was not related at all to compactMap(_:), but it's in the method that you're using for conversion all over your project. Update it to the following:

```
func convertToInt(_ value: Any) -> Int? {
  if let value = value as? String {
    return wordsToInt(value)
  } else if let value = value as? Double {
    return Int(value)
  } else {
    return value as? Int
  }
}
```

This gave your function the ability to convert doubles to integers. The result changed to "[1, 2, 3, 4, 5, 7]".

Later, you can refactor and improve convertToInt(_:) to convert more values without going through many places in your project. This specific example shows a better usage for a function instead of a code block or a closure as a parameter to a higher-order function.

flatMap

As you saw in `compactMap(_:)`, you can have fewer results than in your original array. But what if the operation you want will provide an array for each item? Consider that you want to calculate the square, the cube and the fourth power of each number in an array. Consider the following function:

```
func calculatePowers(_ number: Int) -> [Int] {
  var results: [Int] = []
  var value = number
  for _ in 0...2 {
    value *= number
    results.append(value)
  }
  return results
}
calculatePowers(3) // [9, 27, 81]
```

Now, use this function on a sample array of integers:

```
let exampleList = [1, 2, 3, 4, 5]
let result = exampleList.map(calculatePowers(_:))
// [[1, 1, 1], [4, 8, 16], [9, 27, 81], [16, 64, 256], [25, 125,
625]]
result.count // 5
```

The result contains all the values you want, but it still has the same size as the original array. The only difference is that the array is now an array of arrays `[[Int]]`. For each element in the original collection, you created another collection for it.

If you want to have this in a single, flat array, you can do the additional step of joining them together:

```
let joinedResult = Array(result.joined())
// [1, 1, 1, 4, 8, 16, 9, 27, 81, 16, 64, 256, 25, 125, 625]
```

But the Swift standard library provides a more convenient way to do that using fewer steps. Instead of using `map(_:)` use `flatMap(_:)`:

```
let flatResult = exampleList.flatMap(calculatePowers(_:))
// [1, 1, 1, 4, 8, 16, 9, 27, 81, 16, 64, 256, 25, 125, 625]
```

The two ways are equivalent and provide the same result. The latter is just simpler to write.

filter

`filter(_:)` is one of the simplest higher-order functions. As its name suggests, you want to filter a collection of many items based on criteria. If the element meets the criteria, keep it. But if it doesn't, remove it from the list.

This function expects criteria in the form of a function that returns `true` or `false`. To be in the list or not to be in the list.

Say you want to get the list of number words (numbers in English words, not in digits) that contain only four letters for the numbers between zero and one hundred. First, build the whole list of words:

```
func intToWord(_ number: Int) -> String? {
    let formatter = NumberFormatter()
    formatter.numberStyle = .spellOut
    return formatter.string(from: number as NSNumber)
}

let numbers: [Int] = Array(0...100)
let words = numbers.compactMap(intToWord(_:))
// ["zero", "one", "two", ....., "ninety-nine", "one hundred"]
```

Next, create the function that will decide if this string should stay or not:

```
func shouldKeep(word: String) -> Bool {
    return word.count == 4
}
```

Finally, filter out your array:

```
let filteredWords = words.filter(shouldKeep(word:))
// ["zero", "four", "five", "nine"]
```

As mentioned before, you can use a closure here for simplicity:

```
let filteredWords = words.filter { $0.count == 4 }
```

It's correct. But if your actual check is complex and used all over your application, then it would be better to define it as a function rather than as a closure. Your code will look better and have fewer places to maintain if any changes are needed.

reduce

reduce(_:_:) is a handy method when you want to merge a group of elements.
Common examples include adding or multiplying a group of numbers. But this
doesn't mean it works only on numbers. You also can use it on your own custom
types. Say you have scores for a soccer team and you want to merge them all to see
the team's totals. Consider this Score type:

```
struct Score {
  var wins = 0, draws = 0, losses = 0
  var goalsScored = 0, goalsReceived = 0

  init() {}

  init(goalsScored: Int, goalsReceived: Int) {
    self.goalsScored = goalsScored
    self.goalsReceived = goalsReceived

    if goalsScored == goalsReceived {
      draws = 1
    } else if goalsScored > goalsReceived {
      wins = 1
    } else {
      losses = 1
    }
  }
}
```

Score can represent a single match or a group of matches. The initializer receives
the goals scored and received by the team in one match and sets the wins, draws and
losses values according to this score.

Now, build an array of individual match scores:

```
var teamScores = [
  Score(goalsScored: 1, goalsReceived: 0),
  Score(goalsScored: 2, goalsReceived: 1),
  Score(goalsScored: 0, goalsReceived: 0),
  Score(goalsScored: 1, goalsReceived: 3),
  Score(goalsScored: 2, goalsReceived: 2),
  Score(goalsScored: 3, goalsReceived: 0),
  Score(goalsScored: 4, goalsReceived: 3)
]
```

Next, create a function to easily add the scores of two matches. Using operator
overloading is ideal for this:

```
extension Score {
```

```
static func +(left: Score, right: Score) -> Score {
    var newScore = Score()

    newScore.wins = left.wins + right.wins
    newScore.losses = left.losses + right.losses
    newScore.draws = left.draws + right.draws
    newScore.goalsScored =
        left.goalsScored + right.goalsScored
    newScore.goalsReceived =
        left.goalsReceived + right.goalsReceived

    return newScore
  }
}
```

Finally, reduce this team's scores into a single Score object using reduce(_:_:) and the new operator method you created:

```
let firstSeasonScores = teamScores.reduce(Score(), +)
// Score(wins: 4, draws: 2, losses: 1, goalsScored: 13,
goalsReceived: 9)
```

A nice thing about operators is that you don't need to write the whole signature. The operator symbol by itself is enough, and there's no need to write it like this: +(left:right:).

The first parameter in reduce(_:_:) is the initial value you want to add on top of. In this case, you don't have anything other than the existing matches, so an empty Score object is enough. But if you wanted to add the second season's scores to this season's scores, then this parameter would be quite handy:

```
var secondSeasonMatches = [
    Score(goalsScored: 5, goalsReceived: 3),
    Score(goalsScored: 1, goalsReceived: 1),
    Score(goalsScored: 0, goalsReceived: 2),
    Score(goalsScored: 2, goalsReceived: 0),
    Score(goalsScored: 2, goalsReceived: 2),
    Score(goalsScored: 3, goalsReceived: 2),
    Score(goalsScored: 2, goalsReceived: 3)
]

let totalScores = secondSeasonMatches.reduce(firstSeasonScores,
+)
// Score(wins: 7, draws: 4, losses: 3, goalsScored: 28,
goalsReceived: 22)
```

Instead of supplying an empty score object, you provided the ones from the first season as an initial value, and all the matches from the second season are added to it.

In this example, you couldn't have created separate types for match scores and season scores. The type returned by reduce(_:_:) matches the type of the elements in the array. This is why a single type was used to represent both.

sorted

This might be one of the most frequently used functions in day-to-day work. It sorts an array of elements for you.

Multiple sorting algorithms exist, and each has different complexities and usages. Some are better than others in different situations. For example, the insertion-sort is better for small sets. However, for a larger set, it's not as efficient as others. You can learn about the different sorting algorithms from our book "Data Structures & Algorithms in Swift" — it explains the differences between algorithms.

In the Swift standard library, the sort implementation has changed over the years. With Swift 5.0, the implementation for it uses "Timsort", which is a stable sorting algorithm. Here, stable means that if two elements have the same ordering score, then the order in which they appeared in the original set is maintained in the final ordered result.

To see how sorting works in action, try it on an array of the English words for numbers from zero to ten.

```
let words = ["zero", "one", "two", "three", "four", "five",
"six", "seven", "eight", "nine", "ten"]

let stringOrderedWords = words.sorted()
// ["eight", "five", "four", "nine", "one", "seven", "six",
"ten", "three", "two", "zero"]
```

The sort worked in ascending alphabetical order, starting with "E" and ending with "Z". When the items in the array are comparable, the default ordering is ascending, which is equivalent to words.sorted(<).

sorted(_:) expects an expression that takes two parameters and defines if the first should appear before the second.

Using the same Score as previously defined, create a new method to check if the two provided match scores are ordered:

```
func areMatchesSorted(first: Score, second: Score) -> Bool {
  if first.wins != second.wins { // 1
    return first.wins > second.wins
  } else if first.draws != second.draws { // 2
```

```
      return first.draws > second.draws
  } else { // 3
    let firstDifference = first.goalsScored -
first.goalsReceived
    let secondDifference = second.goalsScored -
second.goalsReceived

    if firstDifference == secondDifference {
      return first.goalsScored > second.goalsScored
    } else {
      return firstDifference > secondDifference
    }
  }
}
}
```

1. This method gives priority to the winning match if only one of them was a win.

2. If there were no winning matches, give priority to the draw match.

3. If both matches were wins, draws, or losses, get the difference between the goals scored and goals received. If both differences were the same, then return the match that had more goals or the match that had a higher difference. Loss matches with a higher difference give a -ve value so they stay at the end of the ordering.

Sorting a set of matches with this function gives the following result:

```
var teamScores = [
  Score(goalsScored: 1, goalsReceived: 0),
  Score(goalsScored: 2, goalsReceived: 1),
  Score(goalsScored: 0, goalsReceived: 0),
  Score(goalsScored: 1, goalsReceived: 3),
  Score(goalsScored: 2, goalsReceived: 2),
  Score(goalsScored: 3, goalsReceived: 0),
  Score(goalsScored: 4, goalsReceived: 3)
]

let sortedMatches = teamScores.sorted(by:
areMatchesSorted(first:second:))
//[Score(wins: 1, draws: 0, losses: 0, goalsScored: 3,
goalsReceived: 0),
// Score(wins: 1, draws: 0, losses: 0, goalsScored: 4,
goalsReceived: 3),
// Score(wins: 1, draws: 0, losses: 0, goalsScored: 2,
goalsReceived: 1),
// Score(wins: 1, draws: 0, losses: 0, goalsScored: 1,
goalsReceived: 0),
// Score(wins: 0, draws: 1, losses: 0, goalsScored: 2,
goalsReceived: 2),
// Score(wins: 0, draws: 1, losses: 0, goalsScored: 0,
```

```
    goalsReceived: 0),
    // Score(wins: 0, draws: 0, losses: 1, goalsScored: 1,
    goalsReceived: 3)]
```

The final result has matches with the largest scoring difference, followed by draws with the highest scoring and finally losses with the smallest difference and then larger difference.

Sorting is not specific to numbers or comparable types. You can implement comparable on any type and use the < and > operators. Or you can have your own comparison method or methods.

As explained earlier, higher-order functions can do a lot for you. They can simplify a complex functionality for you while keeping a tiny, simple part of its overall operation to be provided at the time of calling.

So far, you went deeply through one of the forms of higher-order functions: functions that expect part of their functionality as a parameter. This is the easy part. Before starting the next section, take a break, grab a cup of coffee (strong coffee is advisable) and do whatever you need to give your mind a break. It will help.

Function as a return type

Functions that return other functions are also higher-order functions. This might not be something you're accustomed to. But it can heavily empower your code and make it simple, despite using an indirect approach and looking complicated at first. Make sure you have cleared your mind so it doesn't feel too complicated.

Currying

Earlier, you learned that sending a function directly to a higher-order function requires the signatures to match. Thus, the example below is best done through a closure because the signatures don't match.

```
    aHigherOrderFunction { someOperation($0, "a constant") }
```

Usually, this is fine. But it's not impossible to remove the usage of the closure and send a function directly.

To remove the closure, you'll first need to change the signature of someOperation(_:_:) slightly. The new usage will be something like this:

```
aHigherOrderFunction { curried_SomeOperation("a constant")($0) }
```

And if having the inner function be passed as a parameter instead of closure:

```
aHigherOrderFunction(curried_SomeOperation("a constant"))
```

Now, take a step back and observe `curried_SomeOperation`. There are two major changes:

1. The parameters are now sent separately, each in its own brackets.

2. The parameters are swapped. The constant is passed first.

Currying is breaking down a function that takes multiple parameters into a chain of functions in which each takes a single parameter. To see this in action, you'll practice by implementing the above example, going from `someOperation(_:_:)` to `curried_SomeOperation(_:)`.

Create a new playground page and add the following:

```
func aHigherOrderFunction(_ operation: (Int) -> ()) {
  let numbers = 1...10
  numbers.forEach(operation)
}

func someOperation(_ p1: Int, _ p2: String) {
  print("number is: \(p1), and String is: \(p2)")
}

aHigherOrderFunction { someOperation($0, "a constant") }
```

Now that the abstract has become more concrete, start with the signature of `curried_SomeOperation`. First, break it down: Instead of taking two parameters, create a chain that takes one parameter at a time. Worry about the re-ordering of the two parameters later.

```
func curried_SomeOperation(_ p1: Int) -> ((String) -> ())
```

The first step is done. Well, it's done, but it could still use a cleanup. The signature looks straightforward. The function takes a single parameter and returns another function with the signature `(String) -> ()`.

Now, it's time for the actual body:

```
func curried_SomeOperation(_ p1: Int) -> (String) -> () {
  return { str in
    print("number is: \(p1), and String is: \(str)")
```

```
    }
  }
```

The body returns a closure that takes one parameter of type String. This closure is
(String) -> (), and inside it, the p1 that was sent to the original function is
captured and used.

> **Note**: To avoid retain cycles, you'll need to pay attention to the capture list *if*
> the properties are of reference types and not value types.

So far, you didn't break anything. Try it out:

```
aHigherOrderFunction { curried_SomeOperation($0)("a constant") }
```

The output is:

```
number is: 1, and String is: a constant
.
.
.
number is: 10, and String is: a constant
```

Like before, you're using a closure but it's still needed. To eliminate the usage of the
closure, you'll *need* to re-order the parameters. But before doing that, you should
know *why*.

aHigherOrderFunction(_:) expects the type (Int) -> (). Your function after the
Int parameter is provided doesn't return (). Instead, it returns (String) -> ().

If you change the order of the parameters, you'll have the (Int) -> () signature
that you need to avoid using the closure. Change curried_SomeOperation to this:

```
func curried_SomeOperation(_ str: String) -> (Int) -> () {
  return { p1 in
    print("number is: \(p1), and String is: \(str)")
  }
}
```

Now that the string is expected first, the closure takes the Int as a parameter. This
closure now matches the signature expectations of aHigherOrderFunction(:). The
usage now is:

```
aHigherOrderFunction { curried_SomeOperation("a constant")($0) }
```

You can safely reduce it and eliminate the closure:

```
aHigherOrderFunction(curried_SomeOperation("a constant"))
```

You now understand what currying is and why flipping parameters is useful. But what if there were a way to make a generic curry and flip so you didn't need to create a curried/flipped version for each method you encounter?

Glad you asked!

A generic currying function

Using an original function's signature originalMethod(A, B) -> C, you want to transform it to: (A) -> (B) -> C.

Notice that you mention a return type (C), but in someOperation, there was no return type. Technically, the return type is Void.

The signature of your generic two parameter currying method is:

```
func curry<A, B, C>(
  _ originalMethod: (A, B) -> C
) -> (A) -> (B) -> C
```

Before going through the implementation, there's one *important* difference between what this generic method is doing and what you did in the previous example. Here, you're *generating* what you did yourself in the example, meaning that this will transform the signature of the original function. Although this might be obvious, it's worth pointing out because it introduces two key differences from the previous currying example.

Type the full curry implementation as follows:

```
func curry<A, B, C>(
  _ originalMethod: @escaping (A, B) -> C
) -> (A) -> (B) -> C {
  return { a in
    { b in
      originalMethod(a, b)
    }
  }
}
```

The first difference is that there's an additional closure level. Previously, you returned the closure (Int) -> (). Here, you return a longer chain because the first set of arguments is the actual function that you'll transform.

The second difference is the explicit keyword @escaping. This is needed because the function you pass to it will execute after the curry function itself finishes.

curry is a higher-order function for both of these reasons: It's taking a function as a parameter and it returns a function, too.

Try using this function and compare it with the original someOperation:

```
someOperation(1, "number one")
curry(someOperation)(1)("number one")
```

Using the new method in the playground will give you this expected result, proving that the original function and the curried one are working as expected:

```
number is: 1, and String is: number one
number is: 1, and String is: number one
```

The return type from curry(someOperation) is (Int) -> (String) -> (). This is identical to the first step you did before. Next, you need to flip the arguments to be (String) -> (Int) -> ().

Generic argument flipping

Flipping won't be as confusing as currying because you don't need to make any drastic changes to the signature. Add the following function:

```
func flip<A, B, C>(
  _ originalMethod: @escaping (A) -> (B) -> C
) -> (B) -> (A) -> C {
  return { b in { a in originalMethod(a)(b) } }
}
```

The type of flip(curry(someOperation)) is (String) -> (Int) -> (), which is identical to the final curried_SomeOperation from your previous example. Try this in your playground:

```
aHigherOrderFunction(flip(curry(someOperation))("a constant"))
```

You don't need to write any more code to adapt your existing functions to pass them directly to higher-order functions.

For the specific case of flip, you might feel you can design your APIs to completely avoid needing it. But Swift contains some higher-order functions that make flipping necessary.

Generated class methods by Swift

For each method or instance-function you create, Swift creates a class higher-order function for this method. In a new playground page, add this extension:

```
extension Int {
  func word() -> String? {
    let formatter = NumberFormatter()
    formatter.numberStyle = .spellOut
    return formatter.string(from: self as NSNumber)
  }
}
```

This extension on `Int` generates the word for that number:

```
1.word() // one
10.word() // ten
36.word() // thirty-six
```

By default, Swift will generate a higher-order function for this method for you:

```
Int.word // (Int) -> () -> Optional<String>
```

To use it with the same three numbers used above, your code will look like this:

```
Int.word(1)() // one
Int.word(10)() // ten
Int.word(36)() // thirty-six
```

If you have an array of integers and want to map them to their word equivalents, you can either create a closure and call `word()` on each object or restructure `Int.word` to match the signature requirements for `map(_:)`.

In the same playground, create a new version of `flip`:

```
func flip<A, C>(
  _ originalMethod: @escaping (A) -> () -> C
) -> () -> (A) -> C {
  return { { a in originalMethod(a)() } }
}
```

This overload moves the part that doesn't take any parameters to the beginning, allowing the parameter to be sent at the end.

```
flip(Int.word)()(1) // one
```

You can avoid repeating `flip` by creating a new variable that carries the function `flip(Int.word)()`:

```
var flippedWord = flip(Int.word)()
```

You can use your new property directly as if it were a function:

```
[1, 2, 3, 4, 5].map(flippedWord)
// ["one", "two", "three", "four", "five"]
```

On some occasions, the extra brackets () can be inconvenient. You might want to convert any generated higher-order function for a method/instance-function that doesn't take any parameters and use it if it was a standard class function. Create this new function:

```
func reduce<A, C>(
  _ originalMethod: @escaping (A) -> () -> C
) -> (A) -> C {
  return { a in originalMethod(a)() }
}

var reducedWord = reduce(Int.word)
```

`reducedWord` and `flippedWord` are identical and are both `(Int) -> String?`. But if you pay attention to the declaration of the latter, you'll find that the brackets were already added as if it contains the result of the outer closure of `flip`. But reduce doesn't have an outer closure in the first place.

Merging higher-order functions

An interesting trick you can do with higher-order functions is to merge them. Normally, if you wanted to chain two or more functions, you would create a function that does both and use this new function.

Consider the following extension:

```
extension Int {
  func word() -> String? {
    let formatter = NumberFormatter()
    formatter.numberStyle = .spellOut
```

```
      return formatter.string(from: self as NSNumber)
    }

  func squared() -> Int {
    return self * self
  }
}
```

If you wanted to have one function that would do both, it would look like this:

```
func squareAndWord() -> String? {
  self.squared().word()
}
```

It's definitely not wrong. But you might have many more than just two functions that you want to bundle. There's a nice way to do that. Add this generic function merger:

```
func mergeFunctions<A, B, C>(
  _ f: @escaping (A) -> () -> B,
  _ g: @escaping (B) -> () -> C
) -> (A) -> C {
  return { a in
    let fValue = f(a)()
    return g(fValue)()
  }
}
```

This function is tailored for Swift-generated higher-order functions from methods that take one parameter. It's important to notice how the data types between parameters and return types relate. The return type of the first function matches the parameter of the second. If they don't match, then it wouldn't make sense to chain them. Try it out:

```
var mergedFunctions = mergeFunctions(Int.squared, Int.word)
mergedFunctions(2) // four
```

You might be wondering if there isn't a nicer way to use it. This almost looks like you **added** the two functions. How about doing the same but with operator overloading?

Add the following to your playground:

```
func +<A, B, C>(
  left: @escaping (A) -> () -> B,
  right: @escaping (B) -> () -> C
) -> (A) -> C {
  return { a in
    let leftValue = left(a)()
    return right(leftValue)()
```

```
      }
   }
}
```

Now, the interesting part. Try it out:

```
var addedFunctions = Int.squared + Int.word
addedFunctions(2) // four
(Int.squared + Int.word)(2) // four
```

This is called function composition. You **composed** a function using two smaller functions. This is a bigger topic, but once you understand how you can play with higher-order functions, function composition becomes a lot clearer.

You're free to define the operator you want. But know that once you start having too many operators in your code, it will look unfamiliar to others. Your proprietary conventions will make it complicated for other eyes.

Key points

- A higher-order function is a function that deals with other functions, either as a parameter or as a return type.

- Swift allows the use of a closure or a function signature in a higher-order function, as long as the number of parameters and the return type are identical to the original higher-order function declaration.

- Using a function signature instead of a closure can simplify your code if the operation is complex or gets repeated across your code.

- `map`, `compactMap`, `flatMap`, `filter`, `reduce`, `sorted` and `split` all are examples of higher-order functions in the standard library.

- Higher-order functions also describe functions that return functions as return types.

- Function currying means breaking down a function that takes multiple parameters into a chain of functions that each takes one parameter.

- Currying and argument flipping are ways to alter a function's signature to fit a higher-order function.

- Each instance method can be used as a higher-order function through its containing type.

- Function composition is when you merge higher-order functions to create larger functions.

- You can use operator overloading to create an adding function for higher-order functions, making function composition easier.

Where to go from here?

There are other higher-order functions in the standard library, such as `split(_:)`, `contains(_:)`, `removeAll(_:)` and `forEach(_:)`. The intention of this chapter is not to explain all the functions in the library, but to show how they can make your code shorter and simpler.

You can read about different algorithms in the book **"Data Structures & Algorithms in Swift"** or from the **swift-algorithms-club** on https://github.com/raywenderlich/swift-algorithm-club, which the book is based on.

Chapter 11: Functional Reactive Programming

By Shai Mishali

As a developer, you probably bump into buzzwords daily. Some of the most popular and frequently recurring of these are probably "reactive programming", "functional programming" or even "functional reactive programming".

Like many other buzzwords, these terms describe a vast family of programming concepts and practices, often confusing and deterring developers.

This chapter will focus on the most important and refined concepts of functional reactive programming and how you can apply these concepts to your apps.

Functional? Reactive?

Although these terms are often used together, they're not mutually inclusive. This means that each term stands by itself.

Reactive programming

The idea of reactive programming is that instead of manually and imperatively reading the state or value of some entity, you listen, or **subscribe**, to changes of that entity and get notified whenever your state changes — in which case, you can *react* to the change and update your app accordingly. These changes are *emitted* over time:

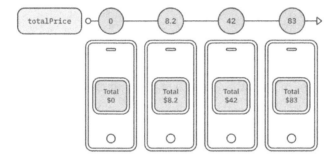

In the example above, there is a *stream* of price values called `totalPrice`. Whenever it emits a new total price, you update your app's UI accordingly.

This minimal concept is powerful in ensuring data integrity, but it also has many other benefits such as **composition** and easy **transformations**, which you'll learn about in this chapter.

Consider this example (there's no need to run this):

```
// 1
var userBalance = 5
let productPrice = 10

// 2
let canMakePurchase = userBalance >= productPrice
print(canMakePurchase)

// 3
userBalance += 20
print(canMakePurchase) // 3
```

In this example, you:

1. Set a user's balance of $5 and a product price of $10.

2. Define a canMakePurchase boolean to make sure the user has a sufficient balance to purchase the product. Its value is false because the user has only $5.

3. Add $20 to the user's balance, which means they should be able to buy the $10 product. But printing canMakePurchase still prints out false. Also, any other views in your app that depend on canMakePurchase still use a wrong false value.

This is the essence of the problem reactive programming aims to solve. canMakePurchase doesn't reflect the latest state of your app because it doesn't know the user's balance changed. It represents a static computation at a previous time, which is hardly useful, and requires that you manually make sure canMakePurchase is updated whenever either of its dependencies changes (in this case productPrice and userBalance).

In a reactive world, this example would look like this in pseudo-code:

```
let userBalance = ?? // Stream of user's balance
let productPrice = ?? // Stream of product's price

let canMakePurchase = userBalance
  .combineLatest(productPrice)
  .map { $0 >= $1 } // Stream of Bool
```

In this pseudo-code example, canMakePurchase will always have the correct boolean value whenever either userBalance *or* productPrice changes. Also, any views depending on canMakePurchase are automatically updated based on that new value:

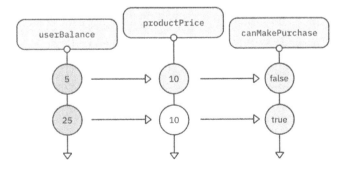

This is how basic composition looks in reactive programming, and it's the key to developing your reactive thinking: "Everything is a stream of values."

Because basically anything that occurs in your app occurs over time, it can easily be represented as a stream of values. When you shift your mind to think of all pieces of data as *streams* of data, the compositional options become endless.

iOS developers have used these concepts with third-party frameworks such as **RxSwift** and **ReactiveSwift**. But became even more widespread with the introduction of **Combine** — Apple's reactive programming framework, built into the SDK.

Functional programming

Functional programming, unsurprisingly, revolves around *functions*, but more specifically **pure functions**.

Pure functions are functions that:

1. **Always produce the same output for the same input**: Consider min(3, 7) — no matter how many times you run it, you'll always get back 3.

2. **Perform no side-effects**: Explaining side-effects broadly is outside the scope of this book. But in essence, a pure function shouldn't affect anything outside its scope. Some examples of this are printing from within your function, performing a network request, or modifying external state: None of these should occur in a pure function.

Why not both?

So why are these terms put together so often, you might ask? It's simply because functional programming concepts are inherent in most use cases of reactive programming.

The most frequently occurring example of this is **operators** — simple functions that transform these reactive pieces you can subscribe to. Most of these operators are pure functions, and many of them are higher-order functions (functions that take other functions, like map, filter and reduce), which you learned about in the previous chapter.

Many of these operators have parallels with the same name in the Swift standard library and also perform the same sort of work. An example of this is map, which transforms each element in a stream:

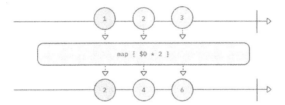

Don't worry if this feels a bit confusing at the moment. You'll work with operators *a lot* throughout this chapter.

Reactive basics

There are many attempts at defining a unified standard for how streams behave. The most common ones are Reactive Streams (https://www.reactive-streams.org/) and Reactive Extensions (Rx) (http://reactivex.io/). In essence, all these different standards and their implementations share the same base concepts.

Naming

The basic streams, or producers, that emit updates to subscribers have different naming across implementations. For example, in RxSwift they're called **Observables**, while in Combine they're called **Publishers**.

Although some minor implementation details differ, all these implementations mostly represent the same notion of pushing updates to consumers.

Events

These producers emit not only values, but something called an **event**.

There are three kinds of events, which might be named a bit differently in each implementation:

- A **value** event, which carries a value of a specific type. You might get an endless stream of these values until completion of the stream occurs.

  Good examples of this would be mouse movements or keystrokes. These are events that occur endlessly and never complete, unlike a network request, which would emit a single value and complete.

- A **failure** or **completion** event. Both of these events are terminating and guarantee no more values will be delivered. A failure event indicates the stream ended with a non-recoverable failure, and a completion event indicates a valid and expected completion of the stream.

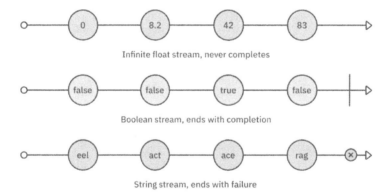

Infinite float stream, never completes

Boolean stream, ends with completion

String stream, ends with failure

Thinking of water

Streams of data are analogous to streams of water. Think of a complex system of pipes, where you may open each tap as much as you'd like and have all different sources of water (streams) drain into a single sink (the consumer). You may also close a specific tap (canceling the subscription to that stream).

These different water sources are the streams, while the multiple points where these water sources connect in the pipes represent the various composition options streams allow.

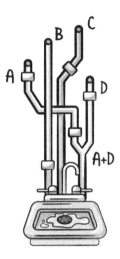

This analogy of a sink is so common that Combine has a `sink(receiveCompletion:receiveValue:)` method, which lets you subscribe to changes on a stream using separate closures for value and completion events.

Streams are just supercharged sequences

When you look at streams and the Swift language, where can you draw a parallel between them? The answer is simple: **Sequences** or, more broadly, **Iterators**.

An iterator lets you *iterate* over a list of values, which could theoretically be either infinite or finite:

```
let events: [Event]
var eventsIterator = events.makeIterator()
while let event = events.next() {
    print(event)
}
```

The code above creates an iterator from an array of `Events` and calls `next()` to retrieve the next event as long as one is available. This is the same as a reactive stream.

The main difference between the two is that streams *push* data to consumers, while an iterator *pulls* data when asked by a consumer. It's still an easy and useful way to understand streams and how simple they are in their most basic form.

The Luthier app

It's time to get practical and write some code. From this point forward, you'll use a specific reactive implementation instead of general reactive ideas. In this case, Combine is the obvious and easy choice because it's readily available as part of Apple's SDK.

You'll build a SwiftUI and Combine-based app that lets you choose guitar parts for a custom guitar and then order it.

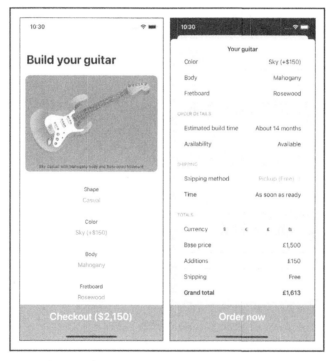

For those about to rock, we salute you!

Exploring the project

Open the starter project. Here's an overview of its structure and what it includes:

- **Build**: In this view, you'll select the various pieces of the guitar and see a preview of the guitar, a price and a checkout button.

- **Checkout**: Here, you'll see an overview of all the parts you've ordered, select a shipping option and finalize your purchase.

- **Services**: This folder includes various API services to fetch guitar information, as well as currency conversions that you'll use in the checkout view.

- **Models**: These are the different models that drive the app. A Guitar may have a specific shape, body wood, fretboard and color attached to it. Each of these additions is represented as an enum with various selections.

- **Helpers**: As the name suggests, this folder includes various helpers you'll use throughout this chapter.

Don't worry about all these bits and pieces right now because you'll use all of them sooner or later in this chapter.

Building a guitar

Build and run the starter project, and you'll notice a preview of the base model guitar along with a dummy "Checkout" button. Nothing too fancy:

In this section, you'll add various SwiftUI `Picker`s and handle the user's selection through the various powers of reactive streams: composition, reactivity, bindings, etc.

For this app, you'll use an **MVVM (Model-View-View Model)** architecture, where each view has a view model that provides the actual business logic, while the view layer only performs drawing. There are many other alternatives, but SwiftUI makes this choice quite a natural fit. The knowledge you'll gain in this chapter isn't tied to a specific architecture, though.

Your first View Model

The view model is the central hub for each of your views. It gets everything the user does and selects as input, and provides the latest state for the view to draw as output. You'll start with making sure you have all the inputs, first.

You're going to use SwiftUI's `Picker` to show the user the possible modifications they can make to the guitar. To track each of the user's selections, you'll need some bindings in your view model.

> **Note**: Some of the terms in this chapter are specific to SwiftUI. Because this chapter's focus is Functional Reactive Programming, you won't dive into the SwiftUI portions except to leverage your reactive streams.

Create a new **BuildViewModel.swift** file in your **Build** folder and add the following code to it:

```swift
import Combine

class BuildViewModel: ObservableObject {
  // Bindings / State
  @Published var selectedShapeIdx = 0
  @Published var selectedColorIdx = 0
  @Published var selectedBodyIdx = 0
  @Published var selectedFretboardIdx = 0
}
```

In the code above, you've defined a new view model that conforms to `ObservableObject`. This means that, using some SwiftUI Black Magic™, your `BuildView` will automatically be notified whenever any `@Published` properties change.

You've also added four @Published properties to act as bindings for the various guitar part pickers. You'll use these in a moment.

Adding guitar addition pickers

Back in **BuildView.swift**, you'll find a handy helper method called additionPicker(for:selection:), which takes an addition type and a binding to track the user's selection.

Because all guitar additions conform to the Addition protocol, you can leverage such a generic method to create all your pickers easily and link them to your new view model.

First, add an instance of your view model at the top of BuildView:

```
@StateObject var viewModel = BuildViewModel()
```

As mentioned earlier, using @StateObject ensures your view keeps itself updated based on the view model.

Then, in body below GuitarView but still inside the ScrollView, add the following code:

```
VStack(alignment: .center) {
  additionPicker(
    for: Guitar.Shape.self,
    selection: $viewModel.selectedShapeIdx
  )

  additionPicker(
    for: Guitar.Color.self,
    selection: $viewModel.selectedColorIdx
  )

  additionPicker(
    for: Guitar.Body.self,
    selection: $viewModel.selectedBodyIdx
  )

  additionPicker(
    for: Guitar.Fretboard.self,
    selection: $viewModel.selectedFretboardIdx
  )

  Spacer()
}
```

You just added a vertical stack view with the four different pickers a user can change in their guitar: shape, color, body wood and fretboard. Each of these is linked to a specific binding in your view model, using the special $ annotation, which lets you use these @Published properties as bindings.

Build and run your project, and you'll notice the four different additions a user can set for their guitar. Tapping each of these will show a list of options per addition, along with any price adjustments:

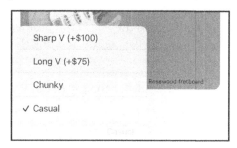

Constructing a Guitar object

Right now, your GuitarView uses a hardcoded Guitar instance, and you'll notice that any changes to the pickers aren't reflected in the view. It's time to change that!

To have a reactive guitar object, you'll want to have it as an output of your view model.

Go back to **BuildViewModel.swift** and add the following code to the end of your current view model:

```
// Outputs
@Published private(set) var guitar = Guitar(
  shape: .casual,
  color: .natural,
  body: .mahogany,
  fretboard: .rosewood
)
```

This new @Published property will be the view's source of truth as to what the current guitar state is for the view to draw. Notice that it's marked as read-only outside the view model and can only be mutated by the view model itself.

How do you connect all the user's choices into a single guitar, though? Not only do you need to track the user's selection, but you also need to make sure it happens **every time a change is made**.

This is quite simple, using a great operator called combineLatest. It tracks multiple publishers and emits whenever *any* of them changes. Because all the user's selections are marked as @Published, you can use them just as if they were Combine Publishers, using the $ prefix.

Add the following initializer to your view model:

```
init() {
  // 1
  $selectedShapeIdx
    .combineLatest($selectedColorIdx,
                   $selectedBodyIdx,
                   $selectedFretboardIdx)
    .map { shapeIdx, colorIdx, bodyIdx, fbIdx in
      // 2
      Guitar(
        shape: Guitar.Shape.allCases[shapeIdx],
        color: Guitar.Color.allCases[colorIdx],
        body: Guitar.Body.allCases[bodyIdx],
        fretboard: Guitar.Fretboard.allCases[fbIdx]
      )
    }
    // 3
    .assign(to: &$guitar)
}
```

This might seem intimidating, but it's quite simple once you get the hang of it. Your new code does the following:

1. Combines the latest values of the selected shape, color, body wood and fretboard indices. Whenever *any* of them changes, this operator will emit the latest values tracked for all four publishers.

2. Uses another useful operator called map. In essence, this is like the map you know from Swift's standard library. Instead of transforming each element in an array, you transform each emission from a publisher. You use it to create a new Guitar object made from the user's latest selection.

3. Uses a special overload of assign that takes an inout reference to a @Published property and essentially *binds* the results of the publisher to that property. This is quite useful because this assignment also takes care of the entire memory handling aspect internally.

Now, your guitar property will always emit the actual latest Guitar object, based on the user's selection.

Using your reactive guitar

To see this in action, go back to **BuildView.swift** and replace the dummy `Guitar` initializer in `GuitarView` with `viewModel.guitar` so it looks like this:

```
GuitarView(viewModel.guitar)
```

Build and run the project, and you'll notice that every change you make to any of the guitar additions is immediately and reactively reflected in the guitar preview image, as well as its caption.

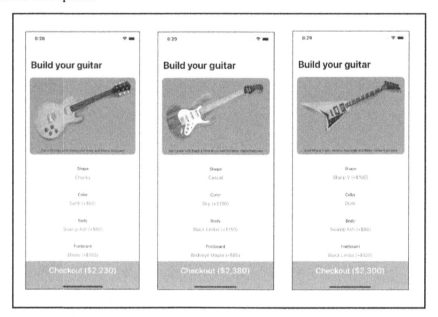

You can now leverage this `Guitar` object for other portions of your view, such as the current price.

Find the checkout `ActionButton`, and replace its text with:

```
"Checkout (\(viewModel.guitar.price.formatted))"
```

Build and run the app, and you'll notice that every change you make updates the guitar price in the checkout button:

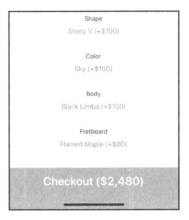

Subscription lifecycle

So far, so good. It seems `viewModel.guitar` is constantly emitting new `Guitar` updates based on your selection. But how can you *confirm* that's the case?

Open **BuildViewModel.swift** and, immediately before `.assign(to: &$guitar)`, add the following operator:

```
.print("guitar")
```

Build and run your app. Then, make a few changes to the selected guitar parts.

You'll notice your console output showing output similar to the following:

```
guitar: receive subscription: (CombineLatest)
guitar: request unlimited
guitar: receive value: (Natural Casual with Mahogany body and
Rosewood fretboard)
guitar: receive value: (Sky Casual with Mahogany body and
Rosewood fretboard)
guitar: receive value: (Sky Casual with Mahogany body and
Birdseye Maple fretboard)
guitar: receive value: (Sky Casual with Koa body and Birdseye
Maple fretboard)
guitar: receive value: (Sky Chunky with Koa body and Birdseye
Maple fretboard)
```

As the name suggests, `print` prints everything that goes through a specific point in your reactive chain. Here, you'll notice that every change you make to your guitar prints a new `value` event with a new computed `Guitar` object.

What do you think would happen if you removed the assignment to `$guitar`, though? The easiest way to find out is simply to try it.

Comment out the `assign(to:)` operator. Then, build and run again and make a few changes to your guitar. What do you expect to happen here?

The most obvious issue you'll notice is that your changes won't be reflected in your UI because you're not assigning them to `$guitar`. But there's a less apparent side-effect going on here.

Open your console, and you'll notice that... nothing printed!

In Combine and other reactive implementations, your chain won't produce any events until you subscribe to it. In *most* cases, it won't even perform the underlying work until there's at least one subscriber.

This makes sense — if there's no one to listen or *subscribe* to a stream, why should it perform work for nothing?

Later, a subscriber could cancel their subscription either actively or implicitly by deallocating whoever is holding it. In this case, deallocating the view model will also throw away the subscription to the user's changes on the view — which is quite a tight-knit memory management model.

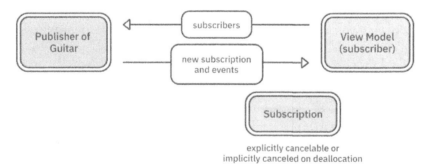

explicitly cancelable or
implicitly canceled on deallocation

Before moving on, uncomment the `assign(to:)` operator and remove the `print` operator.

Getting to checkout

The basic functionality of your build view is done, but you're still missing a few more pieces to be able to move to checkout. Specifically, you'll want to:

- Make sure the user's parts selection is available to order

- Fetch a complete price estimate for the user's selection

- Get possible shipping options for the user to choose from

You'll want to perform all these API calls simultaneously, show a loader and move over to the checkout view when you have all the needed information.

It seems like a lot of work, but you'll take care of it swiftly. Are you ready? Alright!

To start, it could be nice to sketch out a high-level implementation plan. Here goes:

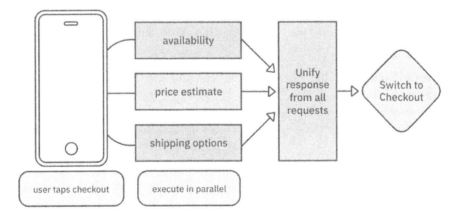

Triggering requests

First, you'll need some way to tell the view model "The user tapped checkout" so you can react to that action and call the three API calls.

Open **GuitarViewModel.swift**. Below your `guitar` output, add the following private property:

```
private let shouldCheckout = PassthroughSubject<Void, Never>()
```

Diving into subjects is unfortunately outside the scope of this book. But, in essence, subjects are simple units that let you imperatively send values to them and have those values published to all their subscribers. You can think of them as manually controlled streams of data.

A `PassthroughSubject` is a perfect candidate to represent events, while a `CurrentValueSubject` is perfect to represent state. You'll use it next to encapsulate the event of a user tapping the checkout button.

Add the following method to your view model:

```
func checkout() {
   shouldCheckout.send()
}
```

All you're doing here is exposing some public interface, the method `checkout`, to send an event to this subject. Next, you'll react to this subject inside your view model to actually perform some work.

Before moving on, you'll also want to trigger this method when the user presses the checkout button.

Back in **BuildView.swift**, find the `ActionButton` and add the following code inside its closure:

```
viewModel.checkout()
```

> **Note**: You won't use a `CurrentValueSubject` in this chapter, but remember `@Published`? All it does is use this `CurrentValueSubject` under the hood. So every time you set or retrieve a value from a `@Published` property, it's internally reaching out to this "manual" subject as its backing storage.

Checkout

As mentioned in the previous section, you'll need to make three separate but parallel API calls to fetch all the data needed for the checkout screen.

All these calls are available to you under `GuitarService`. In `BuildViewModel`, below your `shouldCheckout` subject, add an instance of `GuitarService`:

```
private let guitarService = GuitarService()
```

Preparing your API calls

At the end of your initializer, add the following code to support the guitar availability call:

```
let availability = guitarService
  .ensureAvailability(for: guitar) // 1
  .handleEvents( // 2
    receiveOutput: { print("available? \($0)") }
  )
```

In the above code, you're doing two things:

1. Calling ensureAvailability(for:). This method returns AnyPublisher<Bool, Never>, which means it returns only whether the guitar is available, and it cannot fail.

2. Using an operator called handleEvents, which lets you sort of "peek in the middle of the water flow" to perform side-effects on your stream in the specific point where you add it. In this case, you only print the result.

If you run and build your app, you'll notice this code doesn't do anything. As outlined in the previous section, publishers usually don't *do* anything until subscribed to. But before you do this, you should get the other two calls out of the way. Add the following code below the previous code:

```
let estimate = guitarService
  .getBuildTimeEstimate(for: guitar)
  .handleEvents(
    receiveOutput: { print("estimate: \($0)") }
  )

let shipment = guitarService
  .getShipmentOptions()
  .handleEvents(
    receiveOutput: { print("shipment \($0.map(\.name))") }
  )
```

These two blocks are identical to the previous one, except that they're for fetching a time estimate for the guitar build and shipping options.

> **Note:** In a real application, these publishers wouldn't have a Never failure but rather an actual error type. To keep this chapter more consumable, we've left error handling out.

Connecting the pieces

Now that you have your publishers, it's time to connect them and subscribe to their combined result. But what kind of composition are you looking for here?

There are many ways to connect publishers. For example, `combineLatest`, which you used earlier, would emit all of the publisher values whenever *any* of them changed, whereas `merge` would interleave results of different publishers of the same type.

What you want to do here is run these three requests in parallel and wait for all publishers to emit a value, *interlocked*, and only then emit a single result.

To do this, you'll use an operator with a known counterpart in the Swift standard library — `zip`. To zip all three publishers, all you have to do is:

```
shipment.zip(estimate, availability)
```

Or use the typed publisher directly:

```
Publishers.Zip3(shipment, estimate, availability)
```

But remember, you want to do this as a reaction to the user's tap on the checkout button. In this case, the `shouldCheckout` subject will be quite helpful. Add the following code below your three requests:

```
shouldCheckout
  .flatMap { shipment.zip(estimate, availability) }
  .sink(receiveValue: { print("Got responses: ", $0, $1, $2) })
```

In this subscription chain, you're starting from the trigger `shouldCheckout`. Once it emits, you use an operator called `flatMap` on the zipped emission of the three publishers: `shipment`, `estimate` and `availability`.

In essence, `flatMap` means "*Transform this publisher into a different publisher*". This is exactly what you're doing here: sort of trading a user tap publisher into a network request publisher.

There's still an issue preventing you from actually trying this piece of code, though. If you remember from the **Subscription lifecycle** section, when a subscription is deallocated, it's canceled. In this case, because no one is holding this subscription, it's immediately canceled.

To get over this, add the following temporary property to your class:

```
private var cancellable: Cancellable?
```

`Cancellable` represents the subscription to the publisher and lets you call `cancel()` on it.

Next, store the subscription in `cancellable` so it looks like this:

```
cancellable = shouldCheckout
  .flatMap { shipment.zip(estimate, availability) }
  .sink(receiveValue: { print("Got responses: ", $0, $1, $2) })
```

Now, you're ready to rock! Build and run your app, make some changes and tap the checkout button.

You'll see output like the following in your console:

```
shipment ["Pickup", "Ground", "Express"]
estimate: About 12 months
available? true
Got responses:  [Luthier.ShippingOption(name: "Pickup",
duration: "As soon as ready", price: 0),
Luthier.ShippingOption(name: "Ground", duration: "2-6 weeks",
price: 100), Luthier.ShippingOption(name: "Express", duration:
"1 week", price: 250)] About 12 months true
```

The order of these requests might differ on your side because they run in parallel. But note how the requests are running individually, while the `zip` emits a single value only when all of them complete their work.

Before moving to the next section, remove the temporary `cancellable` property and replace the previous section of code with:

```
let response = shouldCheckout
  .flatMap { shipment.zip(estimate, availability) }
  .map {
    CheckoutInfo(
      guitar: self.guitar,
      shippingOptions: $0,
      buildEstimate: $1,
      isAvailable: $2
    )
  }
```

This is the same code you had earlier but with a `map` operator added to transform the different results into a singular `CheckoutInfo` result.

Showing a loading indicator

Right now, the user can keep tapping the button endlessly. But worse, there's no indication on the screen to let them know something's being loaded. It's time to fix that.

Start by adding a new @Published property below the guitar property in BuildViewModel:

```
@Published private(set) var isLoadingCheckout = false
```

This is a boolean property you'll use to set the loading state of the checkout button in BuildView. But how can you represent something loading?

Simple — user tapped the button? Loading. Any response returned? Not loading. This calls for a different type of composition mentioned in the previous section, using an operator called merge.

Add the following code to the end of your view model's initializer:

```
Publishers
    .Merge(shouldCheckout.map { _ in true },
           response.map { _ in false })
    .assign(to: &$isLoadingCheckout)
```

As mentioned earlier, this code uses Publishers.Merge, the underlying type for the merge operator, to interleave the emissions of two different publishers that emit the same output type. In this case — Bool.

When the user taps the checkout button, an emission of shouldCheckout is immediately replaced with true. Once a valid response is emitted from response, it's immediately mapped to false.

This sort of state machine represents the loading state of the checkout button. Here's the full data flow, so far:

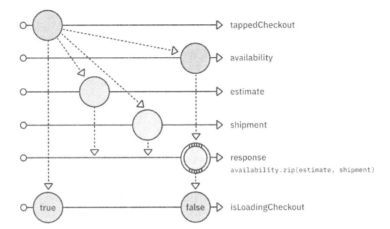

All that's left to do is use your new `isLoadingCheckout` publisher. Back in `BuildView`, replace the definition of the action button with:

```
ActionButton("Checkout (\(viewModel.guitar.price.formatted))",
         isLoading: viewModel.isLoadingCheckout) {
  viewModel.checkout()
}
```

This sets the `isLoading` state of the action button based on the emissions of the view model.

Build and run your project. Then, tap the checkout button. You'll notice the loading state shows up and switches back to an active button when the response is loaded successfully:

Pushing the result to Checkout

The last thing to do in `BuildView` is to use the response and navigate with it to your next view, `CheckoutView`.

In `BuildViewModel`, add one final `@Published` property:

```
@Published var checkoutInfo: CheckoutInfo?
```

This publisher will hold the checkout info once it's available and will tell the build view it's time to switch to the checkout view.

All that's left is to assign your response to this new property. At the end of your initializer, add:

```
response
  .map { $0 as CheckoutInfo? }
  .assign(to: &$checkoutInfo)
```

This simply assigns the response to your new published property while mapping to an optional version of `CheckoutInfo` to match `checkoutInfo`'s type.

Sharing resources

Your code works well right now, but there is a tiny (or yet, quite large) issue with it that is quite hidden.

Notice that `response` is being used in two different streams: the loading state and the assignment to `checkoutInfo`.

Build and run the app, and tap the checkout button. Looking at your logs, you'll see something like:

```
shipment ["Pickup", "Ground", "Express"]
estimate: About 12 months
shipment ["Pickup", "Ground", "Express"]
available? true
estimate: About 18 months
available? true
```

Due to the way Combine and other reactive frameworks work, each subscription gets its own resource.

This means you'll see duplicate network requests in this case:

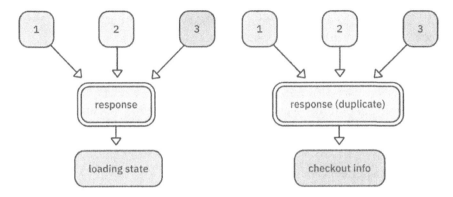

To solve this issue, add the `share()` operator at the end of the `response` stream:

```
let response = shouldCheckout
  .flatMap { ... }
  .map { ... }
  .share() // Add this
```

This will share the `response` resource *among its subscribers*, like so:

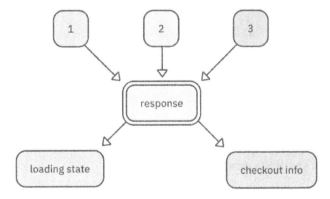

Wrapping up BuildView

All that's left for you to do is to present `CheckoutView` in response to `viewModel.checkoutInfo` firing a value.

SwiftUI has a nifty trick to reactively present a view modally, using a modifier called `sheet`.

It takes a binding of optional type: When it's `nil`, the view is hidden, and when it has a value, it's presented. It will also take care of setting the binding back to `nil` if the user actively dismisses the view.

This seems like a perfect candidate for your use case!

In `BuildView`, immediately before the `navigationTitle` modifier, add the following `sheet` modifier:

```
.sheet(
  item: $viewModel.checkoutInfo,
  onDismiss: nil,
  content: { info in
    CheckoutView(info: info)
  }
)
```

This code accepts three arguments:

- `item` defines the optional binding the sheet works with. Using the $ prefix here provides a `Binding` for the underlying published property.

- `onDismiss` lets you define what happens when the user dismisses the view. You'll come back to this in a moment.

- `content` is where you return the presented view from. `CheckoutView` has a specific initializer to take in the needed checkout info.

With all this done, build and run your app again, make a few changes and tap the checkout button. You'll notice that once the loading is completed, a checkout view is modally presented, waiting for you to implement some new reactive features in it:

Note that if the guitar is unavailable to purchase, the entire screen is not interactable.

Before moving on to checkout, you might notice that if you dismiss the view, the price and the user's selection are still visible on the screen. Usually, you might want to reset the selection to let the user build a new guitar after checkout or an active dismissal.

To do this, add the following method to `BuildViewModel`:

```
func clear() {
  selectedShapeIdx = 0
  selectedColorIdx = 0
  selectedBodyIdx = 0
  selectedFretboardIdx = 0
}
```

This resets the user's selection to the default indices, which is reflected in your view as well.

Then, in `BuildView`, change the `onDismiss` argument in the `sheet` you've just added to:

```
onDismiss: { viewModel.clear() },
```

Build and run your app again, and you'll notice that dismissing the modal sheet also resets your build view to its default state. Awesome!

Performing Checkout

Your checkout view already includes a solid layout of the screen you'll work on, displaying the guitar parts you chose in the previous step, the estimated build time and availability you calculated, as well as available shipping options.

Most of the work has been done for you to not repeat what you learned in the previous section. If you browse through `CheckoutView` and `CheckoutViewModel`, you'll notice it's mostly similar to what you've done so far — connecting various basic inputs and outputs for the view model.

Don't worry though, there are still two big challenges ahead. In this section, you'll:

- Allow changing the currency to one of four available currencies and present updated pricing based on exchange rates fetched from a web service.

- Perform checkout, show a success message to the user and dismiss `CheckoutView`.

Here goes!

Changing the order currency

In this section, you'll add one rather large change. You'll let the user pick one of several currencies to use for their order.

To do this, you'll:

1. Show the user a currency selector along with their current selection.

2. Get the exchange rate from U.S. dollars (USD) to the chosen currency from an API.

3. Update all presented prices to reflect the exchanged currency with an appropriate currency symbol.

Setting up the view model

First things first: Go to **CheckoutViewModel.swift** and add the following @Published property to your "inputs":

```
@Published var currency = Currency.usd
```

You'll use it to track the user's current currency selection.

Next, in the "outputs" section, add the following published properties:

```
@Published var basePrice = ""
@Published var additionsPrice = ""
@Published var totalPrice = ""
@Published var shippingPrice = ""
@Published var isUpdatingCurrency = false
```

You'll use the first four properties to show the appropriate string price, including the correct currency symbol. This is instead of directly accessing guitar.basePrice.formatted, for example. The last isUpdatingCurrency property will be used for the API call's loading state.

Also, below your published properties, add a new instance of CurrencyService:

```
private let currencyService = CurrencyService()
```

Head over to **CurrencyService.swift** and look at getExchangeRate(for:). You'll notice it's quite literally doing nothing and returns an Empty type of publisher, which immediately completes with no results.

You'll fix this next. Replace the entire contents of the method with:

```
URLSession.shared
  // 1
  .dataTaskPublisher(
    for: URL(
      string: "https://api.raywenderlich.com/exchangerates"
    )!
  )
  // 2
  .map(\.data)
  .decode(type: ExchangeResponse.self, decoder: JSONDecoder())
  // 3
  .map { response in
    guard let rate = response.rates[currency.code] else {
      fatalError()
    }

    return rate
  }
  // 4
  .eraseToAnyPublisher()
```

This might seem a bit convoluted, but you just created your first Combine-based network request — hooray! You:

1. Use URLSession.dataTaskPublisher(for:). It works similarly to URLSession.dataTask(for:) but returns a Publisher instead of accepting a closure.

2. Take advantage of a nice Combine operator called decode, which works on Publishers of Data and lets you leverage Decodable right there in your reactive chain. You map the network response to its data portion and then use decode to decode the JSON response to an ExchangeResponse.

3. Retrieve the actual exchange rate from within the decoded object. If it doesn't exist for the provided currency, you crash because this is an invalid state.

4. Erase the publisher so it matches the expected method return type — AnyPublisher<Decimal, Error>.

Taking currency into account

Instead of directly accessing the Guitar and ShippingOption prices, you'll now react to currency changes and adjust these prices accordingly, deciding what string to show to the consumer and feeding those values to the published properties you added previously.

You'll start with reacting to any selection of a currency. Add the following code to `CheckoutViewModel`'s initializer:

```
let currencyAndRate = $currency
  .flatMap { currency
    -> AnyPublisher<(Currency, Decimal), Never> in
    // 1
    guard currency != .usd else {
      return Just((currency, 1.0)).eraseToAnyPublisher()
    }

    return self.currencyService
      .getExchangeRate(for: currency)
      .map { (currency, $0) } // 2
      .replaceError(with: (.usd, 1.0)) // 3
      .eraseToAnyPublisher()
  }
  // 4
  .receive(on: RunLoop.main)
  .share()
```

In this code, you:

1. React to each change of the currency. If the selected currency is USD, you immediately return a rate of `1.0`. Otherwise, you use `currencyService.getExchangeRate(for:)` to fetch the right exchange rate.

2. Map the exchange rate as a tuple along with the requested currency.

3. Return no exchange rate if an error occurred.

4. Use a method called `receive(on:)` to ask the stream to deliver its values on the main run loop and use the `share()` operator as you did before, so multiple subscribers won't cause multiple network requests.

Now, all that's left to do here is to use your new `currencyAndRate` to calculate the right price for each piece.

Add the following code immediately below the code you just added:

```
currencyAndRate
  .map { currency, rate in
    (Guitar.basePrice * rate).formatted(for: currency)
  }
  .assign(to: &$basePrice)

currencyAndRate
  .map { currency, rate in
    (self.guitar.additionsPrice * rate)
      .formatted(for: currency)
```

```
  }
  .assign(to: &$additionsPrice)

currencyAndRate
  .map { [weak self] currency, rate in
    guard let self = self else { return "N/A" }

    let totalPrice = self.guitar.price +
                     self.selectedShippingOption.price
    let exchanged = totalPrice * rate

    return exchanged.formatted(for: currency)
  }
  .assign(to: &$totalPrice)
```

In the portion above, you do the same thing multiple times. Whenever
currencyAndRate emits a new value, you take the guitar base price, the additions
price and the total price and multiply them by the exchange rate to get the correct
price.

You also pass currency to formatted(for:) to get the correct currency symbol
presented to the user.

The last missing piece here is the shipping option prices. All you have to do is replace
the way you're instantiating your shippingPrices property.

At the top of your view model's initializer, find the code of blocks that assigns
shipping options to self.shippingPrices and remove it.

Then, add the following code to the end of your initializer:

```
// 1
currencyAndRate
  .map { [weak self] currency, rate in
    guard let self = self else { return [:] }

    return self.shippingOptions
      .reduce(into: [ShippingOption: String]()) { opts, opt in
        opts[opt] = opt.price == 0
          ? "Free"
          : (opt.price * rate).formatted(for: currency)
      }
  }
  .assign(to: &$shippingPrices)

// 2
$shippingPrices
  .combineLatest($selectedShippingOption, $isUpdatingCurrency)
  .map { pricedOptions, selectedOption, isLoading in
    guard selectedOption.price != 0 else { return "Free" }
```

```
    return pricedOptions[selectedOption] ?? "N/A"
  }
  .assign(to: &$shippingPrice)
```

These two code blocks might look long, but they're pieces of code you've already written before:

1. You use the same code you instantiated `shippingPrices` with before. The only difference is that you multiply the selected option by the exchange rate and use `formatted(for:)` with a specific currency.

2. `combineLatest`, which you used before, will emit whenever either the shipping prices or the selected shipping options change. Then, it would simply pick the pre-calculated and exchanged price for the selected option.

Connecting the view

Phew, that was *a lot* of code — congratulations for getting here! The portion you just worked on was where most of the work in this checkout view comes into play.

Now's the fun part — making your `CheckoutView` use all this data! Head over to `CheckoutView` and find the "Totals" `Section`.

Replace `Text(Currency.usd.symbol)` with:

```
Picker("Currency",
       selection: $viewModel.currency) {
  ForEach(Currency.allCases) {
    Text($0.symbol).tag($0)
  }
}
.pickerStyle(SegmentedPickerStyle())
```

You just allowed the user to pick a specific currency instead of showing only a hard-coded USD currency.

Next, you'll change the USD guitar prices to your new, rate-aware prices.

Replace the last four `TextRows` with the following:

```
TextRow("Base price", viewModel.basePrice)

TextRow("Additions", viewModel.additionsPrice)

TextRow("Shipping", viewModel.shippingPrice)

TextRow("Grand total", viewModel.totalPrice, weight: .semibold)
```

Build and run the app, get to checkout and change the currency. You'll notice that not only the totals but also the prices of the various shipping options are updated:

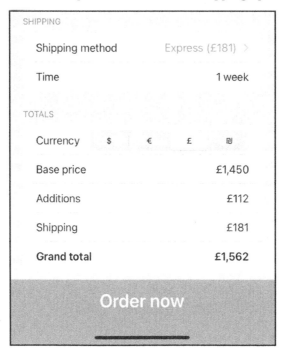

Tidying currency changes

This works quite nicely but misses a final touch.

The first issue is that every change the user makes will cause a network request, and many users tend to just tap around the currencies.

In `CheckoutViewModel`, above `currencyAndRate`, add this code:

```
let currency = $currency
  .debounce(for: 0.5, scheduler: RunLoop.main)
  .removeDuplicates()
```

You're using two operators here — debounce will let through only the last change made within the previous 500 milliseconds, while `removeDuplicates` won't let through duplicate currency changes.

Next, replace:

```
let currencyAndRate = $currency
```

With:

```
let currencyAndRate = currency
```

You do this to leverage your new debounced currency publisher.

Finally, you'll add a loading and disabled state quickly. You already created a
Published property for this. Add the following code to fill it as you did in the build
view:

```
Publishers.Merge(
  currency.dropFirst().map { _ in true },
  currencyAndRate.map { _ in false }
)
.assign(to: &$isUpdatingCurrency)
```

Right before firing a network request, you'll change isUpdatingCurrency to true
while skipping the initial currency value (USD). When you get a response, you'll set it
back to false.

Back in CheckoutView, find the four TextRows of the totals section and add the
following last argument to all four initializers:

```
isLoading: viewModel.isUpdatingCurrency
```

This will set the loading state of the text row accordingly when the currency is being
updated.

It would also be good to disable ordering and other changes while getting a currency.

Find the existing disabled modifier and update it to take isUpdatingCurrency into
account, too:

```
!viewModel.isAvailable || viewModel.isUpdatingCurrency
```

Build and run the app, get to checkout and change the currency.

You'll notice the loading state and network request fires only when the user lets go of the currency picker for over 500 milliseconds and that the various fields are redacted until a valid response returns:

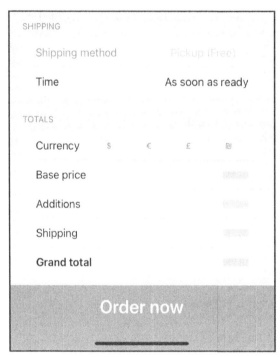

Checking out

All that's left to do is check out. Knock this one out of the park!

In `CheckoutViewModel`, add the following two `@Published` properties and `Subject`:

```
@Published var isOrdering = false
@Published var didOrder = false

private let shouldOrder = PassthroughSubject<Void, Never>()
```

You'll use the first two to track the loading state of the ordering and whether the user performed an order already.

You also use a subject to model the user's tap on the checkout button, just like you did in the build view.

Below currencyService, add an instance of GuitarService:

```
private let guitarService = GuitarService()
```

Then, wrap the shouldOrder subject with a public method:

```
func order() {
   shouldOrder.send()
}
```

All that's left to do is to call the guitar service and update the various states. Add the following code to the end of your view model initializer:

```
// 1
let orderResponse = shouldOrder
   .flatMap { [weak self] _ -> AnyPublisher<Void, Never> in
     self.map { $0.guitarService.order($0.guitar) } ??
     Empty().eraseToAnyPublisher()
   }
   .share()

// 2
Publishers.Merge(
   shouldOrder.map { true },
   orderResponse.map { false }
)
.assign(to: &$isOrdering)

// 3
orderResponse
   .map { true }
   .assign(to: &$didOrder)
```

In the code above, you:

1. React to an emission by shouldOrder by calling guitarService.order(_:). If self is nil, you simply return an empty publisher.

2. Assign isOrdering with the merge of the user's tap on the order button and getting back a response, just like you did before.

3. Once a single orderResponse arrives, you map it to true and assign it to didOrder.

All the work and state are now in place, and all that's left to do is finalize CheckoutView.

Find the .disabled modifier again and add || viewModel.isOrdering to disable the button when the user is performing an order.

And, as cherry on top, find the `.padding(.bottom, 40)` modifier, and add below it:

```
if viewModel.didOrder {
  ConfettiView()
}
```

This code will show a nice surprise for the user (and you) when successfully ordering a guitar.

The last step is showing a successful alert and navigating the user back to the build view.

Add the following modifier immediately above the `navigationTitle` modifier:

```
// 1
.alert(isPresented: $viewModel.didOrder) {
  Alert(
    title: Text("Congratulations!"),
    message: Text("We're working on your new guitar! " +
                  "Hang tight, we'll be in touch"),
    dismissButton: .default(Text("Dismiss")) {
      // 2
      presentationMode.wrappedValue.dismiss()
    }
  )
}
```

In the code above, you:

1. Use the `didOrder` binding to show the alert when `didOrder` turns to `true`.

2. Upon the user tapping the "Dismiss" button, use the view's presentation mode to explicitly ask the view to dismiss itself.

You should also actually call `viewModel.order()` at some point to trigger this entire chain.

Find the view's `ActionButton` and change its `isLoading` argument from `false` to `viewModel.isOrdering`. Then, inside the action closure, add the following line:

```
viewModel.order()
```

That's it! Build and run your app one final time, pick some guitar parts and order a guitar. You'll find the alert you just added, along with a fun surprise:

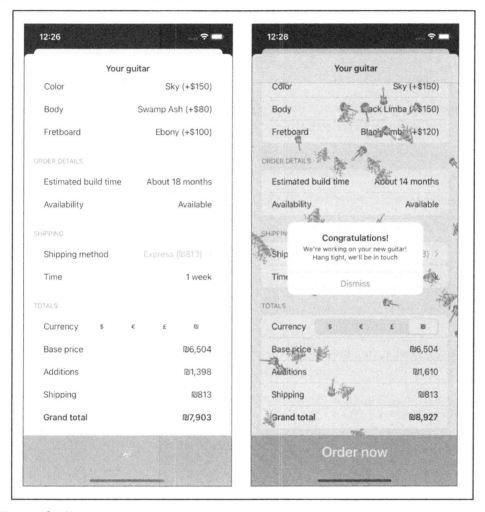

Yay, confetti!

Key points

- Reactive programming is the notion of publishing changes for a specific piece of state so your app can keep itself updated.

- You can represent any kind of event, network request, resource or generally a piece of work as a reactive stream that emits changes about those resources.

- Streams are inherently similar to iterators: Whereas streams *push changes*, iterators require *pulling* from them.

- Many frameworks provide reactive capabilities for Swift developers. The most common ones are Combine, RxSwift and ReactiveSwift.

- Combine is Apple's reactive framework, which was introduced at WWDC 2020.

- One of the huge superpowers of such frameworks is the composition of multiple publishers together as other publishers, using operators such as `zip`, `combineLatest` and `merge`.

- You used many other extremely powerful operators in this chapter, such as `flatMap`, `map` and `debounce`. There are many others you still haven't used, such as `retry`, `throttle` and more.

- Reactive is what you make of it! Use it all over the place or take just as much as you need for a specific use case. It's a tool at your disposal.

- Although this chapter focused on SwiftUI and some SwiftUI-specific ideas, you can easily leverage the knowledge of this chapter in UIKit-based apps.

Where to go from here?

Wow, you've done such wonderful work in this chapter!

You started by learning the basics of reactive programming as a paradigm, and then put your skills to work by building a fully reactive SwiftUI app that uses Combine for encapsulating various pieces of compound logic and state.

Even with this chapter's length, it barely scratches the surface. To dive deeper into Combine, check out our full book on the topic: **Combine: Asynchronous Programming with Swift**.

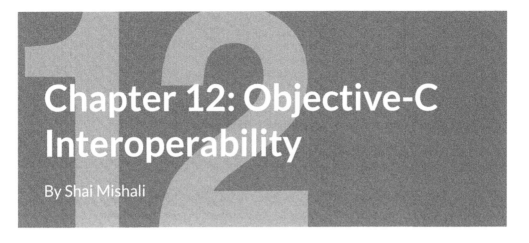

Chapter 12: Objective-C Interoperability

By Shai Mishali

You love Swift. Otherwise, you probably wouldn't be reading this book! Heck, you might've even started your iOS journey with Swift without touching its much more battle-tested ancestor — **Objective-C**.

Objective-C is a Smalltalk-inspired superset on top of the C programming language. Like it or not, Objective-C is still a heavily used language in legacy codebases and apps that have been in production for many years. Put that together with the fact that *most* third-party SDKs are still provided in Objective-C for compatibility reasons, and it could turn out to be quite useful to know at least some key portions of it.

In your own apps, you'll often have a sizable Objective-C codebase that just doesn't feel at home inside your Swift code or want to use some of your shiny new Swift code in your Objective-C code.

Luckily, Apple provides relatively thorough interoperability — hence, the ability for Objective-C code to "*see*" Swift code and vice versa. But there's only so much Apple can do for you automatically, which is where this chapter kicks in!

What you'll learn

As a relatively new father, tracking what my child does takes up a huge part of my day. Like other things that need optimizing, there's an app for that!

In this chapter, you'll work on an app called **BabyTrack**, which lets you track what your baby does: eat, drink, sleep, etc.

The version of the app you'll start with uses its own Objective-C based framework — **BabyKit**. You'll spend this entire chapter creating a wholesome experience for consumers of both the Objective-C and Swift portions of your codebase in a way that feels as if it were designed for either.

Getting started

Open the starter project in the **projects/starter** folder and then **BabyTrack.xcodeproj**.

The project contains two targets:

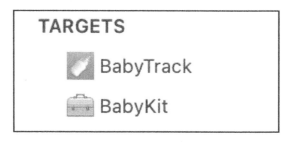

- **BabyTrack** is the main app itself. It has several folders, which you'll explore throughout this chapter. The **UIKit** folder includes the current version of the app, written entirely in Objective-C.

- **BabyKit** is an Objective-C based framework that the main target uses. It features a Feed class and a FeedItem representation of a single item.

Pick the **BabyTrack** scheme. Then, build and run it. You'll see an empty screen momentarily, and then ... darkness falls. Seriously though, it's a black screen. What gives?

Jump over to **Boilerplate/SceneDelegate.swift** and find the first line in `startLegacyApp()`:

```
let navigation = UINavigationController(
  rootViewController: UIViewController()
)
```

An empty `UIViewController` is passed to your navigation controller instead of the Objective-C `ViewController` you actually want. Yikes, that's strange. Change `UIViewController` to `ViewController` and try to build the project.

You'll see the following compiler error:

```
Cannot find ViewController in scope
```

Your `SceneDelegate` is a Swift file, and your `ViewController` is an Objective-C file. It seems your `SceneDelegate` currently can't "*see*" your view controller. Before you fix this, you'll learn about two important kinds of headers.

Bridging and umbrella headers

Bridging and umbrella headers are two headers that do the same thing, in essence: They notify their consumers which portions are exposed to their use, in the header's context.

Umbrella header

You can think of an **umbrella header** as the master header of a framework. In the context of a framework, it tells its consumers which framework portions are publicly available without the headers needing to be manually imported one by one.

Open **BabyKit/BabyKit.h**, which is **BabyKit**'s umbrella header. Notice that it imports the two headers included in the framework:

```
#import <BabyKit/Feed.h>
#import <BabyKit/FeedItem.h>
```

Try to comment these out and build the project, and you'll immediately notice your current code won't build.

You might even see some warnings to the extent of:

```
/<module-includes>:1:1: Umbrella header for module 'BabyKit'
does not include header 'Feed.h'
```

Open **UIKit/FeedCell.h** and look at the second line:

```
#import <BabyKit/BabyKit.h>
```

This is all a consumer needs to do to use **BabyKit**, because its umbrella header already takes care of everything. This is a common practice when creating your own framework and a useful component of defining module maps.

> **Note**: Module maps are not in the scope of this chapter, but as the name suggests they are files that map different modules of a framework to their respective headers. If you're curious, find your **DerivedData** folder and open the folder that starts with **BabyTrack-**. Inside **Build/Products/Debug-iphonesimulator/BabyKit.framework/Modules**, you'll find the coveted **module.modulemap** file.

Although this is useful for your **BabyKit** framework, it still doesn't solve the initial issue. On to the next type of header.

Bridging header

A bridging header belongs to the scope of an app instead of a framework. As its name suggests, it *bridges* Objective-C files into Swift by exposing any headers imported into it to your Swift files.

Eureka! That sounds like exactly what you need here.

Making the app launch

To expose **ViewController.h**, start by right-clicking **Boilerplate** in your project navigator and selecting **New File…**. Then, select **Header File** and name it **BabyKit-Bridging.h**. Make sure you select the **BabyTrack** target.

Replace the contents of the file with this line:

```
#import "ViewController.h"
```

All that's left to do is to actually tell your app to use your new bridging header.

In your project, select the **BabyTrack** target and then the **Build Settings** tab on top.

Use the search bar to find the **Objective-C Bridging Header** field, then set the field's value to $(SRCROOT)/BabyTrack/Boilerplate/BabyKit-Bridging.h:

Finally, go back to **SceneDelegate.swift** and make sure you use ViewController() instead of UIViewController() in startLegacyApp().

Then, try to build again.

Build succeeds, huzzah! Run the app and you'll finally see the basics of it on the screen.

The top bar features buttons to track various activities in your baby's day. Tap a few of the buttons on top, and you'll notice all items show up as "Ate food":

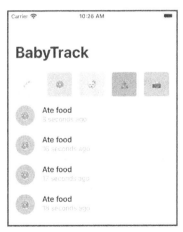

Sounds like a quick bug for you to fix. Time to get to it.

Enriching FeedItem

Open **FeedCell.m** and find `configureWithFeedItem:`. You'll notice that there is absolutely nothing in this configuration method that modifies the title or icon on the left. The only "right" piece is the subtitle — the date itself.

Also, there is code to download an attachment using `dataTaskWithURL:completionHandler:`, but it's using an empty `NSURL`. All these missing pieces need to come from the `FeedItem` passed to the configuration method.

The first option would be to create an Objective-C category as an extension to `FeedItem`, but an easier method you already know is simply using Swift!

Open **FeedItem+Ext.swift** and you'll find several extensions waiting there for you: an `attachmentURL` available on the `FeedItem` as well as an extension on `FeedItemKind` you'll use to get the appropriate `title`, `emoji` and `color` per item kind.

Exposing Swift to Objective-C

Although you needed a fancy bridging header to bridge Objective-C code into Swift, going the other way is quite simple. Simply annotate Swift methods, classes and properties with `@objc`, and they'll be available to your Objective-C code.

For example, replace:

```
extension FeedItem
```

With:

```
@objc extension FeedItem
```

This exposes any properties in this extension to Objective-C as long as Objective-C has a proper representation for it. But how does it actually work?

Press the **Related Items** icon at the top-left of your editor window (or press **Ctrl+1**), and then select **Generated Interfaces ▶ BabyTrack-Swift.h**:

You'll notice a massive, automatically generated Objective-C header file that represents all of the Swift code exposed to your Objective-C code. Build the project to regenerate the file, then search for attachmentURL, and you'll find the following block:

```
@interface FeedItem (SWIFT_EXTENSION(BabyTrack))
@property (nonatomic, readonly, copy) NSURL * _Nullable
attachmentURL;
@end
```

As you see, Swift automatically synthesized this Objective-C property to mirror the Swift counterpart you've annotated.

Now, go back to **FeedItem+Ext.swift** and add the @objc annotation to the second extension on FeedItemKind.

Build the project, and you'll find a compiler error:

> '@objc' can only be applied to an extension of a class

It's not all magic and sparkles. There are some limits to the great bridging capabilities provided to you. In this case, FeedItemKind isn't a regular Swift enum as you may come to expect.

Before continuing, remove the @objc annotation from the FeedItemKind extension again.

Open **FeedItem.h** and you'll notice typedef enum. But how does Swift represent this? Like you did before, press the top-left **Related Items** button, then select **Generated Interface**.

You can now see exactly how your Objective-C code is exposed to Swift. Look at the definition of FeedItemKind:

```
public struct FeedItemKind : Equatable, RawRepresentable {
    public init(_ rawValue: UInt32)

    public init(rawValue: UInt32)

    public var rawValue: UInt32
}
```

It's not a Swift enum at all, as expected! It's actually just a plain C enum represented by a UInt32, which is exactly why you can't extend it from Swift.

No worries, though, because you can still work around this. However, before you do, you'll take a little detour to learn about what *can* and *can't* be directly (or easily) bridged between Swift and Objective-C.

What can and can't be directly bridged

Bridging happens automatically in many cases. For example, when you create a Swift class that inherits from an Objective-C class or write Swift code that extends an Objective-C object, that Swift code is automatically exposed to your Objective-C code as long as you annotate it with @objc. Exceptions to this are Swift-only features, such as:

- Structs

- Enums, unless they have an Int raw value type

- Tuples

- Global functions

- Type aliases

- Variadics (e.g. ... splat operator)

- Nested types

- Curried functions

Also, full-blown generics aren't supported. However, Objective-C has quite robust **lightweight generics**, which support a relatively large set of generic scenarios, such as bridging Array<FeedItem> to NSArray <FeedItem *>*, Dictionary<String, Any> to NSDictionary<NSString*, id>* and vice versa. It will even keep generic constraints of your own Objective-C classes, so the following Objective-C class:

```
@interface BatchArchiver<T: id<NSCoding>> : NSObject
+ (NSArray <NSData *> *) archive:(NSArray<T> *) objects;
+ (NSArray <T> *) unarchiveFromData:(NSArray<NSData *> *) data;
@end
```

Will be perfectly bridged to Swift, like so:

```
open class BatchArchiver<T>: NSObject where T: NSCoding {
  open class func archive(_ object: [T]) -> [Data]
  open class func unarchive(fromData data: [Data]) -> [T]
}
```

Another interesting tidbit is the `throw` keyword. Throwing errors is a Swift feature not supported in Objective-C, so instead an Objective-C error pointer reference (`NSError **`) is provided as an argument to your Objective-C method. That method would also automatically get a `BOOL` return type if it didn't have any other return type, so you can get both a yes/no failure as well as a detailed error object.

You can wrangle many of these unsupported Swift language features by wrapping them in Objective-C supported types. For example, you can wrap a `struct` in a lightweight class or type-erase a generic object that can't easily be bridged.

Bridging back from Objective-C to Swift is also automatic as long as you import the required headers into your bridging header. But similar rules apply here as well. For example, you cannot annotate a non-class extension as `@objc` as you just noticed when trying to use the extension on `FeedItemKind`.

Extending without extending

To still support accessing the Swift-based extensions on `FeedItemKind`, you can simply wrap the properties in methods. Go back to **FeedItem+Ext.swift** and add the following static methods to the `FeedItem` extension:

```swift
static func color(for kind: FeedItemKind) -> UIColor {
  kind.color
}

static func emoji(for kind: FeedItemKind) -> String {
  kind.emoji
}

static func title(for kind: FeedItemKind) -> String {
  kind.title
}
```

These three static methods let you get the color, emoji and title for a specified kind. Because they're part of an `@objc`-annotated extension, they will also be exposed to your Objective-C code.

Time for you to use them!

Switch over to **FeedCell.m** and add the following import to the top of the file:

```objc
#import "BabyTrack-Swift.h"
```

This exposes all Swift content in the BabyTrack target to your `FeedCell`.

Next, add the following three lines to the beginning of `configureWithFeedItem::`

```
self.lblKindEmoji.text = [FeedItem emojiFor:feedItem.kind];
self.lblKindEmoji.backgroundColor = [FeedItem
colorFor:feedItem.kind];
self.lblKindTitle.text = [FeedItem titleFor:feedItem.kind];
```

These lines simply configure the emoji and title elements in the cell with the right contents.

Then, find:

```
[NSURL new]
```

Replace it with:

```
feedItem.attachmentURL
```

All ready to go. Build and run your project, and you'll finally see the items you've added get listed correctly:

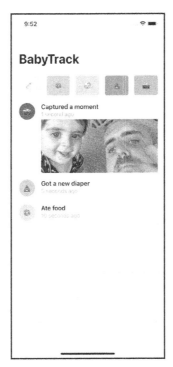

However, there is still some oddity in your extension worth fixing.

Setting explicit names for @objc members

Although a method called emoji(for:) makes sense for Swift, Objective-C consumers would expect a method simply called emojiForKind:. The automatic bridging doesn't really get this correctly, but no worries!

In **FeedItem+Ext.swift**, replace the three static methods with the following:

```
@objc(colorForKind:)
static func color(for kind: FeedItemKind) -> UIColor {
  kind.color
}

@objc(emojiForKind:)
static func emoji(for kind: FeedItemKind) -> String {
  kind.emoji
}

@objc(titleForKind:)
static func title(for kind: FeedItemKind) -> String {
  kind.title
}
```

You just used a variation of @objc in which you explicitly provide the full name exposed to your Objective-C code.

Go back to **FeedCell.m** and fix the three existing calls to emojiForKind:, colorForKind: and titleForKind:, accordingly.

Then, build your code to confirm that it still works.

Neat! As you just learned, Swift gets you most of the way there. But when you need that granular level of control, it's right there at your fingertips.

> **Note**: There is one more variation of the @objc annotation, which you won't use in this chapter but is worth mentioning, called @objcMembers. Annotate a class with it, and all of its members are automatically exposed to Objective-C without having to attach @objc by hand to each member.

Improving Objective-C enums

As you noticed before, your FeedItemKind enum is bridged as a non-finite standard C enum, which is not optimal when working in a Swift codebase where you're used to working with a finite set of strongly typed cases.

Luckily, Objective-C provides a modern way to define an enum that is favorable for Swift.

Go to **FeedItem.h** and replace:

```
typedef enum {
```

With:

```
typedef NS_CLOSED_ENUM(NSInteger, FeedItemKind) {
```

Also, at the closing line of the enum, remove the redundant `FeedItemKind`, leaving only `};`.

Using `NS_CLOSED_ENUM` lets you define a Swift-bridgeable enum represented by the type in the first argument (`NSInteger`) named as the second argument (`FeedItemKind`).

Switch to the generated Swift interface for this header like you did before, and you'll notice your enum looks a lot different now:

```
@frozen public enum FeedItemKind: Int {
    case bottle = 0
    case food = 1
    case sleep = 2
    case diaper = 3
    case moment = 4
    case awake = 5
}
```

Wow, the difference is like night and day! Not only do you get a real Swift enum, but your cases no longer include the `FeedItemKind` prefix, exactly like you would expect in a native Swift codebase. Also, each case is represented by a regular `Int` and not a `UInt32`.

Build your project, and you'll discover a dozen or so compilation errors caused by your enum case names having changed.

Unfortunately, there's nothing much to do but manually replace the `FeedItemKind` prefix with a dot in each of the cases as well as make the the first letter lowercase. Go ahead and take care of it — I'll wait for you right here.

Once you have fixed all your compilation errors, you'll need to make one minor fix.

Head over to **ViewController.m** and find the for loop inside `reload`.

Add the following line at the *beginning* of the loop:

```
UIButton *button = self.actionButtons[kind];
```

Then, add the next two lines to the *end* of the loop:

```
[button setTitle:[FeedItem emojiForKind:kind]
        forState:UIControlStateNormal];
[button setBackgroundColor:[FeedItem colorForKind:kind]];
```

These added lines ensure the buttons in the top action bar are also fed by your new extensions.

Build and run. You'll notice everything is working as expected. More impressive than that, though, is that your Objective-C enum cases are still called FeedItemKindBottle and the like, while your Swift case is simply called .bottle. You just created an entirely native experience for consumers of your framework from either side of the language war, and you'll keep perfecting your code this way throughout this chapter.

Objective-C and ... SwiftUI ?!

You heard it. In this section, you're going to pretend your Objective-C app doesn't exist. You've just been handed this Objective-C framework, and you want to build a brand new SwiftUI app that uses it.

Before you get to the SwiftUI-specific part, you'll take some time improving the Swift-related part of your interaction with the **BabyKit** framework.

Improving nullability

Nullability in Objective-C is the parallel of using Optional in Swift. Generally speaking, these nullability constraints are automatically bridged in a decent way but not good enough for a demanding developer, such as yourself.

Open **FeedCell.swift** and add the following print statement inside the initializer:

```
print(feedItem.date)
```

You'll immediately see the following warning:

> Coercion of implicitly unwrappable value of type 'Date?' to 'Any' does not unwrap optional

Wait, unwrap *optional*? All feed items **must** have a date attached to them, so why is the date property optional to begin with?

To understand this, remove the print statement and switch over to **FeedItem.h**. Take a look at the generated Swift interface as you've done earlier:

```
open class FeedItem: NSObject {
  public init!(kind: FeedItemKind)
  public init!(kind: FeedItemKind, date: Date!)
  public init!(kind: FeedItemKind,
               date: Date!,
               attachmentId: UUID!)

  open var kind: FeedItemKind
  open var date: Date!
  open var attachmentId: UUID!
}

public func FeedItemKindDescription(_: FeedItemKind) -> String!
```

Notice the alarming force-unwrap sign ! scattered all over the place to denote an implicitly unwrapped optional in your initializers, properties and return types.

Some of these *should* be optional, but most of them should not. The problem arises because Objective-C types are implicitly unwrapped by default. Think about it: If you've ever worked with Objective-C, you never thought *too much* about nullability at the compiler level, because there is no compile-time nullability, just runtime nullability, as is fit for a dynamic language.

Because there's no obvious bridging to be done here, Swift marks all these various pieces as implicitly unwrapped, as they are in Objective-C. It's time for you to improve this.

Head back to **FeedItem.h**. The portions that should be optional are attachmentId and the date in the third initializer.

Replace:

```
@property (nonatomic, strong) NSUUID * attachmentId;
```

With:

```
@property (nonatomic, strong) NSUUID * _Nullable attachmentId;
```

The _Nullable annotation on the NSUUID pointer marks attachmentId as optional, and Swift should treat it as such.

Note that as soon as you add a single nullability type specifier, the compiler will start emitting warnings until you resolve all pointers without one in that specific header file.

Replace the third initializer definition with the following:

```
- (FeedItem *) initWithKind: (FeedItemKind) kind
                      date: (NSDate * _Nullable) date
               attachmentId: (NSUUID * _Nullable) attachmentId;
```

In this case, the date and attachmentId parameters are both marked as nullable. What's the opposite of _Nullable, though? Simply — _Nonnull.

Replace the return type of the first method from FeedItem * to FeedItem * _Nonnull, so it looks like this:

```
- (FeedItem * _Nonnull) initWithKind: (FeedItemKind) kind;
```

This annotation tells Swift that this initializer will return a non-optional FeedItem.

You're probably flooded with warnings at this point and not too eager to add non-null definitions to all the remaining code. Fortunately, the good folks at Apple have you covered.

At the top of the file, immediately below the import statement, add:

```
NS_ASSUME_NONNULL_BEGIN
```

Then, add to the very bottom of the file:

```
NS_ASSUME_NONNULL_END
```

Build your app, and you'll see that all your warnings are gone!

This statement is the equivalent of "*innocent until proven guilty*" — or, in this case, "*non null until defined otherwise*".

Feel free to remove the single _Nonnull you've added at this point.

If you switch back to the generated Swift interface for the header, you should see the following definition for FeedItem:

```
open class FeedItem: NSObject {
    public init(kind: FeedItemKind)
    public init(kind: FeedItemKind, date: Date)
    public init(kind: FeedItemKind,
                date: Date?,
                attachmentId: UUID?)

    open var kind: FeedItemKind
    open var date: Date
    open var attachmentId: UUID?
}
```

Notice how clean everything looks now. Everything is non-optional, except for the few occurrences you've defined, as if you'd written this in Swift to begin with (I won't tell if you won't!).

Similar optionality fixes have already been done for you in **Feed.h**. Feel free to jump over and check those out if you're curious.

Setting up SwiftUI

With Feed optimized, it's time for you to start working on the SwiftUI part of your app.

Go to **SceneDelegate.swift**. Below startLegacyApp(), add the following method:

```
private func startNewApp() {
  self.window?.rootViewController = UIHostingController(
    rootView: FeedView()
  )
  self.window?.makeKeyAndVisible()
}
```

In this code, you use a UIHostingController to wrap FeedView — a SwiftUI View — and use it as the root view controller of your window.

Finally, in scene(_:willConnectTo:options:), replace startLegacyApp() with startNewApp().

Build and run:

Hello World!

Nothing too exciting; just a simple "Hello, World!" view. Time for you to build the SwiftUI counterpart of your Objective-C **ViewController**.

You'll start by creating the top bar with the different kinds of activities you can track in the app. Open **AddFeedItemBar.swift** and add the following two properties to AddFeedItemBar:

```
let isBabySleeping: Bool
let onKindTapped: (FeedItemKind) -> Void
```

AddFeedItemBar uses these two properties like so:

- isBabySleeping determines if you'll show an **awake** or **sleeping** button.

- onKindTapped notifies the consumer when an item is selected.

Next, replace the contents of body with the following code:

```
let kinds: [FeedItemKind] = [.bottle, .food, .sleep,
                             .diaper, .moment]

// 1
HStack(spacing: 16) {
  // 2
  ForEach(kinds, id: \.self) { kind in
    // 3
    let type = kind == .sleep && isBabySleeping ? .awake : kind

    Button(type.emoji) {
      // 4
      onKindTapped(type)
    }
    .frame(minWidth: 52, maxWidth: .infinity,
           minHeight: 52, idealHeight: 52)
    .background(Color(kind.color))
    .cornerRadius(4)
  }
}
.padding([.leading, .trailing])
```

In that code, you:

1. Define a horizontal stack to contain the various action icons

2. Use `ForEach` to iterate over the list of kinds

3. If `kind` is `sleep` but the baby is currently sleeping, you'll decide to show the awake action instead.

4. Display a `button` with the appropriate emoji and color, invoking `onKindTapped` with the appropriate kind once tapped by the user.

Next, you'll focus on getting this screen on the view.

Improving FeedItemKind's naming

There is already some room for improvement here from the Swift perspective. Notice the type `FeedItemKind`.

In Objective-C, it is quite common to have such verbose naming, but in Swift, you might have wanted to structure your code as follows:

```
struct FeedItem { ... }

extension FeedItem {
  enum Kind {
    // cases
  }
}
```

This would result in a nested `FeedItem.Kind`. Luckily, Objective-C provides a nice way to achieve this level of granularity, using `NS_SWIFT_NAME`.

Head over to **FeedItem.h** and find the `FeedItemKind` enum. Replace the ending curly brace, e.g. `};` with:

```
} NS_SWIFT_NAME(FeedItem.Kind);
```

With this tiny macro, you tell your code to still use `FeedItemKind` for Objective-C, but — specifically for Swift — to expose this type as `FeedItem.Kind`. This is the sort of attention to detail that makes your consumers not even notice they're using an underlying Objective-C framework.

Build your app, and you'll notice a bunch of compiler errors. The quickest way to deal with these would be to do a quick **Find and replace** for `FeedItemKind` to `FeedItem.Kind` in all Swift source files, but you can also fix these quickly by hand.

There will be a bunch of additional opportunities to use this trick throughout the rest of this chapter, so keep reading!

It's time to put something on the screen. Go to **FeedView.swift**, and replace the contents of body with the following:

```
NavigationView {
  VStack {
    AddFeedItemBar(isBabySleeping: false) { kind in

    }
    .padding([.top, .bottom], 8)

    List(1..<5) { i in
      FeedCell(feedItem: .init(kind: .food))
    }
  }
  .navigationTitle("BabyTrack")
}
.navigationViewStyle(StackNavigationViewStyle())
```

In this code, you wrap two items in a vertical stack — the AddFeedItemBar you just created and a List with five fake FeedCells. You also wrap your screen in a NavigationView.

> **Note**: To save you time, FeedCell was already provided for you. Feel free to check it out in **FeedCell.swift**.

Build and run, and you'll see the following:

Nice! You've got the basics looking good, but you're still not doing anything or feeding this UI with real data. You'll take care of this next.

Understanding the problem with BabyKit.Feed

Although your UIKit-based Objective-C code uses a regular UITableView with an associated delegate and imperatively reloads the table and reads items from a Feed object, SwiftUI is quite different.

With SwiftUI, the information the user sees in the UI is always a **function of your state**. This means that SwiftUI should be notified when the feed changes and update the UI accordingly. But how?

If you were to build this entire app from scratch, making your Feed an ObservableObject would be a sure choice — because your SwiftUI Views could immediately be fed and updated by it.

Unfortunately, you already have a bunch of existing code in **Feed.m**, which you definitely won't want to rewrite. In a perfect world, you could have both a Swift Feed and an Objective-C Feed, each tailored to its specific needs.

Is that even possible?! Why yes, it is, with NS_REFINED_FOR_SWIFT.

You can use this macro to *hide* Objective-C code from Swift consumers while providing your own, Swifty alternative to it. This sounds like exactly what you need!

Refining the Feed object

Open **Feed.h**. Above the @interface line, add the following line:

```
NS_REFINED_FOR_SWIFT
```

That's it! It's quite common to use this on individual properties or methods. But in this case, refining the entire class would prove quite useful.

Build your project, and you'll see a compiler error:

```
Cannot find 'Feed' in scope
```

More interestingly, if you start typing Feed, you'll notice it doesn't show up in auto-complete anymore:

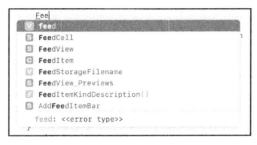

So where is it? The macro hid it for you using a neat trick — prepending two underscores (__) to the class name. This prevents the auto-complete engine from seeing it while still giving you access to it for refinement purposes.

In **FeedView.swift**, replace:

```
let feed = Feed()
```

With:

```
let feed = __Feed()
```

Your code will now build with no issues. This also frees up the Feed symbol for your Swift code, so you could make your own just like defined earlier.

In the project navigator, right-click the **BabyKit** folder and pick **New file…**. Then, choose **Swift File** and name it **Feed.swift**. Make sure you have the **BabyKit** target selected.

Next, replace the content of your new file with the following code:

```
import Foundation
import Combine
import SwiftUI

// 1
public class Feed: ObservableObject {
  // 2
  @Published public var items: [FeedItem] = []
  // 3
  private let legacyFeed = __Feed()

  public init() {
    // 4
    items = legacyFeed.loadItems()
  }
```

```
// 5
public var isBabySleeping: Bool {
  legacyFeed.babySleeping
}

public func addItem(of kind: FeedItem.Kind) {
  items.insert(legacyFeed.addItem(of: kind), at: 0)
}

public func addMoment(with attachmentId: UUID) {
  items.insert(
    legacyFeed.add(FeedItem(kind: .moment,
                            date: nil,
                            attachmentId: attachmentId)),
                at: 0
  )
}

public func storeImage(_ image: UIImage) -> UUID? {
  legacyFeed.store(image)
}
}
}
```

This code is quite long, but all it does is wrap the original Objective-C Feed in a SwiftUI-friendly shell. You:

1. Define a new Feed class that conforms to ObservableObject.

2. Use an @Published property to store the current feed items. Thanks to ObservableObject, changes to this property will automatically update SwiftUI consumers.

3. Instantiate a copy of __Feed, your Objective-C feed. You'll relay any of the heavy work to it.

4. In your initializer, you initialize your @Published property by calling loadItems() on the Objective-C feed.

5. From here on, you simply mirror calls to the Objective-C feed while wrapping each call in a SwiftUI-friendly way, making sure to update your @Published items property as you go.

All done! Before moving on, there are two pieces that stand out as non-Swifty: legacyFeed.babySleeping and legacyFeed.store(). You can use the same NS_SWIFT_NAME trick here, as well.

Go to **Feed.h** and replace:

```
@property (nonatomic, readonly) BOOL babySleeping;
```

With:

```
@property (nonatomic, readonly) BOOL babySleeping
NS_SWIFT_NAME(isBabySleeping);
```

Also, replace

```
- (NSUUID * _Nullable) storeImage:(UIImage *) image;
```

With:

```
- (NSUUID * _Nullable) storeImage:(UIImage *) image
NS_SWIFT_NAME(storeImage(_:));
```

You've now configured Swifty names for both of these entities. Build your project, spot the compiler errors and make the appropriate renames.

Improving property mirroring with @dynamicMemberLookup

Right now, isBabySleeping simply mirrors legacyFeed.isBabySleeping. This is fine for a single item, but it can become quite tedious and full of boilerplate as you add more and more properties to your Objective-C Feed.

Fortunately, because Feed is a Swift class now, you can leverage some powerful Swift tricks, such as @dynamicMemberLookup.

Add the @dynamicMemberLookup annotation to Feed so it looks like this:

```
@dynamicMemberLookup
public class Feed: ObservableObject {
```

Then, add the missing subscript method to the class:

```
public subscript<T>(
  dynamicMember keyPath: KeyPath<__Feed, T>) -> T {
  legacyFeed[keyPath: keyPath]
}
```

This lets you perform a dynamic lookup to *any* Key Path between __Feed and a generic T, meaning any property of __Feed.

Finally, remove the isBabySleeping property from Feed. With the power of dynamic member lookup, you can now access every property of the Objective-C Feed directly through the Swift Feed, with no additional boilerplate.

Finalizing FeedView

You have almost everything ready to go to finalize FeedView. Head over to
FeedView.swift.

Replace:

```
let feed = __Feed()
```

With:

```
@StateObject var feed = Feed()
```

You've just replaced the legacy Objective-C Feed with your newly created SwiftUI-
centric Feed, which is annotated with @StateObject so it can automatically keep the
view up to date.

Then, replace the List in the view with:

```
List(feed.items, id: \.date) { item in
  FeedCell(feedItem: item)
}
```

This code uses your Feed's @Published items and creates a cell for each. This will
automatically be re-invoked whenever the items change.

Build and run your app, and you'll finally see your feed items show up on the screen:

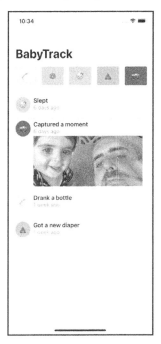

If you look at the screenshot, you'll notice that even though the baby is currently sleeping, you're seeing the **sleep** action instead of **awake** action. This is because you're still passing a hard-coded `false` to `AddFeedItemBar`.

Replace:

```
AddFeedItemBar(isBabySleeping: false) { kind in
```

With:

```
AddFeedItemBar(isBabySleeping: feed.isBabySleeping) { kind in
```

This property actually uses the @dynamicMemberLookup implementation you've added earlier.

Build and run again, and your toolbar should show up correctly:

You'll notice that tapping the buttons doesn't do anything, yet. It's time for you to wrap this chapter up with two final changes.

Reacting to tapping the action bar

Inside the AddFeedItemBar closure, add the following code:

```
// 1
print("Selected \(FeedItemKindDescription(kind))")

// 2
if kind == .moment {
  // ???
  return
}

// 3
feed.addItem(of: kind)
```

In this code you:

1. Print out the description of the selected kind using `FeedItemKindDescription`, a global function from **Feed.h**.

2. If the user selects a moment, you'll have them pick a photo. You still don't have all the parts to do this, so you'll skip this for now.

3. If the user selected a non-moment action, you ask the `Feed` to add an item of the selected kind.

Build and run, and tap some of the buttons on top.

You'll see output similar to the following:

```
Selected Awake
Selected Bottle
Selected Diaper
Selected Food
Selected Sleeping
```

You'll also notice that, finally, items are shown in your list as you tap the buttons on the action bar. Everything is working in sync and reactively updated by your `Feed`, which is an `ObservableObject`.

As long as you're here, how about taking care of this ugly global `FeedItemKindDescription` function?

Head over to **FeedItem.h** and find the definition of the global function at the bottom of the file:

```
NSString * FeedItemKindDescription(FeedItemKind);
```

How can you make this nicer? Wrap it in a different object? Refine it using `NS_REFINED_FOR_SWIFT`? You could. But there's a nicer way.

Replace the line with:

```
NSString * FeedItemKindDescription(FeedItemKind)
NS_SWIFT_NAME(getter:FeedItemKind.description(self:));
```

You just used a specialized version of `NS_SWIFT_NAME` that lets you define not only your own name but also this global function as a getter of a different type. In this case, `FeedItemKindDescription(kind)` is now simply `kind.description`, as you'd expect. How magical!

Build your project, and you'll get this informative compiler error:

> 'FeedItemKindDescription' has been replaced by property
> 'FeedItemKind.description'. Replace 'FeedItemKindDescription(kind)' with
> 'kind.description'.

You can use the **Fix** button to automatically use your new Swifty naming, while your existing Objective-C code can still use the regularly named global function.

Finally, to wrap up this massive undertaking, you'll take care of adding a new moment.

Letting the user pick a moment photo

When the user wants to add a new moment, the Objective-C version of the app modally presents a PHPickerViewController to let the user pick a photo.

There are two problems with this in your new SwiftUI app:

1. Funnily, even though PHPicker is an iOS 14 and up API, there is no SwiftUI-specific handling for it, and it is only provided as a UIViewController.

2. There is no way to do a simple modal presentation with a UIViewController, but only using SwiftUI-specific views.

To alleviate these problems, you'll need to wrap PHPickerViewController with a UIViewControllerRepresentable — a protocol that lets you bridge UIViewControllers into SwiftUI.

Open **AddMomentView.swift**, where the basic shell of this has already been provided for you with an AddMomentView struct conforming to UIViewControllerRepresentable.

This struct includes a few important pieces:

- An isPresented @Binding used to show and hide the view

- makeUIViewController(context:) from which you return a new PHPickerViewController limited to a single image, with the object's coordinator as the delegate

- `makeCoordinator` is responsible for returning a new instance of `Coordinator`.

- A `Coordinator` definition. The coordinator is responsible for communicating changes from your view controller to your SwiftUI views. In this case, it is also the delegate for `PHPickerViewController`.

Everything is done except for handling the user's photo selection. At the end of `picker(_:didFinishPicking)`, add:

```
// 1
result.itemProvider
  .loadObject(ofClass: UIImage.self) { [weak self] obj, err in
  // 2
  defer { self?.parent.isPresented = false }

  // 3
  guard let image = obj as? UIImage,
        let parent = self?.parent else { return }

  // 4
  if let err = err {
    print("Error in picked image: \(err)")
    return
  }

  guard let attachmentId = parent.feed.storeImage(image) else {
    print("Failed storing, no UUID")
    return
  }

  // 5
  DispatchQueue.main.async {
    parent.feed.addMoment(with: attachmentId)
  }
}
```

In the above code, which won't compile yet, you handle the user's picked photo by:

1. Using the `PHPickerResult`'s item provider to try to load an object of type `UIImage`

2. Using a `defer` statement to set `isPresented` back to `false` at the end of the current scope. This will cause the view to be dismissed.

3. Making sure you can unwrap the resolved `object` as a `UIImage` and that the `parent` object (e.g. `AddMomentView`) is accessible

4. Printing an appropriate message, if there is an error or you're unable to store the selected image

5. Using the resulting `attachmentId` to add a new moment.

To make the code compile, add the following property before the `isPresented` binding at the top of the struct:

```
let feed: Feed
```

All that's left to do is to use your new view. Head back over to **FeedView.swift**.

Above the feed `@StateObject`, add:

```
@State private var isPickingMoment = false
```

You'll use this `@State` property to keep track of whether the add moment view is currently displayed.

Next, replace `// ???` inside the `.moment` conditional with:

```
isPickingMoment = true
```

This sets the presentation state to `true` if the user tapped the **moment** action button.

Finally, before the `.navigationViewStyle` modifier, add the following modifier:

```
.sheet(isPresented: $isPickingMoment) {
  AddMomentView(feed: feed,
               isPresented: $isPickingMoment)
}
```

You used the `sheet(isPresented:)` modifier and passed it the `$isPickingMoment` binding to define when the `AddMomentView` is presented and dismissed.

Inside the closure, you create a new `AddMomentView`, passing the feed so it can add the new moment and passing the binding so the view can set it back to `false` when it's time for it to be dismissed.

Before you build and run, go to **Feed.h** one final time.
addMomentOnPresenter:completion: isn't useful for your Swift codebase at all, so
it would be better to hide it.

You could use NS_REFINED_FOR_SWIFT, but there is actually a much more fitting
macro to use here. Add the following macro at the end of
addMomentOnPresenter:completion:, before the ;:

```
NS_SWIFT_UNAVAILABLE("Use `AddMomentView` instead")
```

This makes addMomentOnPresenter:completion: entirely unavailable to Swiftand
provides a migration warning to any consumers who might use it.

For the final time, build and run the project and press the **Add moment** button in
the actions bar. A photo picker is shown to you:

Once you select a photo, a new moment is added to your feed with the photo attached:

Before wrapping up, head over to **SceneDelegate.swift**. In `scene(_:willConnectTo:options:)`, replace `startNewApp()` with `startLegacyApp()` to launch your Objective-C app. Build and run, and you'll see everything is working as it did before.

Two languages (Objective-C and Swift), two UI Frameworks (UIKit and SwiftUI), working in harmony, each served by its own naming conventions and APIs. This is the essence of a perfectly implemented interoperability.

Key points

- Objective-C is a powerful language, with relatively comprehensive bridging to Swift. When that automatic bridging isn't enough, you can get as granular as you want with your Swift-specific customizations.

- A bridging header exposes Objective-C headers inside your app, while an umbrella header exposes all Objective-C headers for a given framework.

- Because nullability is a given in Objective-C's dynamic nature, you can use `_Nullable` or `_Nonnull` to define the appropriate nullability or use `NS_ASSUME_NONNULL_BEGIN` and `NS_ASSUME_NONNULL_END` to make an entire definition block non-nullable.

- You can use the `@objc` or `@objc(name)` annotation to expose Swift types to Objective-C.

- You can use `NS_CLOSED_ENUM` to bridge Objective-C enums into entirely Swifty enums.

- Although full-blown generics aren't fully supported, lightweight generics pack quite a powerful punch for most common needs.

- If you want to have Swift-specific names for properties, objects or even global functions as getters, use `NS_SWIFT_NAME`.

- If you want to hide an Objective-C implementation so you can wrap it in an improved Swift interface, use `NS_REFINED_FOR_SWIFT`. This allows you to leverage Swift-specific features that are otherwise inaccessible to your Objective-C based code.

- If you want to make a method or property entirely unavailable to Swift, use `NS_SWIFT_UNAVAILABLE`.

- Don't give up on Objective-C — it's here to stay.

Where to go from here?

Congratulations on completing the **BabyTrack** app! You've modernized an old-school Objective-C SDK and app, while wrapping most SDK components with modern Swift-centric APIs and keeping the same interface for your Objective-C consumers, creating a wholesome experience that feels as if you designed the code for either language.

You've also entirely replaced and wrapped the Objective-C Feed with your own Swift Feed and used it in a SwiftUI app, leveraging features such as `ObservableObject` and `@dynamicMemberLookup` that aren't available to Objective-C, but still leveraging the underlying logic of the SDK.

We highly recommend further exploring how you can stretch the boundaries of bridging, and also explore Apple's great documentation on the topic available at https://developer.apple.com/documentation/swift/objective-c_and_c_code_customization.

Chapter 13: Instrumentation

By Ehab Amer

Being a great iOS software engineer isn't only about being a grandmaster of the Swift language. It's also about knowing which tools the platform puts at your disposal, how to use them to sharpen your skills and how to identify areas of improvement in your code.

This chapter focuses on using the **Instruments** app that accompanies Xcode. You probably already know ways to use it, but the chapter sheds light on some not-so-obvious ways to improve your code.

As you read along, you'll cover some interesting topics:

- Common memory issues and how to resolve them.

- How to measure performance and identify bottlenecks in your code.

- How to measure and improve the performance of CoreData.

- How to identify lines in your code that take too much time to build.

- An interesting instrument called **Timelane**, which you can install as a plugin to Instruments.

- How you can use os_signpost to send your information on Instruments.

Getting started

In the starter folder, you'll find multiple projects. You'll use them all throughout this chapter. To begin, open the project **"TheExhibition"**. Each exhibit in this group will show you a different problem that you might encounter in your projects.

Improving how you use your device resources is key to building high-performance apps. For the first section, you'll cover memory.

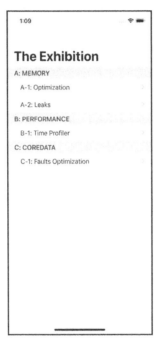

Memory optimization

The first exhibit, **A-1: Optimization**, is a gallery of wonderful images from NASA.

These are high-quality photos. One of them has a resolution higher than 6,000×6,000 pixels!

This exhibit has an effect on the app's memory. You'll use **Instruments** to identify what's causing this memory problem.

From Xcode, press **Command-I** to start profiling the app. Choose **Allocations** in Instruments. Then press the **Record** button at the top-left corner.

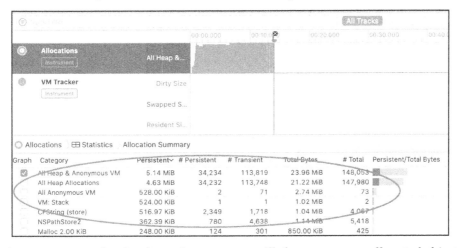

As the app runs on the simulator, Instruments will show you every allocated object in memory. The very top item in the list, **All Heap & Anonymous VM**, shows all your app's memory usage.

While Instruments is recording, tap the first item in the simulator. The app will freeze for a few seconds and Instruments will show a huge spike in memory usage.

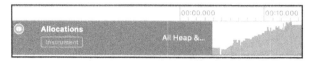

One new allocation entry responsible for this large increase is **VM: ImageIO_AppleJPEG_Data**. It has *21* allocations of almost *800 MB*.

Category	Persistent⌄	# Persistent	# Transient	Total Bytes	# Total
All Heap & Anonymous VM	950.68 MiB	41,426	162,815	4.85 GiB	204,241
All Heap Allocations	9.62 MiB	41,398	162,687	3.55 GiB	204,085
All Anonymous VM	941.06 MiB	28	128	1.31 GiB	156
VM: ImageIO_AppleJP... ⊙	792.89 MiB	21	0	792.89 MiB	21
VM: CoreAnimation	147.56 MiB	4	1	147.61 MiB	5

It might seem strange that your images can take up so much space when the overall file sizes are much much smaller. You'll find out why that happens in the next section.

Calculating memory usage for images

The space that images take up in memory isn't equal to their file size. Rather, images allocate memory that fits their resolution size. An example:

The first image has a resolution of 5011×3341 pixels. The size of each pixel is 4 bytes, meaning that when this image is loaded in memory, it occupies almost 64 MB. Images with such large resolution come at a cost.

But the gallery has only *12* images. Why does Instruments list *21* allocations? To answer that, open **MemoryOptimizationViewController.swift**. Reduce the value of totalImages to 11. Profile and record the app again.

Open the first screen and notice the new number of allocations on **VM: ImageIO_AppleJPEG_Data**.

Category	Persistent⌄	# Persistent	# Transient	Total Bytes	# Total
All Heap & Anonymou... ⊙	654.86 MiB	41,523	158,058	4.17 GiB	199,581
All Heap Allocations	8.91 MiB	41,506	157,947	3.36 GiB	199,453
All Anonymous VM	645.96 MiB	17	111	835.00 MiB	128
VM: ImageIO_AppleJP... ⊙	645.32 MiB	11	0	645.32 MiB	11
VM: Stack	524.00 KiB	1	1	1.02 MiB	2

It's 11, as it should be. How did that one image make a difference in *10* allocations? The answer lies in the image itself.

The last image has a resolution of **6228×6198 pixels**. This takes over *147 MB* of memory to load! But the OS didn't load this large amount of memory under one object. It broke it down to 10 objects, which is why there are 21 total objects.

0	0x12e6be000	VM: ImageIO_AppleJPEG_Da...	00:04.989.645	•	14.76 MiB
1	0x12f581000	VM: ImageIO_AppleJPEG_Da...	00:05.585.092	•	14.76 MiB
2	0x130444000	VM: ImageIO_AppleJPEG_Da...	00:05.673.657	•	14.76 MiB
3	0x131307000	VM: ImageIO_AppleJPEG_Da...	00:05.765.982	•	14.76 MiB
4	0x1321ca000	VM: ImageIO_AppleJPEG_Da...	00:05.858.940	•	14.76 MiB
5	0x13308d000	VM: ImageIO_AppleJPEG_Da...	00:05.945.508	•	14.76 MiB
6	0x133f50000	VM: ImageIO_AppleJPEG_Da...	00:06.028.422	•	14.76 MiB
7	0x134e13000	VM: ImageIO_AppleJPEG_Da...	00:06.116.670	•	14.76 MiB
8	0x135cd6000	VM: ImageIO_AppleJPEG_Da...	00:06.211.134	•	14.76 MiB
9	0x136b99000	VM: ImageIO_AppleJPEG_Da...	00:06.303.617	•	14.71 MiB

Next, you'll see how you can change your app to use memory more thoughtfully.

The solution

Now that you've established that the problem is caused by the high resolution of the photos, you'll reduce their size to something more friendly to the gallery screen.

Open each image with the **Preview** app. Resize it from **Tools ▸ Adjust Size**. Change the unit to **pixels** and the width to **1024**. Leave the padlock closed to maintain the aspect ratio of the image.

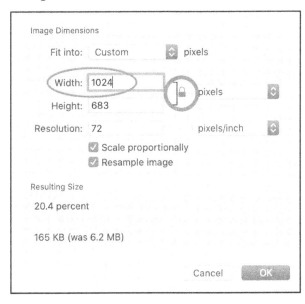

It's helpful to know the resolutions of the devices that will run your app. The resolution of the iPhone 11 Pro Max is 2688×1242 pixels. A 12.9-inch iPad has a resolution of 2732×2048 pixels. Knowing those numbers can help you fine-tune the images so they look good but don't take up unnecessary space.

Once you finish updating the sizes, profile and record your app on Instruments and open the first screen.

You'll notice that there was barely any freeze while the gallery loaded, and the increase in memory use is much smaller.

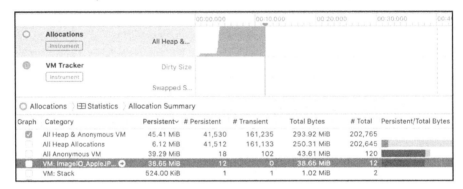

Congratulations, you reduced the memory use of the gallery screen without having to change any code. You can see that it's worth paying attention to the assets you use in your project. Higher-quality images mean a better-looking app, but they might use too much memory. In this case, that extra improvement no longer adds value — rather, it affects your app negatively.

In the next part, you'll continue to improve your app's memory usage. But now it's time to make sure all references to an object are cleaned from memory when you finish with them. This sounds basic, but there are many details around the tools that help you improve your object handling.

Memory leaks

Handling leaks is like the ABC's of memory management. "Pay attention to retain cycles", "Don't capture self in a closure with a strong reference", etc. So what's new to say about the issue?

It's the same story. But it might not always be as clear as you think!

In exhibit **A-2: Leaks**, you'll see a memory leak that Instruments doesn't capture at all.

The exhibit shows a very basic screen. It has a single button and a joke above it. Each tap on the button fetches a random, awesome joke from https://icanhazdadjoke.com/.

In your current Instruments window, add the **Leaks** item from the library. If the + button is greyed out, you'll need to stop recording first.

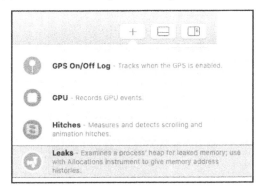

Profile and start recording the app, then open the second screen. Wait a few seconds, then tap **Back** to close the screen, then open it again. Wait a few seconds and repeat a couple more times.

Notice that Instruments didn't flag anything.

Here's where this gets interesting. Select the **Allocations** section and search for **MemoryLeaksViewController**.

Those are all instances of `MemoryLeaksViewController` still available in your memory. The total number depends on how many times you opened the screen.

How is that possible? Take it even farther. Build and run the app from Xcode this time. Repeat the same process of opening and closing the second screen. Then open the **Debug Memory Graph** from Xcode.

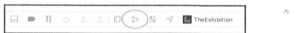

Filter memory objects of `MemoryLeaksViewController`, in the filter input box at the bottom-left corner. You'll find there are a few objects from that view controller that are still alive.

They are there! Instruments knew about them. Xcode knew about them. And yet the Leaks meter knew nothing about them? Why not?

To find out, look at the code. In Xcode, open **MemoryLeaksViewController.swift**. Inside viewDidLoad(), you'll see it creates an instance of InformationWriter. That instance takes the view controller itself as a parameter, then it calls doSomething:

```
override func viewDidLoad() {
  super.viewDidLoad()
  infoWriter = InformationWriter(writer: self)
  infoWriter?.doSomething()
}
```

Moreover, MemoryLeaksViewController conforms to the protocol WriterProtocol, which only defines the method writeText(_:):

```
protocol WriterProtocol {
  func writeText(_ text: String)
}
```

Now, look at **InformationWriter.swift**. Its init takes a writer as the parameter and creates a closure that calls writeText(_:) on that writer:

```
init(writer: WriterProtocol) {
  writeOperation = { info in
    writer.writeText(info)
  }
}
```

You probably already noticed where the problem lies. The closure created in the init(:) captures a strong reference to the writer. So adding [weak writer] should do the trick.

But before you fix anything, build and run the app and open and close the leaks screen a few times. Then, open the **Debug Memory Graph** and choose one of the MemoryLeaksViewController instances that are still allocated.

Memory graph is conservative

The memory graph isn't part of the Swift language. It's a tool that analyzes the app in memory during runtime. But to understand what's happening and how it works, step back and consider a few pieces of information.

You're familiar with ARC, short for **Automatic Reference Count**. It's the system Apple uses to manage memory, and it's been around since iOS 4. You know about weak, unowned and strong references. Those are the only possible combinations for any reference type. The compiler tracks the count of references for each object. When the count reaches zero, the compiler releases the object from memory.

The Debug Memory Graph works in a different way, however. It uses an approach that's much closer to a garbage collector than it is to ARC.

A garbage collector needs to build a memory graph of an app at a specific moment. It then identifies the orphaned objects or cycles to delete. Those are objects that aren't linked to the main app anymore.

A graph can be precise or conservative, depending on how the collector constructs its memory graph. To construct a **precise** graph, a collector must identify all pointers. And for that, the code generator or compiler must keep pointers or any information needed for the graph in an accessible and obvious way.

A **conservative** approach is different. It explores memory and starts building the graph. But at some points, it won't be sure if something is a value or a pointer, raising the possibility of false positives or false negatives.

Xcode's Debug Memory Graph is conservative. It's built on top of the Leaks instrument. In fact, they're practically the same thing, just represented differently. The Debug Memory Graph analyzes a snapshot of your app's memory, regardless of whether the app was built in Swift, Objective-C or even C. But the graph can identify if the reference found was weak or strong.

In the scenario you're debugging, the memory leak is present, but the memory graph is confused. It's not sure if some references to the view controller are valid references or not.

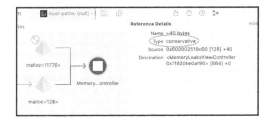

Fixing the leak

Now, it's time to fix the leak. In **InformationWriter.swift**, update the creation of the closure to the following:

```
writeOperation = { [weak writer] info in
    writer?.writeText(info)
}
```

In **WriterProtocol.swift**, add the AnyObject constraint on the protocol.

```
protocol WriterProtocol: AnyObject
```

You can't capture weak references for value types, and because protocols work for value types and reference types, the [weak writer] part won't be valid unless it's clear that WriterProtocol instances are always reference types.

Now that you know how to measure your memory usage, optimize it and make sure that it's cleaned up and nothing stays there longer than it should, it's time to move to the other valuable device resource you need to be aware of: the CPU.

You deserve to grab a drink and have a break before jumping to the next section.

Performance

B-1 Time profiler, the 3rd cell in **The Exhibition** app, is a collection view of random numbers along with how many times that number was generated. It doesn't do anything fancy. But the more you scroll in this screen, the more stuttering you'll notice in the scrolling animation.

You'll use the Time Profiler instrument to help you identify what's causing this effect.

3:38		
‹ Back		
Time Profiler		
7997	2238	8504
2	2	1
5518	8119	8170
1	1	1
391	1526	7696
3	1	2
2551	3809	4002
1	1	1
2893	7527	6201
3	1	1
5119	8031	4438
1	1	1

The number with the large font is the random number and the small digit in the lower-right corner tells you how many times that number was generated.

The more you scroll, the rougher the scrolling gets. It might not be very obvious that your app has a performance issue, especially in the beginning. But it's worth making sure either way.

Profile and record the app using the **Time Profiler** instrument. Open the third screen and spend some time scrolling.

Before looking at Instruments' data, filter what it's showing so you don't get lost in all the stack traces.

At the very bottom of the Instruments window, click **Call Tree** and check **Hide System Libraries**. This will filter the call stack to calls related to your app, keeping out system calls.

The Time Profiler should show something like this:

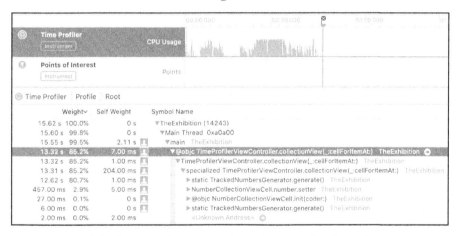

You can see something's wrong here. For about 40 seconds of scrolling, `TimeProfilerViewController.collectionView(_:cellForItemAt:)` is taking over *80 percent* of the execution time. And `TrackedNumbersGenerator.generate()` is contributing to nearly all the CPU time.

Now, expand `TrackedNumbersGenerator.generate()`.

12.62 s	80.7%	1.00 ms		▼static TrackedNumbersGenerator.generate() TheExhibition
12.62 s	80.7%	1.00 ms		▼TrackedNumbersGenerator.generate() TheExhibition
12.61 s	80.7%	12.39 s		▶TrackedNumbersGenerator.saveTrackedNumbers() TheExhibition
7.00 ms	0.0%	0 s		▶specialized static FixedWidthInteger.random(in:) TheExhibition

As you can see, `saveTrackedNumbers()` is the cause of all that CPU time.

Measuring the impact

Now that you've identified where the issue is, how about measuring the impact directly from your app? You'll show it among the other information in the collection.

Go to **MachineTimer.swift** and check the first line after the declaration of the struct:

```
let startTime = mach_absolute_time()
```

This gets the processor time at the moment of initializing an instance of `MachineTimer`.

Now, take a look at `mark()`:

```
func mark() -> Int {
  var baseInfo = mach_timebase_info_data_t(numer: 0, denom: 0)

  guard mach_timebase_info(&baseInfo) == KERN_SUCCESS else {
    return -1
  }

  let finishTime = mach_absolute_time()
  let nano = (finishTime - startTime) *
    UInt64(baseInfo.numer / baseInfo.denom)

  return Int(nano / 1000)
}
```

This method calculates the time spent between the creation of the timer and the moment this method was called. The original value is measured in nanoseconds, so to make it more human-friendly, it returns it in microseconds.

Go to **TimeProfilerViewController.swift** and add the following line at the very beginning of `collectionView(_:cellForItemAt:)`:

```
let timer = MachineTimer()
```

And add this line to just before `return cell`:

```
cell.time = "\(timer.mark())µs"
```

Build and run. Open the third screen and see the new values:

Those numbers seem tiny in the beginning. Each is just a few milliseconds. Doesn't seem like much, right? But those few milliseconds are repeated for each cell, and as you scroll, this spent time repeats over and over again.

Instruments already pointed out that this area accounts for over 80 percent of your whole app's CPU usage. You can definitely improve something here.

Open **TrackedNumbersGenerator.swift**. At the top of the class, change the value of `shouldAlwaysSave` to `false`.

Build and run. Open the third screen and see how the numbers changed:

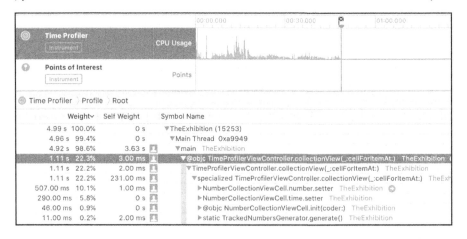

Now, you see a few hundred instead of several thousand. Look at Instruments, too.

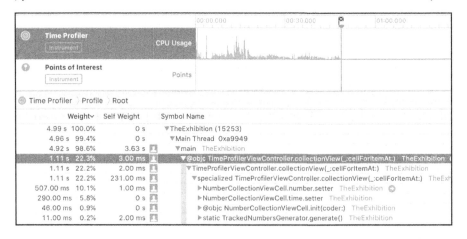

`collectionView(_:cellForItemAt:)` now takes less than **25 percent** of the execution time. This is a major improvement.

You just turned off the saving feature, but your app still needs to save all the generated numbers to the file. You'll solve this in the next step.

Solving the problem

Your app was saving new information to the file every time you generated a new number. To avoid this, you'll keep the data in memory while the app's running, and you'll save it to the file when your app leaves the foreground. In other words, you'll:

- Load data if it was previously saved.

- Manipulate the data as much as you want.

- Write it back to disk when you're done using it.

The user will enjoy your fast and responsive app, and you're safely storing the data when the user is done.

Open **AppDelegate.swift** and add this method at the end of the class:

```
func applicationDidEnterBackground(_ application: UIApplication)
{
  TrackedNumbersGenerator.saveTrackedNumbers()
}
```

Disk access is an important performance factor, and you've just solved one more issue on your app. Way to go!

In the next section, you'll use Core Data to read info from the disk. Although Core Data abstracts that operation for you, a few changes can highly improve how many times you fetch data from the disk.

Core Data

C-1: Faults Optimization lists all the countries in the world and the continent where each resides. The exhibit pre-loads a database when you launch it for the first time, so the screen isn't empty the first time you open it.

The database schema has three tables: `Countries`, `Continents` and `Languages`:

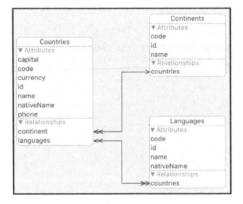

`Countries` has a many-to-one relationship with `Continents`. Each country has only one continent, but each continent can have many countries. It also has a many-to-many relationship with `Languages`.

Profile and record the app with the **Core Data** Instruments template, or add **Faults** to your existing one. Open the last screen.

Before you scroll through the content, Instruments will show you six Core Data Faults. Once you start scrolling, a seventh will appear, and that's it! No matter how long you scroll, up or down, no more faults will appear.

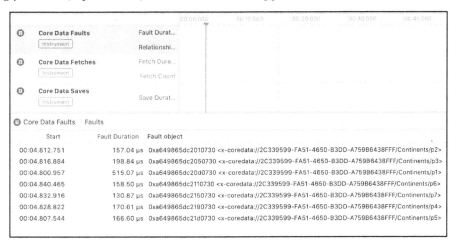

You might ask why they were seven faults? That's easy. It's because there are seven continents, at least in this database.

So what is a **fault**? To explain quickly, it means that the app attempts to read an object from memory, because that's the first location and has a higher I/O speed. However, that object is not present, so it automatically tries to read from another location — the disk, with a slower I/O speed. It then updates the first location with that information in case it was requested again.

Processors already use the concept of fault. When you launch an app, not all of it is loaded in memory to be executed. Instead, the processor loads only the parts that are needed at the time, and it will automatically bring in more parts of your app from the disk as you continue to use it. Memory is much faster than disks, but also much smaller — and, therefore, more expensive.

When you initialize Core Data, it won't load all of its data to memory. It will load only the information you fetch, which in this case is the list of countries.

Although each country has other relationships, those aren't loaded in memory at first. Reading each continent's information for the first time triggers a fault to read that object from the database and store it in memory.

Each fault takes some time to resolve, and Instruments can show you how long each fault took.

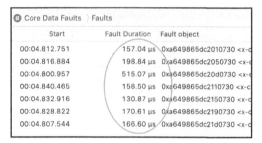

Those faults aren't causing any performance impact, but as you saw in the previous example, even tiny impacts can become a problem when they're repeated too often.

Open **CoreDataOptimizationViewController.swift**, and at the very top, right before the class declaration, you'll find the constant shouldShowLanguages. Set its value to true. This will show the languages people speak in each country.

Profile and record the app. Open the last screen.

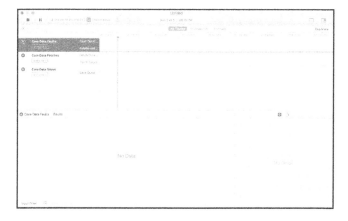

Now you can see there are many more faults going on. When each language object is accessed for the first time, it's read from the database. As you scroll, more faults will appear.

Core Data pre-fetching

Core Data offers a way to pre-fetch objects in relationships within the fetch request. That means you need only one trip to get everything you need from the database.

Open **CoreDataManager.swift**, and in allCountries(), add this line right after the creation of request:

```
request.relationshipKeyPathsForPrefetching =
  ["languages", "continent"]
```

Profile, record the app and open the last screen. You won't see any faults occurring at all on Instruments.

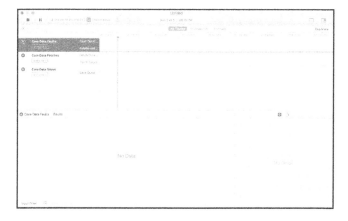

That's because you specified on the fetch request to pre-load the objects in those relationship properties.

If you have a large operation on your database, this could greatly improve your performance.

However, it's also good to know that you can unload objects from memory. This is not deallocation. This is the opposite of loading a fault. You are unloading the object while maintaining its reference. When it's accessed again, a fault will trigger.

Add this method at the end of `CoreDataManager`:

```
func clearMemory() {
  context.refreshAllObjects()
}
```

Then in **CoreDataOptimizationViewController.swift**, add the following at the end of `viewDidLoad()`:

```
DispatchQueue.main.asyncAfter(deadline: .now() + 1) {
  CoreDataManager.shared.clearMemory()
}
```

Profile and record the app. Open the last screen and start scrolling as soon as the screen opens.

Start	Fault Duration	Fault object
00:06.641.811	293.94 μs	0xd996ddbe74021b51 <x-coredata://2
00:04.898.263	206.69 μs	0xd996ddbe740e1b51 <x-coredata://2
00:05.532.994	209.03 μs	0xd996ddbe74121b51 <x-coredata://2
00:07.403.366	240.68 μs	0xd996ddbe74161b51 <x-coredata://2
00:07.347.561	265.60 μs	0xd996ddbe741e1b51 <x-coredata://2
00:06.823.976	276.03 μs	0xd996ddbe742a1b51 <x-coredata://2
00:06.757.934	304.41 μs	0xd996ddbe742e1b51 <x-coredata://2
00:07.498.141	328.21 μs	0xd996ddbe743e1b51 <x-coredata://2
00:07.564.023	231.21 μs	0xd996ddbe74421b51 <x-coredata://2
00:07.744.923	489.89 μs	0xd996ddbe74461b51 <x-coredata://2

Notice that faults only started to appear exactly one second from the fetch request. `clearMemory()` returned all pre-fetched objects to their original state as faults.

So far, you've learned about optimizing your app for the user, making it run faster and smoother. So far, 99% of the optimizations you learned about benefit the user. What about optimizing the app for yourself, the developer? You'll cover that next.

Build times

In this section, you'll learn about optimizing the code for yourself! Yes, that's right. You can reduce the time you spend waiting for your app to build.

You might feel that the time you spend waiting for a build to be ready is barely noticeable. That's often true, because most of the time, you're doing incremental builds. Xcode is only building the parts that you've modified since the last time you built the app. But do a clean build and you'll notice that takes much longer.

If you work in a big team, and you have a build server with a CI/CD pipeline with unit tests and a lot of fancy, automated stuff, you know a thing or two about waiting for a build to complete.

Of course, the more your project grows, the longer it takes to build. However, this isn't the only factor affecting build times.

Some parts of your code, such as long equations or lots of chained commands, might require a little extra effort for the compiler to compile as they might be long statements or many things that need to be resolved or inferred before the compiler knows what are you talking about similar to this sentence you are just reading now that feels long and should be broken down into smaller sentences to be easier to understand!

See what I did there? That long sentence probably took you a little longer to understand. If I had split it into a few smaller sentences, it would have been easier to read.

In this sample project, you'll cover how to measure the build times of your code.

The **SlowBuilder** project demonstrates a few different slow building methods. The project doesn't do anything and you won't need to run it.

Open the project and build it. Nothing special happens. Open the Report Navigator (**Cmd+9**), and click on the first entry in the list (that's the latest build), then choose **All Messages** if it's not already chosen. Expand the information under Compile Swift source files (x86_64) and under Compile SlowMath.swift (x86_64).

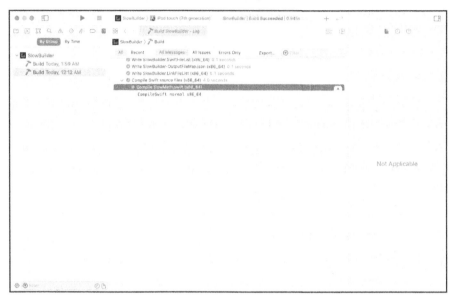

Nothing helpful here. Now, in your target's **Build Settings**, search for **Other Swift Flags** and add this flag for the **Debug**:

```
-Xfrontend -debug-time-function-bodies
```

Build the project again and look at the same part in the build log.

```
771.92ms
    instance method calculatePoint()
27.72ms
    instance method calculateEquation()
0.01ms
    deinitializer deinit
0.01ms
    initializer init()
```

It shows you the time it took to build each method in that file. The rest of the files will also have the same new information. Add this flag, too:

```
-Xfrontend -debug-time-expression-type-checking
```

Then, build and look at the same part of the build log.

Even more information is written in the log. It now shows the time it took to build each expression along with the time for each method. This is very informative but not very user-friendly.

In Xcode, you can specify a threshold to show a warning if an expression or a function took too long to build.

Add those two flags with the previous two:

```
-Xfrontend -warn-long-expression-type-checking=25
-Xfrontend -warn-long-function-bodies=25
```

The first will display a warning when an **expression** exceeds the threshold. The second will show a warning when a **function** or a **method** took too long. The threshold for each is set for 25 milliseconds.

> **Note**: 25 milliseconds is a small number. However, that's what this chapter uses. In your own projects, feel free to specify the threshold you think suffices to help you identify spikes.

Clean the build folder, then build the project again. Notice the presence of a few new warnings.

Chaining & build times

Take those warnings on one by one. Open **SlowArray.swift**. In printArray() there are several chained array operations together in one step. These operations can be broken down into multiple steps:

```swift
func printArray() {
  var doubleArray = Array(repeating: 1.123, count: 100)
  doubleArray = doubleArray.map { $0 * Double.random(in: 0 ..<
1000) }
  var intArray = Array(repeating: 1, count: 100)
  intArray = intArray.map { $0 * Int.random(in: 0 ..< 1000) }
  let doubleMultiply = zip(doubleArray, intArray)
    .map { $0 * Double($1) }
  let sum = doubleMultiply.sorted()
    .map { $0 * 123 }
    .reduce(0, +)
  print(doubleMultiply)
  print(sum)
}
```

Open **SlowMath.swift**. In calculatePoint(), a new CGPoint is constructed, but each parameter looks to be a long and confusing equation. And calculateEquation() is not less confusing at all!

```swift
func calculatePoint() -> CGPoint {
  CGPoint(
    x: (UIApplication.shared.windows.first?.frame.size.width ??
300 / 3)
      + CGFloat.random(in: 0...1000) / CGFloat(100),
    y: (UIApplication.shared.windows.first?.frame.size.height ??
300 / 3)
      + CGFloat.random(in: 0...1000) / CGFloat(100)
  )
}

func calculateEquation() -> Double {
  (Bool.random() ?
    (pow(pow(Double.random(in: 100...1000), 2.0), 6.0) / 5.5
      + Double.random(in: 100...1000)) * 25 / 3
    + Double.random(in: 100...1000)
    :
    (pow(pow(Double.random(in: 1...100), 2.0), 6.0) / 5.5
      + Double.random(in: 1...100)) * 25 / 3 + Double.random(in:
1...100))
    +
  Double(UIApplication.shared.windows.first?.frame.size.width ??
      CGFloat(400) / 2 * 500 * CGFloat.random(in: 100...1000))
}
```

What seems to be common between all those slow building methods and expressions is chaining operations together.

Look at **SuspiciousChain.swift** and check `getSuspiciousStruct()`:

```
static func getSuspiciousStruct() -> Self {
  SuspiciousStruct()
    .setting(\.name) { "SomeName" }
    .setting(\.phone) { "0123456789" }
    .setting(\.email) { "email@somewhere.com" }
    .setting(\.country) { "Earth-Country" }
    .setting(\.city) { "Earth-Country-City" }
    .setting(\.address) { "A place on earth, beside that shop" }
    .setting(\.job) { "Super-Duper iOS Developer" }
}
```

Xcode doesn't seem to be complaining at all about how long this method took to build. If you check the build log to make sure, you'll find it took a very tiny amount of time. For me, it took half a millisecond. So the theory that chaining expressions causes long build times is not 100% accurate.

The factor most affecting the build time here is the chaining of different operations that have different precedence and associativity. It probably took you awhile to read it yourself.

In `getSuspiciousStruct()`, the chain is a clear order of methods. Despite the many methods, you didn't have any problem reading the chain, unlike the other methods.

Breaking down expressions with large build times into smaller ones is an improvement. Sometimes you can save actual seconds, while in other instances the time saved may not be noticeable. But it is worth measuring occasionally, especially if you're using a build server and have a large team.

The possible causes of a build-time spike are many, and the significance of this impact will vary from one Xcode version to another. However, the way to identify and measure the time taken for your code to compile is the same.

Now, you've learned how to use existing instruments to measure defined meters on your app. In the next section, you'll see how you can use a new instrument to measure something new — and even measure anything you want, at your discretion.

Timelane

Tracking the progress of asynchronous code is usually not a trivial feat. To help with that, Marin Todorov developed a fantastic instrument called **Timelane**. You can download it from: http://timelane.tools.

Timelane is a plugin that you install on Instruments, and it works like the other templates you already have.

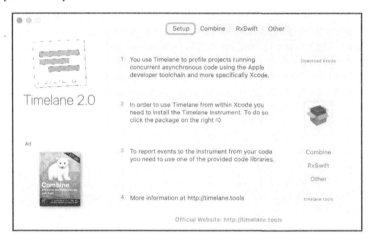

In this section, you'll learn how to use Timelane to help you measure and track asynchronous code. The **FarOutPhotos** project has a bigger gallery of NASA pictures. You use the image library, **Nuke**, to download the images asynchronously.

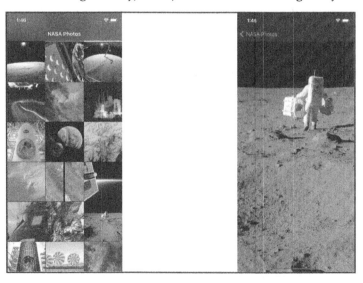

The project uses the standard Nuke library to download the gallery images. When you tap one of them to open the details, the Combine extension for the library opens the image in full size. The full-sized image displays over two steps. First, the extension downloads the resized image from the gallery. Then, it shows the full-sized image right after.

You'll use Timelane to track when each image was requested, how long it took to be retrieved, if it was completed or canceled and its download progress.

Putting Timelane to work

Build and run the project and look at the console log in Xcode. It shows a lot of **started** logs, a lot more **progress** and **completed** — but it's very hard to track them. Timelane does that magic for you.

```
progress for clouds_amo_2018238_lrg.jpg: 94
progress for clouds_amo_2018238_lrg.jpg: 94
progress for clouds_amo_2018238_lrg.jpg: 95
progress for clouds_amo_2018238_lrg.jpg: 95
progress for clouds_amo_2018238_lrg.jpg: 95
progress for clouds_amo_2018238_lrg.jpg: 95
progress for clouds_amo_2018238_lrg.jpg: 96
progress for clouds_amo_2018238_lrg.jpg: 96
progress for clouds_amo_2018238_lrg.jpg: 96
progress for clouds_amo_2018238_lrg.jpg: 96
progress for clouds_amo_2018238_lrg.jpg: 96
progress for clouds_amo_2018238_lrg.jpg: 97
progress for clouds_amo_2018238_lrg.jpg: 97
progress for clouds_amo_2018238_lrg.jpg: 97
progress for clouds_amo_2018238_lrg.jpg: 97
progress for clouds_amo_2018238_lrg.jpg: 98
progress for clouds_amo_2018238_lrg.jpg: 98
progress for clouds_amo_2018238_lrg.jpg: 98
progress for clouds_amo_2018238_lrg.jpg: 98
progress for clouds_amo_2018238_lrg.jpg: 99
progress for clouds_amo_2018238_lrg.jpg: 99
progress for clouds_amo_2018238_lrg.jpg: 99
progress for clouds_amo_2018238_lrg.jpg: 99
progress for clouds_amo_2018238_lrg.jpg: 100
completed clouds_amo_2018238_lrg.jpg
completed atmosphere_geo5_2018235_eq.jpg

All Output ≎
```

To add **Timelane**'s Swift package, open the menu **File ▸ Swift Packages ▸ Add Package Dependency**.

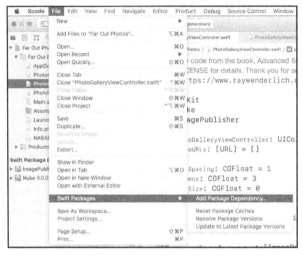

Add the URL **"https://github.com/icanzilb/TimelaneCombine"** then click next. When prompted for the rules choose **Version**, from the drop-down choose **Exact** and write **2.0.0** in the version number text field.

> **Note**: At the time of writing this chapter Timelane 2.0.0 was the latest version.

This will download two packages: **TimeLaneCombine** and **TimeLaneCore**. Open **PhotoGalleryViewController.swift** and import TimelaneCore with the other imports:

```
import TimelaneCore
```

Right after the declaration of the class, define a new subscription lane labeled **Gallery** to log the events on:

```
var galleryLane = Timelane.Subscription(name: "Gallery")
```

At the very end of the file, you'll find `ImagePipelineObserving.pipeline(_:imageTask:didReceiveEvent:)`. It's the delegate method that's responsible for all the logs you see on the console.

Add those three lines in their correct locations in the `switch` statement:

```
// for .started
galleryLane.begin()

// for .cancelled
galleryLane.end(state: .cancelled)

// for .completed
galleryLane.end(state: .completed)
```

Profile and record the app. Use the `Timelane` template in Instruments.

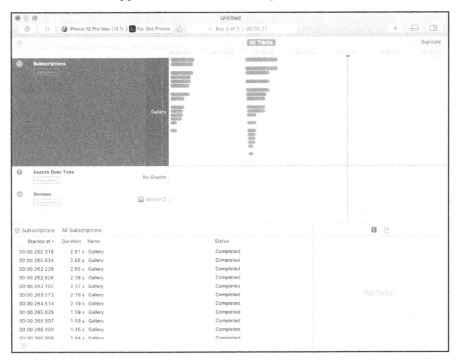

This instrument now shows you **visually** the duration of each `begin()` and `end(:)`. However, it's not clear from this graph which line represents which image.

There's also a slight problem with the code you added. You only defined one lane named **Gallery**, and all the events are logged onto this lane. Because your code is asynchronous, the order of begin() doesn't need to call the same as end(:). For that, you need to have a lane for each request.

Multiple lanes

Replace the lane you defined at the beginning of the class with a dictionary of lanes:

```
var galleryLanes: [ImageTask: Timelane.Subscription] = [:]
```

Then update the implementation of
ImagePipelineObserving.pipeline(_:imageTask:didReceiveEvent:) to the following:

```
let imageName =
imageTask.request.urlRequest.url?.lastPathComponent ?? ""

switch event {
case .started:
  let lane = Timelane.Subscription(name: "Request " + imageName)
  lane.begin()
  galleryLanes[imageTask] = lane
  print("started " + imageName)
case .cancelled:
  let lane = galleryLanes[imageTask]
  lane?.end(state: .cancelled)
  galleryLanes[imageTask] = nil
  print("canceled " + imageName)
case .completed(result: _):
  let lane = galleryLanes[imageTask]
  lane?.end(state: .completed)
  galleryLanes[imageTask] = nil
  print("completed " + imageName)
case .progressUpdated(
      completedUnitCount: let completed,
      totalUnitCount: let total
):
  let lane = galleryLanes[imageTask]
  let percent = completed * 100 / total
  lane?.event(value: .value("progress: \(percent)"))
  print("progress for \(imageName): \(percent)")
default:
  print("default")
}
```

Uninstall the app from the simulator to remove any cached images. Profile, record the app and look at Instruments again.

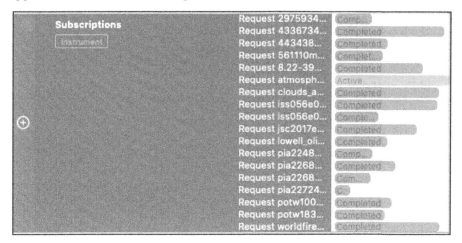

Also, under the subscriptions group, there's another group for the events. You'll find all the progress events you triggered are grouped for each subscription. In the graphical view, select the **Events over time** graph, then in the bottom select **All Events by Subscription**.

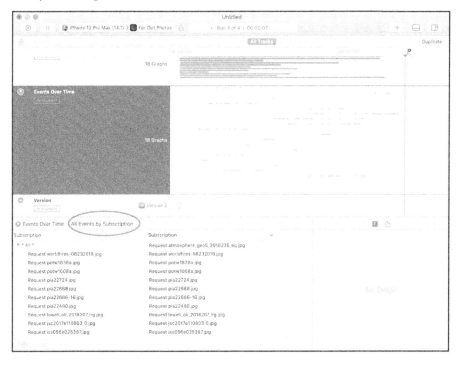

When you select one of the events in the list, the time marker at the top moves to the location of that event to show you the moment that this happened.

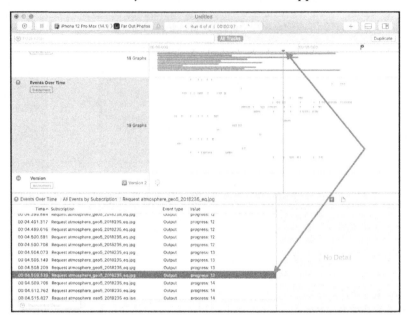

Profile and record the app again. This time, scroll quickly up and down.

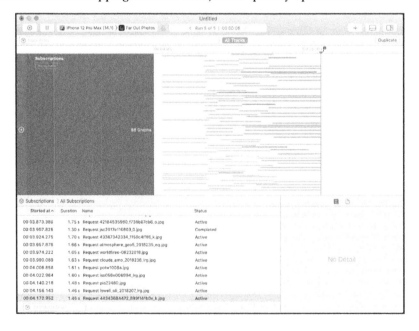

Blue bars represent completed operations, green represents operations that are still in progress and orange represents canceled operations.

When you scroll quickly, Nuke automatically optimizes requests. When a request for an image on a cell isn't completed and another one is triggered for that same cell, Nuke cancels the first one in favor of the latter — hence the cancel event. A picture is worth a thousand words, isn't it?

TimelaneCombine

Open **PhotoViewController.swift** and import `TimelaneCombine`:

```
import TimelaneCombine
```

For Combine usage, it is simpler. Go to `loadImage(url:)` and change the declaration of `resizedImagePublisher` & `originalImagePublisher` variables to the following:

```
let resizedImagePublisher =
  ImagePipeline.shared.imagePublisher(with: resizedImageRequest)
  .lane("Resized Image")
let originalImagePublisher =
  ImagePipeline.shared.imagePublisher(with: url)
  .lane("Full Image")
```

Profile and record the app. Select any of the images in the gallery and notice the addition of two new lanes in the subscriptions group.

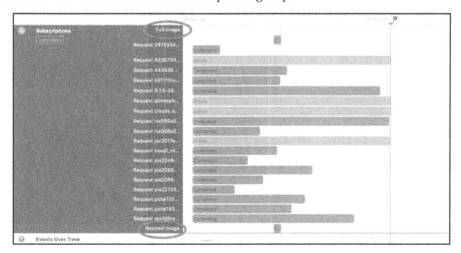

The begin and end calls were automatically executed for the Combine subscriber, and you didn't need to track anything.

Showing information visually is much easier than searching for it in a console log. You can see how crowded operations were and when they all ended with a glance.

Visual representation can help you do much more than this. You can quickly spot anything wrong with the order of your operations, or if something was supposed to finish but gave an error instead.

To learn more about Timelane, visit http://timelane.tools. The more you learn about it, the better you will use it — especially with Combine and RxSwift.

Signpost

Now that you saw a custom instrument, explore what made it possible and how the events are **logged** from your app to instruments.

Two key points are used on the app side: OSLog & os_signpost.

The first uses the system's log to write any logs directly from your app. The second is a type of log entry to write down.

Open the project **FarOutPhotos-Signposts**. It's identical to **FarOutPhotos** but with a clean start just before you integrated Timelane.

Go to **PhotoGalleryViewController.swift**, and add this to the imports:

```
import os.signpost
```

Then, right after the class declaration, add this line:

```
let log = OSLog(
  subsystem: "com.raywenderlich.Far-Out-Photos",
  category: "PhotoGallery")
```

This created an instance of a new log, with the AppID for its subsystem, and the category PhotoGallery. The category can be anything, but it's always helpful to have relevant names.

Tracking image downloads

Similar to what you did with Timelane earlier, you want to track the image downloads. Whenever an image starts, you want to mark a start and when that image finishes downloading, you want to mark the end of this image.

In `pipeline(_:imageTask:didReceiveEvent:)`, add this line in the `.started` case:

```
os_signpost(.begin, log: log, name: "ImageDownload")
```

And this line in the `.completed` case:

```
os_signpost(.end, log: log, name: "ImageDownload")
```

Profile the project, create a new **Blank** Instruments project and add the **os_signpost** instrument from the library.

Record the project and right away you'll see entries. You don't want all of them, so expand the instrument until you find the row/lane called **com.raywenderlich.Far-Out-Photos**. Inside, you'll find **PhotoGallery**. Those were the names you used to define the log object. You'll also see several ImageDownload intervals.

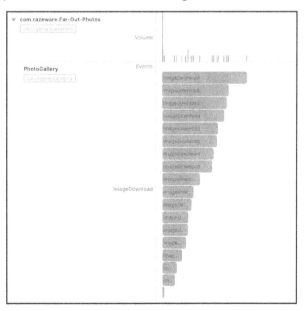

Each `os_signpost` end call pairs with a begin call that has the same value in the name parameter. But because they all have the same name, Instruments seems to have just paired them in reverse order: The last one that began is the first to end. Also, this is not the order of the images loaded on the screen.

You could think that this is easy: Why not just put the image name as that string?

> ⊗   Cannot convert value of type 'String' to expected argument type 'StaticString'

But when you try that, Xcode complains. The name parameter must be a static string. The way to disambiguate between different begin and end signposts is by using OSSignpostID.

Providing this ID along with the name in the begin and end calls means that matching is done when a begin and an end both have the same name and the same SignPostID.

In pipeline(_:imageTask:didReceiveEvent:), add the line at the top of the function:

```
let signpostID = OSSignpostID(log: log, object: imageTask)
```

This created an OSSignpostID object with the image task. This makes sure that you have the same ID for the same image task.

Update the two os_signpost calls to include the new ID:

```
os_signpost(.begin, log: log, name: "ImageDownload", signpostID:
signpostID)
.

.

.
os_signpost(.end, log: log, name: "ImageDownload", signpostID:
signpostID)
```

Remove the app from the simulator to delete the cached images, then profile and record.

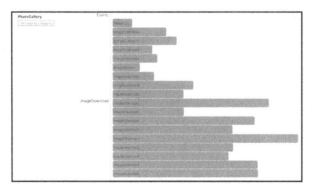

It doesn't look like an upside-down pyramid anymore, so this solved the matching problem. But it doesn't show much information on which image has which bar.

Displaying more information

Each signpost can have metadata attached to it. For now, it's enough to include the name of the image in the begin signpost. Update the begin call to the following:

```
os_signpost(
  .begin,
  log: log,
  name: "ImageDownload",
  signpostID: signpostID,
  "%{public}s",
  imageName)
```

The parameters right after the signpost ID are a format string followed by the arguments needed. The format string follows the same formatting rules used by the Logging. Here, you only want to log the image name as a public string.

Delete the app, then profile and record.

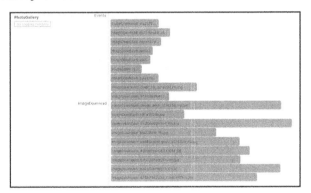

Now, the bars are much more informative. The next part is to track if the image was completed or canceled. For that, you'll add different metadata on their signposts. The signpost you already have for the completed case should have "completed" as its metadata, and the canceled one to have "canceled".

Update the end call for the completed case as follows:

```
os_signpost(
  .end,
  log: log,
  name: "ImageDownload",
  signpostID: signpostID,
  "completed")
```

And add a new end call in case of a cancelation:

```
os_signpost(.end,
log: log,
name: "ImageDownload",
signpostID: signpostID,
"canceled")
```

Delete the app again, then profile and record. Scroll up and down a couple times as soon as the app starts on the simulator.

The information on the bars might not be very clear, especially for the canceled items, because the bar will be rather narrow — which is a good thing. Look at the table below the graph.

You'll see signposts that began, how many times, total duration, min and average duration — some very useful statistics. Most importantly, they will also show you the metadata you received with the end signposts. The screenshot shows two canceled and one completed for this image. That's a lot of useful info right there!

Using signposts as events

Signposts can also be an event — they don't need to always represent the beginning and the end of an operation. You can have a .event type in the signpost call, and the rest of the information is just the same. However, no matches occur because this event is a standalone signpost. Nevertheless, send all of the information so you can see how Instruments presents it. Add a new signpost call in .progressUpdated, right after the percentage calculation:

```
os_signpost(.event, log: log, name: "ImageProgress", signpostID:
signpostID, "%{public}s progress: percentd", imageName, percent)
```

Delete the app, then profile and record.

Your events are present in the graph, but it might be difficult to identify them. It's better to see them from the table below in the **List: Events** section.

This only scratches the surface of what you can do with `os_signpost`. You can provide metadata that Instruments can understand so it automatically creates useful statistics for you.

You can create custom instruments that give you more control over the UI and how the information is provided.

The **Instruments Developer Help** is an awesome place to find more about what you can do with Instruments. The more you understand the tool and what it has to offer, the more you'll find yourself already knowing solutions to challenges you come across.

Key points

In this chapter, you learned a lot about some of the tools available to understand and measure what's happening inside your app. You learned how to:

- Understand and observe how your app allocates memory size.

- Discovered allocated objects in the memory graph and Instruments.

- Measure the performance of your code and the time it takes to execute it.

- Understand how faults work in Core Data, how to avoid them and how to reduce the memory usage when you're done using fault objects.

- Measure the compile time of your expressions and methods.

- Use the fantastic measurement instrument, **Timelane**, which shows the progress of your asynchronous code.

- Send custom events to instruments using `os_signpost`.

Chapter 14: API Design Tips & Tricks

By Shai Mishali

Welcome to the last chapter of the book!

You've spent most of your time in this book diving into specific topics, learning how they work, writing code to sharpen your instincts around them and working through real-life examples.

Although using Swift and all its incredible capabilities is a wonderful skill to have, it doesn't help much without actually shipping code with it. More often than not, though, you'll find yourself creating code that's used not *only* by you but also by your team, or even other teams if you're creating an open-source project.

In those cases, just knowing Swift as a language isn't enough, and neither is just practicing a specific language feature. That's why this chapter is going to be a bit different.

In this chapter, you'll explore a few different topics. Each of these isn't directly related to the previous one, but they all tie into enhancing your skillset and intuition for designing great APIs. You may freely explore each of these individual topics based on your interest:

- What developers consider a *good* API.

- How to separate and encapsulate your implementation details from your public API using access levels.

- Powerful language features with examples you can leverage for your APIs, including examples from Swift itself: Literals, Dynamic Member Lookup, Dynamic Callable, Property Wrappers and others.

- Documenting your APIs using Swift's powerful markup syntax.

- Finally, a few important concepts and ideas related to the process of shipping your API to the world.

This chapter will also be less code-heavy than previous ones and won't require you to copy-paste code or run any project. It's more of a philosophical and exploratory chapter that doesn't cover one specific topic. You're welcome to stop at any point to experiment with a specific idea in Xcode. We're opening a discussion together, me and you, to hopefully help inspire you with some fresh new ideas and ways of thinking about API design.

> **Note**: API design is a highly opinionated topic. As such, you should take everything in this chapter with a grain of salt and mainly as an inspiration rather than a single truth. Take the portions that make sense for your use case and taste, and discard the ones that don't.

What do developers want?

Wow, that's a tough question. I wish I knew, really; it might've helped bring this book even further! And yet, some things are obvious and universal for developers.

The first time a developer interacts with a new piece of code, they have certain hopes and expectations. It doesn't matter if that code is your app and the person is a new developer on your team, or if it's an open-source library you shared with the community and the person is a new consumer of it.

In essence, developers look for some characteristics that make an API "feel good":

- **It should be obvious**: This means using the API *"makes sense"* for a developer and that your API's design aligns with their expectations. For example, a `Zip` class might have an expected method called `unzip` or `extract` rather than `pullContentsTo(path:)`, which is not common or obvious.

- **It should be well-documented**: People often say Swift is a self-documenting language and, as such, good APIs don't need documentation. I personally disagree with that statement. Even though Swift is a very expressive language, documenting the public portions of your API is language-agnostic and crucial to help self-exploration, reduce ambiguity and make sure your intention is clear to the consumer. It would be good for internal APIs to also be documented well, but public-facing documentation is the bare minimum.

- **Reduces mental load**: This ties to being obvious but is a bit broader and more open to interpretation. Some things that fall into this category include trying to use the minimum obvious naming for APIs, using prior art if a convention exists in the domain you're developing for (you might use `View` instead of `Screen` if it makes sense in that domain, for example) and using abstractions that are simple to the consumer. As the Swift API guidelines sharply note: "Don't surprise an expert. Don't confuse a beginner."

- **Being modern**: This point touches a wide range of topics. Using proper language-specific conventions, leveraging the correct language features a consumer would expect to see and inspiring proper usage and creativity from the consumer are all small parts of this point.

What is the core of your API?

When the raywenderlich.com team works on a tutorial or a book, it always asks: "What is the most important 80 percent of this topic?"

When exposing some API or functionality to the outside world, you should ask yourself the same question, in a way: "What is the core functionality of this framework or API?"

This starting point might seem obvious, but it's *so* crucial because it helps dictate where you'll spend most of your effort forging an easy-to-use and explorable API.

It's the exact point when you start differentiating your public-facing API from your implementation details that aren't quite relevant to the majority of your consumers.

A great way to enforce this separation is by using **access levels**.

Using access levels properly

Access levels define which entities of your code are exposed and to which scopes they're exposed. Swift specifically provides a relatively fine-grained set of *five* access levels (from most permissive to most restrictive): open, public, internal, fileprivate and private.

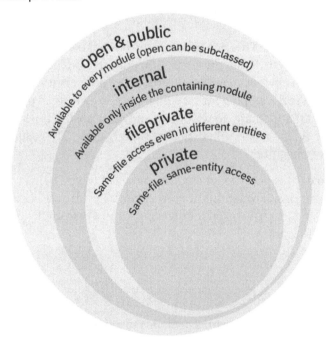

If you've never written code meant to be consumed outside your app, you might not understand the need for such a level of control over your code and its entities. But it's crucial to understanding what each level means and when to use it.

Internal by default

Every piece of code that doesn't have an explicit access level set is internal by default. This means other files in *the same* module can access it, but files *outside* of the module can't.

If `Module2` defines `func getThings()`, a different `Module1` won't be able to access `getThings()`, unless it's annotated with `public`.

```
// In Module2
func getThings() {

}

// In Module1
Module2.getThings()
// Error: Module 'Module2' has no member named 'getThings'
```

This is great for most apps. It means every piece of code you write is accessible for every part of your app because it's usually a single module. But what if you want to split your app into several modules or share code as a public library/framework?

The public world

In cases where `internal` doesn't suffice, you'll want to use either `open` or `public`. These levels mean the same thing in essence: This entity is available to every piece of code inside *or outside* the module it was defined in.

This means you might want to make your `UserService` public to let anyone consume it but keep `NetworkService` internal because only your module cares about it.

```
// In Module1
public class AmazingClass {
  public init() { }
}

open class WonderfulClass {
  public init() { }
}

// In Module2
AmazingClass() // OK
WonderfulClass() // OK
```

`open` lifts an additional limitation and allows overriding or subclassing a class marked with that access level. This makes open relevant only for classes and not other types, where `public` would have the same effect.

```
class AmazingSubclass: AmazingClass { } // Error: Cannot inherit
from non-open class 'AmazingClass' outside of its defining
module

class WonderfulSubclass: WonderfulClass { } // OK
```

Keeping it private

With `public` and `open` representing the more permissive side of the possible access levels, it's also critical to properly limit access to the private portions of your code. These pieces of code are often implementation details and don't concern consumers of your public interface or even your internal interfaces.

Swift offers two private access levels:

- `private` makes an entity available only to the file it was defined in, and in the specific scope it was defined in.

- In contrast, `fileprivate` makes an entity available only to the file it was defined in but also in different object scopes.

For example, imagine an `Encrypter` type that can encrypt various types:

```
struct Encrypter<Encrypted> {
  let base: Encrypted
}
```

Then, imagine you have a `Person` struct with a `private` property called `password`:

```
struct Person {
  let id: UUID
  let name: String
  private let password: String
}
```

If you extend `Encrypter` in the same file to provide encryption for `Person`, like so:

```
extension Encrypter where Encrypted == Person {
  func encrypt() -> String {
    sha256(base.password)
  }
}
```

You'll get an error because `password` is only accessible in `Person`'s scope within the file:

'password' is inaccessible due to 'private' protection level.

If you change `private` to `fileprivate`, the code will work, extending `password`'s access scope to other types in the same file.

Finally...

No, this isn't the end of the chapter, but *final* has a different meaning you should know. I mentioned that `public` means an entity is public outside of a module but can't be overridden and subclassed.

Another useful keyword is `final`, which essentially means the same thing but also applies to the module scope. This means a `final` class can't be overridden or subclassed, inside or outside of the module.

This is more useful in an app's scope or a tightly-held module because it limits what can be done with that class. It also helps the compiler perform optimizations because it can know *for a fact* that none of the methods can be overridden and the class will remain unchanged:

```
final public class Network {
  // Code here...
}

class SpecializedNetwork: Network { } // Error: Inheritance from
a final class 'Network'
```

Some of this information might be harder to figure out in a large class or code base. Luckily, Xcode can help out a bit with generated interface previews.

Exploring your interface

A great feature built into Xcode is the ability to view the generated interface of source files. You used this a bit earlier in this book, in the "Objective-C Interoperability" chapter, but you can use the same capability for Swift files, too.

If you put the following code in a Swift file:

```
import Foundation

public struct Student {
  public let id: UUID
  public let name: String
  public let grade: Int
  let previousTests: [Test]

  public func sendMessage(_ message: String) throws -> Bool {
    // Implementation
  }
```

```
    private func expel() throws -> Bool {
      // Implementation
    }
  }
}

struct Test {
  let id: UUID
  let name: String
  let topic: String
}
```

And then go to the **Related Items** icon and pick the generated interface for your Swift file:

You'll see the full interface generated from your Swift source:

```
public struct Student {
  public let id: UUID
  public let name: String
```

```
    public let grade: Int
    internal let previousTests: [Test]
    public func sendMessage(_ message: String) throws -> Bool
  }

  internal struct Test {
    internal let id: UUID
    internal let name: String
    internal let topic: String
  }
```

Notice how the private methods aren't part of the interface and all the implicitly internal definitions show `internal` explicitly.

This a great way to get an "eagle's eye" view of your codebase, stripping out the implementation details and anything in the private scope.

Now that you have a good grasp of the higher-level ideas of good API design and encapsulation, you'll also want to know how to leverage specific Swift language features to enrich your API.

Language features

This section will focus on some interesting language features you can leverage to improve your API surface, and provides short examples of how API designers and developers commonly use them.

Although using the latest and greatest language features isn't a hard requirement for API design, it's extremely valuable to know the tools at your disposal to forge the most natural and modern-feeling API possible for your consumers. You'll learn more about this throughout this section.

Literals

Literals are a great abstraction to let consumers initialize your types using typed literals, such as `String`, `Bool`, `Array` and many others.

A great example of this is a `Path` type, using `ExpressibleByStringLiteral`:

```
public struct Path: ExpressibleByStringLiteral {
  private let path: String

  public init(stringLiteral value: StringLiteralType) {
    self.path = value
```

```
  }

  public func relativePath(to path: Path) -> Path {
    // Implementation ...
  }
}
```

You can then initialize it by simply using a string literal:

```
// Option 1
Path("/Users/freak4pc/Work/")

// Option 2
let path: Path = "/Users/freak4pc/Work/"
```

The great power of this feature is that it creates a relatively smooth and seamless developer experience while still providing type safety and additional features related to the specific initialized type. In Path's case, it can expose a relativePath(to:) method that isn't relevant for any String but is interesting for Paths.

You can do the same with other expressible types, such as Arrays:

```
public struct AlphabeticArray<Element: Comparable>: Collection,
ExpressibleByArrayLiteral {
  // Additional collection boilerplate here
  let values: [Element]

  public init(arrayLiteral elements: Element...) {
    self.values = elements.sorted(by: <)
  }
}

public func presentContacts(_ contacts: AlphabeticArray<String>)
{
  print(contacts)
}

presentContacts(["Shai", "Elia", "Ethan"]) // Prints Elia,
Ethan, Shai
```

This example is a bit contrived, as you could achieve the same effect by simply using sorted(by: <) internally. But it does provide a type-safe guarantee that you can always expect values in that array to be sorted alphabetically, which improves clarity in the API surface.

Another possible use case for literals is for a headers object in a networking library:

```
public struct Headers {
  private let headers: [String: String]
```

```
  // Many other pieces of headers-specific functionality
}

extension Headers: ExpressibleByDictionaryLiteral {
  public init(dictionaryLiteral elements: (Header, String)...) {
    self.headers = Dictionary(uniqueKeysWithValues: elements.map
{ ($0.rawValue, $1) })
  }

  public enum Header: String {
    case accept = "Accept"
    case contentType = "Content-Type"
    case authorization = "Authorization"
    case language = "Accept-Language"
    // Additional headers
  }
}
```

This implementation lets you initialize a new Headers object from a dictionary with strictly typed keys, like so:

```
class HTTPRequest {
  func addingHeaders(_ headers: Headers) -> Self {
    // Implementation ...
  }
}

let request = HTTPRequest(...)
  .addingHeaders([.accept: "text/html",
                  .authorization: "Basic freak4pc:b4n4n4ph0n3"])
```

You can take this a step further and add ExpressibleByArrayLiteral conformance *in addition* to the dictionary literal conformance and count on enums with associated values:

```
extension Headers: ExpressibleByArrayLiteral {
  public init(arrayLiteral elements: TypedHeader...) {
    self.headers = Dictionary(uniqueKeysWithValues:
      elements.map(\.value))
  }

  public enum TypedHeader {
    case accept(AcceptType)
    case jwtAuthorization(Token)
    case basicAuthorization(user: String, password: String)

    var value: (String, String) {
      switch self {
      case .accept(let type):
        return ("Accept", type)
```

```
      case .jwtAuthorization(let token):
        return ("Authorization", "Bearer \(token)")
      case let .basicAuthorization(user, password):
        return ("Authorization", "Basic \(user):\(password)")
      }
    }
  }
}
```

This lets you use the following code:

```
let request = HTTPRequest(...)
  .addingHeaders([.jwtAuthorization("AmazingToken"),
            .basicAuthorization(user: "freak4pc",
                                password: "b4n4n4ph0n3"),
            .accept("text/html")])
```

Because these both are literals, you can also instantiate them simply by providing an explicit type when using an array or dictionary:

```
let headersFromDict: Headers = [
  .accept: "text/html",
  .authorization: "Basic freak4pc:b4n4n4ph0n3"
]

let headersFromArray: Headers = [
  .jwtAuthorization("AmazingToken"),
  .basicAuthorization(user: "freak4pc",
                      password: "b4n4n4ph0n3"),
  .accept("text/html")
]
```

Both of these are actual `Headers` objects, not a `Dictionary` or `Array`.

The options around literals are quite endless, but they're all about making your API surface pleasant and seamless to use while still providing a specialized experience for the typed use case in question.

Take your time to experiment with the full list of possible literal conformances on Apple's documentation.

Dynamic member lookup

Dynamic member lookup was initially shipped in Swift 4.2 (SE-0195) and meant to provide a somewhat type-safe way to access arbitrary string keys for a type. This was relatively helpful to bridge dynamic languages, such as Python, or create proxy APIs. Unfortunately, it lacked *real* type-safety when it came to abstracting existing Swift code as well as providing actual runtime safety.

Luckily, Swift 5.1 introduced **key path member lookup** (SE-0252), which gives you the same dynamic handling capabilities but for a key path to an object. This is one of the most underrated and useful language features brought into Swift in recent years, and it unlocks a wide range of opportunities to improve your APIs.

Wrapping types naturally

It's quite common to create types that would wrap existing types. An example of this might be trying to create your own `SearchBar` view that wraps a regular `UITextField`:

```
class SearchBar: UIControl {
  private let textField: UITextField
}
```

You might notice there's a 1-to-1 relationship between a search bar and a text field. For example, you might want `SearchBar.isEnabled` to disable the text field itself, or `SearchBar.keyboardType` to change the underlying `textField`.

You could consider doing this manually:

```
extension SearchBar {
  var isEnabled: Bool {
    get { textField.isEnabled }
    set { textField.isEnabled = newValue }
  }

  var keyboardType: UIKeyboardType {
    get { textField.keyboardType }
    set { textField.keyboardType = newValue }
  }

  // About 20 more of these ...
}
```

But this is quite tedious, and it can also hinder maintainability and require a lot of manual work. What if `UITextField` gets some new properties in the future?

Luckily, there's a way to get rid of all this boilerplate:

```
@dynamicMemberLookup
class SearchBar: UIControl {
  private var textField: UITextField

  subscript<T>(
    dynamicMember keyPath: WritableKeyPath<UITextField, T>
  ) -> T {
    get { textField[keyPath: keyPath] }
    set { textField[keyPath: keyPath] = newValue }
  }
}
```

Once you add the @dynamicMemberLookup annotation to SearchBar, Swift will look for both the string-based and key path-based subscripts.

In this case, a generic writable key path from UITextField to *any* of its properties means you can access any property of UITextField directly from SearchBar without more boilerplate code. For example:

```
let searchBar = SearchBar(...)
searchBar.isEnabled = true
searchBar.returnKeyType = .go
searchBar.keyboardType = .emailAddress
// etc, etc...
```

Enriching key paths

Exposing or mirroring the key paths of a linked object is extremely useful, but you can return *anything you want* from the dynamic member subscript method.

This means you can wrap the typed key path in any other type to enrich the original property with more capabilities.

A good example of this is RxSwift's use of @dynamicMemberLookup to expose Binders, a RxSwift-specific abstraction, for every property of an object on top of RxSwift's .rx namespace:

```
@dynamicMemberLookup
struct Reactive<Base> {
  // Additional implementation details...

  subscript<Property>(
    dynamicMember keyPath: WritableKeyPath<Base, Property>
  ) -> Binder<Property> where Base: AnyObject {
    Binder(base) { base, value in
      base[keyPath: keyPath] = value
```

```
      }
    }
  }
}
```

This example lives under the `.rx` namespace in RxSwift and allows regular (as opposed to "enriched") access to the property:

```
myView.isEnabled // Bool
myView.rx.isEnabled // Binder<Bool>
```

Dynamic callable

Dynamic callable was introduced in Swift 5 (SE-0216) to provide syntactic sugar when creating wrappers around dynamic languages/calls inside Swift and allows to naturally invoke values as if they're functions.

A common example of this is trying to represent a shell command:

```
@dynamicCallable
struct Command {
  let base: String

  init(_ base: String) {
    self.base = base
  }

  func dynamicallyCall(withArguments args: [String]) {
    print(#line, base, args.joined(separator: " "))
  }
}

struct Shell {
  static let swift = Command("swift")
}
```

`dynamicallyCall(withArguments:)` would be invoked whenever you "call" the `swift` property.

So calling:

```
Shell.swift("--version")
```

Produces:

```
swift --version
```

You can use the `Process` API to execute the command, but it's outside the scope of this chapter.

You can even leverage string-based dynamic member lookup to make this a bit more robust. Combining `@dynamicMemberLookup` with `@dynamicCallable` and adding the following subscript to `Command`:

```
subscript(dynamicMember member: String) -> Command {
  Command("\(base) \(member)")
}
```

Will concatenate the dynamically accessed member of a command as a continuation of the previous command. So you can write something like this, quite naturally:

```
Shell.swift.build("--verbose")
```

And `dynamicallyCall(withArguments:)` would print out:

```
swift build --verbose
```

Property wrappers

Property wrappers, introduced in Swift 5.1 (SE-0258), provide a way to abstract the handling of the get/set accessor portions of properties. Some of the common built-in ones are `@Published`, `@State` and `@Binding`, which you used in the **Functional Reactive Programming** chapter.

When designing your APIs, property wrappers serve as a powerful tool in two ways: abstracted reusability and capability layering.

Reusing accessor logic

A property wrapper's primary goal is encapsulating the get/set accessors for properties, both internally for you as a developer and for other people contributing to your codebase. But also, if this sort of abstraction is powerful *outside* your module, you might want to make it `public`.

A common use case of this is for abstracting `UserDefaults`, similarly to SwiftUI's `@AppStorage` property wrapper:

```
@propertyWrapper
struct AppStorage<Value> {
  var wrappedValue: Value {
    get { defaults.object(forKey: key) as? Value ?? fallback }
    set { defaults.setValue(newValue, forKey: key) }
```

```
  }

  private let key: String
  private let defaults: UserDefaults
  private let fallback: Value

  init(wrappedValue fallback: Value,
       _ key: String,
       store: UserDefaults = .standard) {
    self.key = key
    self.defaults = store
    self.fallback = fallback

    if defaults.object(forKey: key) == nil {
      self.wrappedValue = fallback
    }
  }
}
```

This property wrapper lets you encapsulate reading and writing from `UserDefaults` simply by writing:

```
@AppStorage("counter") var counter = 4
@AppStorage("thing", store: customDefaults) var thing = "hello"
```

You can make this a bit nicer by also allowing string-based `RawRepresentables` if you add the following initializer to `AppStorage`:

```
init<R: RawRepresentable>(
  wrappedValue fallback: Value,
  _ key: R,
  store: UserDefaults = .standard
) where R.RawValue == String {
  self.init(wrappedValue: fallback,
            key.rawValue,
            store: store)
}
```

This lets you provide `RawRepresentable` keys with string values, such as enums:

```
enum Key: String {
  case counter
  case thing
}

@AppStorage(Key.counter) var counter = 4
@AppStorage(Key.thing, store: customDefaults) var thing = "hi"
```

If there's no value in the provided user defaults key, the assigned value will be used as the default one and written to the user's defaults.

The main points to note here are how the consumer doesn't care about `UserDefaults` necessarily being used under the hood and that the property wrapper entirely removes the unneeded repetition when accessing the value through the wrapper's `wrappedValue` property.

You can also use property wrappers to transform or limit the input of a consumer. For example, an `Assert` or `Clamped` property wrapper:

```swift
@propertyWrapper
struct Clamped<T: Comparable> {
  var wrappedValue: T {
    get { storage }
    set {
      storage = min(max(range.lowerBound, newValue),
                    range.upperBound)
    }
  }

  private var storage: T
  private let range: ClosedRange<T>

  init(wrappedValue: T, _ range: ClosedRange<T>) {
    assert(range.contains(wrappedValue))
    self.storage = wrappedValue
    self.range = range
  }
}
```

This lets you clamp a property into a specific range. Consider a human temperature given in degrees Celsius:

```swift
struct Patient {
  let id = UUID()
  let name: String
  @Clamped(35...42) var temperature = 37.5
}

var p = Patient(name: "Shai")
p.temperature = 39
// Temperature is unmodified as 39, since it's within range

p.temperature = 100
// Temperature is 42, the maximum value in the range

p.temperature = 20
// Temperature is 35, the minimum value in the range
```

You could easily create a similar wrapper to `fatalError` or `assert` on an invalid value instead of simply clamping the value to a range.

The use cases are endless. **swift-argument-parser**, for example, uses it to define arguments and their properties for command-line arguments.

Layering with projection

A somewhat hidden superpower of property wrappers is their **projected value**. It's an auxiliary value you can access for the wrapped property using the $ prefix. This feature is heavily used in Combine and SwiftUI.

For example, using the $ prefix on a Published property projects it as a publisher of the value's type:

```
@Published var counter = 1
counter // Int
$counter // Publisher<Int, Never>
```

Implementing your own naive @Published might look like this:

```
@propertyWrapper
struct MyPublished<Value> {
  var wrappedValue: Value {
    get { storage.value }
    set { storage.send(newValue) }
  }

  var projectedValue: AnyPublisher<Value, Never> {
    storage.eraseToAnyPublisher()
  }

  private let storage: CurrentValueSubject<Value, Never>

  init(wrappedValue: Value) {
    self.storage = CurrentValueSubject(wrappedValue)
  }
}
```

This uses Combine's CurrentValueSubject as a storage mechanism you can access imperatively but also use as a publisher.

You can then use this the same way you'd use @Published:

```
@MyPublished var count = 1

count // Int
$count // AnyPublisher<Int, Never>
```

Another great example is `@ObservedObject`, which uses a clever combination of `@dynamicMemberLookup` with a projected value to let you produce bindings of its properties:

```
class MyViewModel: ObservableObject {
  @Published var counter = 5
}

// In a different class
@ObservedObject var viewModel = MyViewModel()

viewModel // MyViewModel
$viewModel // MyViewModel.Wrapper (which has
@dynamicMemberLookup)

viewModel.counter // Int
$viewModel.counter // Binding<Int>
```

`ObservedObject.Wrapper`'s dynamic member lookup uses the same trick in the **Enriching key paths** section of this chapter to transform properties to `Binding`-wrapped versions of themselves.

All these examples are here to show that designing your APIs using fancy language features isn't the end goal but only means to achieve great ergonomics and overall experience for the end-user.

But now that you have a beautiful API designed, it might be helpful to write some documentation on how to properly use it!

Documenting your code

As mentioned earlier in this chapter, documenting at least the public-facing portions of your code is crucial for new consumers of your code. Documenting your internal code is just as important because a different kind of consumer (developers) will use it later on.

Symbol documentation

Back in Objective-C days, Apple used a variation of **Headerdoc** for documentation.
Luckily, with Swift, you can now use (*almost*) full-blown markdown to write
documentation. Apple calls this Swift-flavored markdown **Markup**.

Starting with the basics, documentation starts with three forward-slashes (///) or
lives between the /** ... */ delimiters:

```
/// This method does a thing.
///
/// This can easily become a multi-line comment as well,
/// and span as many lines as possible.
func performThing() {
  // Implementation
}


/**
 This method does a different thing.

 Multi-line works using these Javadoc-styled delimiters as
 well, and it's mainly a matter of taste and preference.
 */
func performOtherThing() {
  // Implementation
}
```

Xcode also handles and recognizes some specific metadata fields for information
such as parameters, return values and thrown errors:

```
/// This method does a thing.
///
/// This can easily become a multi-line comment as well,
/// and span as many lines as possible
///
/// - parameter userId: Identifier of user to fetch things for
///
/// - throws: `User.Error` if user doesn't exist or
///           `id` is invalid
///
/// - returns: An array of `Thing`s for the user with
///            the provided ID
func fetchThings(for userId: UUID) throws -> [Thing] {
  // Implementation
}
```

The quick-look for this method will look like this:

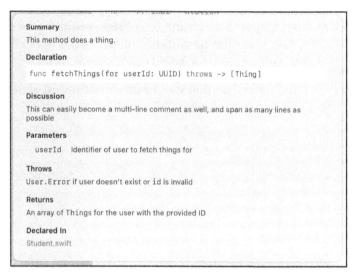

As you see, the first sentence is the primary portion of the documentation, whereas the rest (separated by an empty line) is split into the **Discussion** section. Also, all metadata is presented in its own "fields" as expected.

When documenting individual properties, or even enum cases, you can use a subset of the same metadata fields. For example, note:

```
/// Represents a single node in a linked list
indirect enum LinkedNode<T> {
  /// A node with a value of type `T`
  case value(T)

  /// A node with a value of type `T`, linked
  /// to the next node in a linked list
  ///
  /// - note: `next` is simply another case of the
  ///         same indirect `Node` enum
  case link(value: T, next: LinkedNode)

  /// The value associated with the current node
  var value: T {
    switch self {
    case .link(let value, _),
         .value(let value):
      return value
    }
  }

  /// The next node, if one exists
  var next: LinkedNode? {
```

```
    if case .link(_, let next) = self {
      return next
    }

    return nil
  }
}
```

Quick-looking over the `link` case looks like this:

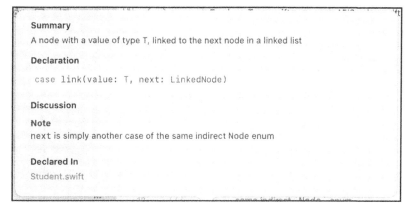

And of course, as you might expect, you can embed code blocks right into your documentation.

You can choose from three options to add a code block. The first is simply indenting your code by four spaces:

```
/// This is a function
///
/// A proper usage of this method is:
///
///     myFunction(
///       a: 1,
///       b: "Hello"
///     )
///
func myFunction(a: Int, b: String) -> Bool {

}
```

The second option is using triple-backtick (```) before and after the code-block like you would do in regular Markdown:

```
/// This is a function
///
/// - parameter a: A number
```

```
/// - parameter b: A String
///
/// A proper usage of this method is:
///
/// ```
/// myFunction(
///    a: 1,
///    b: "Hello"
/// )
/// ```
func myFunction(a: Int, b: String) -> Bool {

}
```

And a third, less common option, is using triple-tilde instead of backticks (~~~).

All three options will produce an identical quick-look:

Summary
This is a function

Declaration
```
func myFunction(a: Int, b: String) -> Bool
```

Discussion
A proper usage of this method is:
```
myFunction(
   a: 1,
   b: "Hello"
)
```

Parameters
a   A number
b   A String

Declared In
Student.swift

Finally, as mentioned earlier, you can use most portions of markdown in a comment: paragraphs, ordered and unordered lists, headers, links and others. This allows you to create quite detailed and rich documentation:

```
/// This is a function
///
/// It might have a single paragraph, with **bold**
/// words or even _italic text_
///
/// - parameters:
///     - a: A number
///     - b: A string
///
/// - returns: A boolean value
```

```
///
/// But it might have more points to discuss, such as:
///
///    * Item 1
///    * Item 2
///
/// # H1 header
/// Some descriptive text with ordered list:
///    1. First item
///    2. [Second link item](https://raywenderlich.com)
func myFunction(a: Int, b: String) {
  // Implementation
}
```

The quick-look for this will look as follows:

Summary

This is a function

Declaration

```
func myFunction(a: Int, b: String)
```

Discussion

It might have a single paragraph, with **bold** words or even *italic text*

But it might have more points to discuss, such as:

- Item 1
- Item 2

H1 header

Some descriptive text with ordered list:

1. First item
2. Second link item

Parameters

a   A number

b   A string

Returns

A boolean value

Additional metadata fields

Like `parameters`, `returns` or even `note`, Xcode supports a wide range of metadata fields you can use in your documentation:

GENERAL	METADATA	RUNTIME INFO
attention bug experiment note remark todo	author authors copyright date seealso since version	complexity invariant important precondition postcondition requires warning

> **Note**: Some additional fields specifically available for playgrounds exist, but they're out of scope for this chapter. You can read more about all the available fields on Apple's Markup Functionality documentation (https://apple.co/3rqAFQA).

Code markers

Aside from symbol-specific documentation, you can also divide your code using code markers. Xcode supports three of these: `MARK`, `TODO` and `FIXME`:

```
// TODO: - Finalize this class later on
class MyClass {
  // MARK: - Properties
  var a = 33
  var b = "Hello"

  // FIXME: - There's some issue here that needs attention
  func badMethod() {

  }
}
```

Here's how this looks in the file structure:

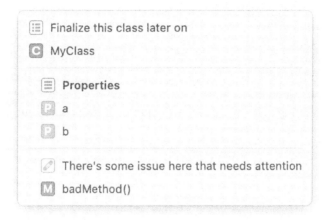

Specifically, MARKs are also visible in Xcode's minimap:

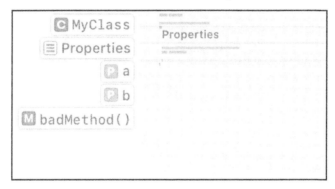

Your code is now *amazingly* documented! But there are still some final parting thoughts to share with you before you publish your code to the rest of the world.

Publishing to the world

In this section, you'll explore some ideas and important tidbits about how to release a library or other piece of code to the outside world. It doesn't matter if you're open-sourcing your code to the entire world or publishing it as an internal library in your company, some guidelines exist that you should follow to make fellow developers' lives easier.

Although this section applies more to library developers than to app developers, it's still a great reference because even app developers might need to understand why library authors work a certain way.

Versioning

When writing code for yourself, versioning doesn't matter much. But as soon as a piece of code is bundled into some reusable dependency and consumed by other developers, versioning becomes quite critical in ensuring consistency and expectability.

Most frameworks use **semantic versioning** to indicate changes to the framework's codebase. The most basic format looks like this:

$$2 \ . \ 7 \ . \ 1$$

major   minor   patch

A basic version consists of three components:

- **Major**: You should bump this version component whenever you make a breaking change to your code. It usually doesn't matter how small that change is. As soon as your consumer won't be able to compile their code "as-is" due to changes in your library, a major version bump is due.

- **Minor**: Use a minor bump to indicate non-breaking, additive features or changes to your library. For example, if you have a network library that adds a *new* method, bumping a minor version is the way to go.

- **Patch**: Whenever you fix bugs in your codebase, you should bump the patch component of your framework.

You'd consider either a minor or patch version change **safe to update** because it would not (or should not) cause any issues to an existing codebase. But you'd consider a major version change **breaking** because you'd likely need to modify your interaction with the framework after updating.

> **Note**: During initial development, you may use a `0.minor.patch` versioning (meaning the major component is 0). This indicates to consumers that the library is still under development and may break its API surface at any time, even with a minor or patch bump.

There are two more useful portions of a full-blown semantic version that are sometimes used: the **pre-release** and **metadata** labels:

$$2 \;.\; 7 \;.\; 1 - rc.1 + meta$$

major   minor   patch   pre-release   metadata

- **Pre-release**: Use the pre-release portion of the version to indicate the version isn't final yet. Some common values to use here are rc (release candidate), beta and alpha with an associated number (e.g. rc.1, beta.3, alpha.12).

- **Metadata**: You can assign additional build information to the metadata portion of the semantic version. This is seldom used, but when it is, most commonly it's for the build number (e.g., 4.1.7-rc.1+113245).

Deprecation

In the lifetime of every piece of code, you might need to retire some classes or methods. First, you should *almost always* bump the major version of your framework if you deprecate a piece of code because it means you're making a breaking change to your API contract with your consumer.

The nicest way to note this deprecation to consumers is using Swift's @available annotation. You can simply attach it to a specific method or even an entire class:

```
@available(*, deprecated)
func myOldMethod(value: Int) {
  // implementation
}
```

This results in the following warning:

```
'myOldMethod(value:)' is deprecated
```

You can also provide a specific message to describe the deprecation:

```
@available(*, deprecated, message: "Don't use me anymore")
func myOldMethod(value: Int) {
  // implementation
}
```

Which shows the following warning:

```
'myOldMethod(value:)' is deprecated: Don't use me anymore
```

Or optimally, if there is a new symbol to replace the old one, you can provide an automatic fixit for your consumer by providing the renamed argument:

```
@available(*, deprecated, renamed: "myNewMethod(number:)")
func myOldMethod(value: Int) {
  // implementation
}
```

This results in the following fixit:

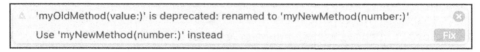

Using these statements correctly can help evolve your APIs because proper usage enhances communication between you and your API consumers as well as defines the developer experience (in case of an automatic fixit).

Key points

Great work on finishing this chapter!

You've learned quite a lot about how to think and go about creating great, expected and modern APIs. Hopefully, you'll keep some of this chapter's points in mind when designing your next APIs. But don't forget there are probably endless opinions about API design, and you should try to find your voice and aesthetic preference to it.

Here's a quick recap of some of the key points you learned today:

- Knowing Swift as a language is one thing, but designing an API well is an entirely different skill.

- Developers get a "feel" for how good an API is based on various characteristics: how obvious, well documented and modern it is, and how much the API developer focused on reducing the consumer's mental load.

- You should use access levels to properly separate the implementation details (`private`, `fileprivate` and `internal`) from the public-facing API portions (`public` and `open`). You should focus on the "core" of your API and not needlessly expose APIs to your consumer, because they might confuse the consumer when exploring.

- Fully understanding the tools and language features Swift offers is extremely helpful in designing APIs because they give you some creative freedom in crafting the best possible API a developer would expect in its domain. You've explored some such features and seen some usage examples: literals, dynamic member lookup, dynamic callable, property wrappers and more. Mixing these features (like in the case of `@ObservedObject`) can prove quite powerful.

- Although Swift is an easy to read language, you still should properly document your APIs and especially their public-facing properties. You can use powerful markup syntax as well as special metadata fields and markers to enrich the documentation experience for consumers.

- Finally, although you can simply release your code to the world without any "release etiquette", it's usually a good idea to provide proper versioning and to deprecate code correctly to not frustrate consumers.

Where to go from here?

As mentioned at the beginning of this chapter, API design is the subject of many opinions. As such, the best way to gain intuition as to what *you* like is to learn as much as possible about different perspectives, combined with the official guidelines from Apple, and experiment with different creative options! There is usually more than a single way to expose functionality, and the process of finding the right API is part of the fun of designing code!

You can also read Swift's API Design Guidelines (https://bit.ly/39uvYPD) document to better understand what Apple expects you to name your APIs, along with other useful pieces of information. As you can imagine, Apple's expectations often align with those of fellow developers and consumers of your APIs, so it's a great idea to dive into this document, which is well thought out and quite detailed.

To wrap up, congratulations on completing the last chapter of this book! The team thanks you for reading and hopes you've enjoyed the various chapters, examples and perspectives this book aims to showcase. Thank you for coming along on this ride!

Conclusion

We hope you learned a lot about the advanced features of Swift in this book — and had some fun in the process!

With the advanced knowledge you've acquired, you're ready to write better Swift code and improve your existing apps. If you want to read more, there are several books to check out. For building apps in the Apple ecosystem, look at *SwiftUI by Tutorials* and *Combine: Asynchronous Programming with Swift*. If you need to support older platforms, you might want to check out *RxSwift: Reactive Programming with Swift*. If you are interested in learning about classic data structures and algorithms, check out: *Data Structures & Algorithms in Swift*. Finally, if you want to look at another advanced framework that extends beyond the Apple ecosystem, check out: *Server-Side Swift with Vapor*.

If you have any questions or comments as you continue to use Swift, please stop by our forums at https://forums.raywenderlich.com.

Thank you again for purchasing this book. Your continued support is what makes the tutorials, books, videos, conferences and other things we do at raywenderlich.com possible — we truly appreciate it!

Wishing you all the best in your continued Swift adventures,

– The *Expert Swift* team

Made in the USA
Coppell, TX
04 February 2023